☞ W9-ASE-154

REGIS COLLEGE LIBRARY
100 Wellesley Street West
Toronto, Ontario
Canada M5S 2Z5

Hosea—Micah

Regis College Library
15 ST. MARY STREET
TORONTO, ONTARIO, CANADA
M4Y 2R5

WITHDRAWN

INTERPRETATION

A Bible Commentary for Teaching and Preaching

INTERPRETATION
A BIBLE COMMENTARY FOR TEACHING AND PREACHING

James Luther Mays, *Editor*
Patrick D. Miller, Jr., *Old Testament Editor*
Paul J. Achtemeier, *New Testament Editor*

JAMES LIMBURG

Hosea—Micah

REGIS COLLEGE LIBRARY
100 Wellesley Street West
Toronto, Ontario
Canada M5S 2Z5

INTERPRETATION

A Bible Commentary
for Teaching and Preaching

BS
1560
L55
1988

Regis College Library
15 ST. MARY STREET
TORONTO, ONTARIO, CANADA
M4Y 2R5

John Knox Press
ATLANTA

95919

Unless otherwise indicated Scripture quotations are from the Revised Standard Version of the Holy Bible, copyright, 1946, 1952, and © 1971, 1973 by the Division of Christian Education, National Council of the Churches of Christ in the U.S.A. and used by permission. Translations from the Hebrew are the author's.

Library of Congress Cataloging-in-Publication Data

Limburg, James, 1935–
  Hosea—Micah.

  (Interpretation, a Bible commentary for teaching and preaching)
  Bibliography: p.
  1. Bible. O.T.—Minor Prophets—Commentaries.
I. Title.   II. Series.
BS1560.L553 1988   224'.907   87-46293
ISBN 0-8042-3128-1

© copyright John Knox Press 1988
10 9 8 7 6 5 4 3 2 1
Printed in the United States of America
John Knox Press
Atlanta, Georgia 30365

SERIES PREFACE

This series of commentaries offers an interpretation of the books of the Bible. It is designed to meet the need of students, teachers, ministers, and priests for a contemporary expository commentary. These volumes will not replace the historical critical commentary or homiletical aids to preaching. The purpose of this series is rather to provide a third kind of resource, a commentary which presents the integrated result of historical and theological work with the biblical text.

An interpretation in the full sense of the term involves a text, an interpreter, and someone for whom the interpretation is made. Here, the text is what stands written in the Bible in its full identity as literature from the time of "the prophets and apostles," the literature which is read to inform, inspire, and guide the life of faith. The interpreters are scholars who seek to create an interpretation which is both faithful to the text and useful to the church. The series is written for those who teach, preach, and study the Bible in the community of faith.

The comment generally takes the form of expository essays. It is planned and written in the light of the needs and questions which arise in the use of the Bible as Holy Scripture. The insights and results of contemporary scholarly research are used for the sake of the exposition. The commentators write as exegetes and theologians. The task which they undertake is both to deal with what the texts say and to discern their meaning for faith and life. The exposition is the unified work of one interpreter.

The text on which the comment is based is the Revised Standard Version of the Bible. The general availability of this translation makes the printing of a translation unnecessary and saves the space for comment. The text is divided into sections appropriate to the particular book; comment deals with passages as a whole, rather than proceeding word by word, or verse by verse.

Writers have planned their volumes in light of the requirements set by the exposition of the book assigned to them. Biblical books differ in character, content, and arrangement. They also differ in the way they have been and are used in the liturgy, thought, and devotion of the church. The distinctiveness and use of particular books have been taken into account in decisions about the approach, emphasis, and use of space in the commentaries. The goal has been to allow writers to develop the format which provides for the best presentation of their interpretation.

The result, writers and editors hope, is a commentary which both explains and applies, an interpretation which deals with both the meaning and the significance of biblical texts. Each commentary reflects, of course, the writer's own approach and perception of the church and world. It could and should not be otherwise. Every interpretation of any kind is individual in that sense; it is one reading of the text. But all who work at the interpretation of Scripture in the church need the help and stimulation of a colleague's reading and understanding of the text. If these volumes serve and encourage interpretation in that way, their preparation and publication will realize their purpose.

The Editors

PREFACE

The world of these prophets was a real world, marked by joys and sorrows, hopes and fears, peace and war. As we enter that world through their words, we discover people buying and selling in their shops, working in their fields, building their homes, worshiping in their sanctuaries (Amos). We find them engaged in urban renewal projects and making plans to buy yet another farm (Micah). We hear of abundant harvests (Hosea) but also of blight and mildew (Amos) and of a rural crisis such as had not before been seen (Joel). We experience the sounds and sights of war: The bugle sounds the alarm, the chariots and horses charge, the smoke of fire and the stench of death go up from the camp (Hosea, Micah, Amos). We learn about people who failed to help refugees (Obadiah), and we find hints of the toll war takes on young people and on children (Amos, Joel).

The prophets themselves were real people, whose presence was not always welcome, we discover. Amos was ejected from the royal chapel at Bethel. Micah was told flat out, "Do not preach!" Hosea was called a fool and a madman. We sense something of the pain that went with the prophetic calling; Hosea experienced the breakup of his marriage and had to function as a single parent for a time. We also feel the passion that drove them to speak the truth no matter what the consequences: "I am filled with power, with the Spirit of the LORD, and with justice and might," said Micah.

This was their world and these were the prophets. But that world and those individuals are thousands of years removed from our own. Why should we pay attention to their words today? To a world as torn and troubled as any, these prophets brought a word which they identified as a word from God. They took up the cause of the powerless, calling for justice to roll through the land like a mighty stream and challenging their hearers to *do* justice (Amos, Micah). They spoke of peace, promising a day when nations would no longer be engaged in an arms race but would beat swords into plowshares. They spoke of a ruler who would bring peace, a Messiah who would come from Bethlehem (Micah). They told of the remarkable forgiving, nurturing, and healing love of God (Hosea), who would take up the people's sins and throw them into the depths of the sea (Micah). The single story *about* a prophet in this collection tells about

God's amazing grace and issues a challenge to get the word about that grace out to the teeming cities of the world (Jonah).

Peace and justice, Messiah and mission, love and forgiveness—these are the major themes of the Minor Prophets. The purpose of this commentary is to introduce these books and then to provide comments that will assist in bringing their words to our world.

A word about the design of this commentary: Each Introduction offers a summary of the book as a whole; those wishing to get a thorough grasp of one of these prophets should begin by reading through the entire biblical book with the help of the summary. Then, in the case of each book except Jonah, which is of a different sort than the rest, comments on the book's title introduce the prophet and locate him in his setting. The main part of the commentary consists of short essays on those sections of each book which seem to be of particular value and interest for preaching and teaching. Not every text is dealt with in these expositions, but it is hoped that the major themes of each book are considered. Finally, two bibliographies are included, one suggesting further reading and the other listing the works cited in the text.

I want to thank a number of people for their help along the way. Professors Patrick D. Miller and James Luther Mays have been wise and patient in their editorial counsel. Professor Siegfried Mittmann of Tuebingen University was a gracious host who provided a fine place to work in the *Theologicum* during a sabbatical year in Germany. Students at Luther Northwestern Theological Seminary and people in a variety of churches, camps, and classrooms have listened to these prophetic words with me; their questions and comments have been of great value. My assistant, Kai Nilsen, carefully checked the Scripture references.

I am grateful to Luther Northwestern Seminary for a generous sabbatical program, and to the Aid Association for Lutherans and Lutheran Brotherhood for further sabbatical support.

Finally, this book is dedicated to my wife Martha, whose laughter, wisdom, and love have been for me an interpretation of Proverbs 31:29: "Many women have done excellently, but you surpass them all!"

James Limburg

CONTENTS

INTERPRETATION

To Martha

THE BOOK OF

Hosea

Introduction

Hosea is the first book in the collection called the Minor Prophets or the Book of the Twelve. *The Wisdom of Jesus the Son of Sirach,* a second-century B.C. apocryphal book, says this about these prophets:

> May the bones of the twelve prophets
> revive from where they lie,
> for they comforted the people of Jacob
> and delivered them with confident hope.
> (Sirach 49:10)

Hosea makes a major contribution to the message of hope and comfort about which Sirach speaks. As such it provides an excellent entrance into the Book of the Twelve, telling in unforgettable imagery of God's love which will not let God's people go. The book falls into three major sections:

1—3: After the title in 1:1, the first three chapters have to do with Hosea and his family. The materials have been arranged topically in three groups, with sayings of doom alternating with hopeful sayings. The tone of 1:2–9 is of doom and that of 1:10—2:1 is of hope. The verses in 2:2–13 consist of accusations and announcements of future punishment; these are followed by words of hope in 2:14–23. In chapter 3, words of doom in verses 3 and 4 are framed by hopeful sayings in verses 1–2 and 5.

Another factor determines the arrangement of these materials. Reading through these first chapters, one almost has the sense of reading a story interrupted by a long middle sec-

1

tion containing sayings. The "story" may be summarized as follows:

Obeying the Lord's command, Hosea marries a woman of known promiscuous nature. She bears three children, each of whom is given an ominous name that announces doom for the nation's future (1:2–9). After this doom, a brighter day will bring the reverse of what these names announce (1:10—2:1).

Why should the nation be punished? The answer is given in the accusations of 2:2, 5, 8, and 13: Israel has been unfaithful to the Lord. These accusations provide reasons for the punishment announced in 2:3–4, 6–7, and 9–12. Once again, beyond this immediate tragedy will be a brighter future. The Lord will court Israel like a young lover courting his beloved (2:14–15); their marriage will be marked by fidelity (2:16–20); and the doom announced in the ominous names will be reversed (2:21–23).

Then comes a rerun of the command given at the beginning of the story. The Lord tells Hosea, "Go again, and show your love for a woman who is committing adultery with a lover. You must love her just as I still love the people of Israel, even though they turn to other gods" (3:1, GNB). In the context of this story, that woman can be no other than Hosea's wife Gomer, whom he purchases for the price of a slave. The prophet's experience with his wife is a model of the Lord's experience with Israel. Just as Hosea could still love his unfaithful wife, so God still loves unfaithful Israel. Similarly, on some day in the future, Israel will once again return and enjoy the goodness of the Lord (3:5).

The editor of the book intends that this story provide an entrance to the Hosea material. It illustrates God's *forgiving love,* portrayed in the account of Hosea's love for his wife and succinctly expressed in the statement, ". . . the Lord loves the people of Israel, though they turn to other gods . . ." (3:1).

4:1—11:11: This central section of the book is framed by the divine speech formulas, "Hear the word of the Lord" in 4:1 and "says the Lord" in 11:11. Once again the doom/hope pattern is a factor in the arrangement of the materials. The sayings in chapters 4—10 are mostly words of doom, with the promise of a hopeful future announced in chapter 11.

Again in this section, chronological sequence plays a part in the arrangement of the materials. Verses 1–3 in chapter 4 sound the theme for the whole. Because there is no faithfulness, no love, and no knowledge of God in the land, the Lord has a legal complaint against the people of Israel and announces that punishment will come. The sayings which follow, through 5:7, reflect the time of stable government during the last years of Jeroboam and develop the themes announced in 4:1–3. The fault for the lack of knowledge about God lies with the priests, the theologians who have failed at their task (4:4–10). Since the people have not been properly instructed and nurtured in their own religious traditions, they have become fascinated with another religion and have become caught up in Baalism (4:11–19). Again, the fault for this religious breakdown lies with the theological leadership (5:1–7).

About 735 B.C., the winds of war began to blow across Israel. The section 5:8—9:9 begins with a bugle call sounding the alarm and continues with sayings which reflect the chaotic period of the Syro-Ephraimitic war (see on Hosea 1:1, part 2). We hear echoes of assassinations and futile attempts to set up a stable government (7:7; 8:4). We catch hints of a frantic foreign policy that shifts allegiance from one superpower to another (5:13; 7:11). The sayings beginning with 5:8 lead to the call for steadfast love and knowledge of God in 6:6, a return to the themes announced in 4:1–3. The materials from 6:7 to 7:16 move away from that pivotal verse and continue to furnish evidence that there is neither steadfast love nor knowledge of God in the land. Yet another trumpet call is sounded in 8:1, announcing the enemy's coming (cf. 5:8). Returning to the themes of 4:1–3, the prophet says that the people claim knowledge of God (8:2) but in fact have forgotten their Maker (8:14; cf. 8:4b–6). Punishment will follow. Soon will come the whirlwind and the fire (8:7, 14). When the prophet tries to warn the people of the coming danger, they consider him to be crazy (9:1–9).

Hosea 9:10–17 looks back at Israel's past, charging that the people have carried on a flirtation with Baalism since early in their history. The sayings in chapter 10 reflect the last years of the nation's life, providing further evidence for the charge of faithlessness and lack of love and knowledge of God (4:1) and announcing the end of the monarchy (10:7, 15). Finally, chapter 11 also looks back, recalling God's *nurturing love* in Israel's past; "When Israel was a child, I loved him . . ." (11:1). This parental love becomes the basis for the announcement of a hopeful future for God's children (vv. 10–11).

3

11:12—14:9: Again, the materials here have been arranged according to a broad doom/hope pattern. Chapter 12 charges Ephraim/Israel with deceit and 13 announces the death of the nation. Chapter 14 then speaks of God's *healing love,* concluding the book with the image of the Lord as physician and with the statement, "I will heal their faithlessness; I will love them freely . . ." (14:4). Chronologically, all of the materials in this final section of the book reflect the situation under Hoshea, Israel's last king.

In sum, each section of the book contains accusations against Israel and announces that punishment will come. However, each section also concludes on a positive note, telling of the Lord's forgiving, nurturing, and healing love and thus contributing to the message of comfort and hope which Sirach recalled centuries later.

The book opens by locating the prophet in his historical setting, thus indicating that the prophetic word must first be heard in its particularity. After some comments on this opening sentence, the expositions will focus on those sayings which are central to the prophet's message and which seem especially promising for preaching and teaching.

Hosea 1:1
The Prophet Hosea

The Book of Hosea begins, "The word of the Lord that came to Hosea. . . ." The books of Joel, Micah, and Zephaniah in the Book of the Twelve are introduced in the same way, immediately identifying that which follows as a word from God.

1. Hosea the Son of Beeri

Hosea is identified in relationship to his father, like Joel, Jonah, Zephaniah, and Zechariah in the Book of the Twelve, rather than in connection with his hometown, like Amos, Micah, and Nahum. He was called to be a prophet while of marriageable age (1:2), thus presumably while still young, perhaps as a late teenager. He was married to a woman named Gomer who gave birth to two sons and a daughter (1:3–9). Chapter 3 indicates that Hosea bought a woman and took her as his wife; this was apparently Gomer, whom he took back after she had been unfaithful to him. All the evidence in the book suggests that the prophet lived his life in Israel, the Northern Kingdom. Places named are in the north: Samaria, the capital city (7:1; 8:5–6; 10:5, 7; 13:16), Bethel (or Beth-Aven; 4:15; 5:8; 10:5; 12:4), Gilgal (4:15; 9:15; 12:11). References to "the land" (4:1) and "our king" (7:5) indicate that Hosea was a citizen of the land to which he delivered his message.

Behind the sayings in the Hosea book is a person of unusual imagination. The imagery used to speak of God and people is astonishing in its power and variety. Two major metaphors describe the God/people relationship: God as husband and the people as unfaithful wife (chapters 1—3, and throughout the book) and God as parent and the people as rebelling child/ children (11:1–4; cf. 11:10). In addition to these there are a number of other pictures used for God and people. Some are personal ones: God is a farmer, the people a trained heifer (10:11); God is a hiker, coming upon his people as one comes upon sweet grapes in the wilderness (9:10); God is a bird catcher, the people like a dove without any sense (7:11); God is a physician, the people a sin-sick patient (14:4); God is the one who provides shade and protection (14:7). Other pictures for God are taken from animal life: God is like a moth (5:12), a lion (5:14; 11:10; 13:7–8), a leopard or a bear robbed of her cubs (13:7–8). Imagery is taken from plant life: God is like a cypress tree (14:8). Or images come from other natural phenomena: God is like dry rot (5:12) or the showers in the springtime (6:3) or the dew (14:5).

Pictures used to describe the people are equally varied. From the personal sphere: The people are like a sick person (5:13; 14:4) or a gray-haired old man who does not act his age (7:9) or a man who has hired a prostitute (8:9) or even like an unborn child who does not have the sense to emerge from the womb (13:13). From animal life: The people are like a stubborn heifer (4:16; cf. 10:11), a lamb (4:16), a silly dove (7:11–12), a wild ass (8:9), or a flock of birds (11:11). From plant life: The people are like grapes (9:10), a vine (10:1), or a garden (14:7). From other spheres: The people are like a heated oven (7:4–7), a half-baked cake (7:8), a defective bow (7:16), the morning mist, dew, chaff, or smoke (13:3).

Like Jesus who told stories and used a variety of images, the prophet finds pictures for God and people everywhere.

5

His imaginative creativity in speaking about God stands as an example for artists, musicians, theologians, and all others who try to express traditional biblical teachings in fresh and effective ways.

Behind these sayings is also a person of unusual sensitivity. Because of his own heart-wrenching experiences with his family, Hosea is able to describe the anguish in the heart of God like no other prophet. Abraham Heschel said, "Amos dwells on what God has done . . . Hosea dwells on what God has felt for Israel" (*The Prophets,* p. 60). The anguish of God over a faithless people is like that of a husband over a wife who is ungrateful and unfaithful (2:8, 13). The pain in the heart of God is like the pain in the heart of a parent who has invested decades in child rearing only to have that child turn out to be a rebel (11:1–4).

2. The Days of Uzziah, Jotham, Ahaz, Hezekiah, and Jeroboam

The fact that the introductory sentence first names four kings of Judah suggests that the book was edited in Judah some time after the fall of Samaria in 722 B.C. had confirmed Hosea's announcement of the end of Israel. Uzziah ruled from 783–742 B.C., Jotham from 742–735, Ahaz from 735–715, and Hezekiah from 715 to 687. We may ask why only one king from Israel, Jeroboam II who ruled from 786–746, should be mentioned, with no mention of the other half dozen kings who ruled in the north up until its fall in 722. Once again, this omission would seem to point to a final editing in Judah. Since Israel began to fall apart politically after the death of Jeroboam, the editor may have been saying that the kings who followed were not even worth mentioning!

The administrations of Jeroboam and Uzziah were times of peace and prosperity for Israel and Judah; this period is described in connection with the setting for Amos (see Amos 1:1, part 2.). With the death of Jeroboam in 746, however, the process leading to the fall of Israel began. A powerful new ruler, Tiglath-Pileser III, took the throne in Assyria (745–727 B.C.). Eager to extend his empire, he was taking tribute from Menahem of Israel by 738 B.C., thus indicating Israel's subjection to Assyria by that time (II Kings 15:19). He was succeeded by Shalmaneser V (726–722) who began the siege of Israel's capital. Sargon II (721–705) finally captured Samaria and deported its inhabitants, bringing the existence of the Northern Kingdom to an end just a bicentennial after it had begun at the time of Solomon's death in 922.

During the decades leading up to its fall in 722, Israel was plagued by political anarchy. John Bright describes the nation's leadership during this period: "Each turn of the helm brought the ship of state closer to the rocks" (*A History of Israel*, p. 273). A reading of II Kings 15—17 makes the story clear enough: Jeroboam's son Zechariah ruled only six months and was assassinated by Shallum. Shallum ruled for a month, only to be assassinated by Menahem (745–736) who, as we have seen, became a vassal of Assyria. Menahem's son Pekahiah was in office for two years (737–736) before being assassinated by Pekah.

Along with Remaliah of Syria, Pekah began to round up support for a rebellion against Assyria. In 735, when Ahaz of Judah refused to join this anti-Assyrian coalition, Syria and Israel marched on Jerusalem to try to force Ahaz to join. These events are called the "Syro-Ephraimitic war" (Ephraim as a name for Israel). Ahaz still refused, choosing rather to ask Assyria for help against Israel and Syria and to submit as a vassal to Assyria's rule. In response to this appeal, the Assyrian armies moved into the west. Portions of the population of Israel were deported, most likely in 733 (II Kings 15:29, 37; 16:5–9; Isa. 7:1–17; see Bright, *History,* pp. 273–4). These events provide the background for a number of Hosea's sayings collected in 5:8—9:9.

In 732 Pekah was assassinated by Hoshea, who first submitted to Assyria but then rebelled (II Kings 17:3–4). Hoshea was then imprisoned and thus presided over the downfall of the nation and the deportation of its inhabitants in 722 B.C.

In the pages which follow, we shall see that Hosea's sayings often reflect the political crises through which the prophet lived. For example: The lack of stable government during these years is evident in 8:4 and 13:10–11. The inconsistent foreign policy, with Israel flitting now to Egypt, now to Assyria, finds expression in 7:11 and 12:1.

A careful reading of the Hosea book indicates that during these final chaotic years there was also a crisis in religion. The saying that introduces the central section of the book points to a general breakdown of morality in the land (4:2). Priests and prophets alike have failed in their tasks (4:4–6). The people have substituted trust in military strength (10:13) or in other gods (4:11–14; 10:1; 13:2) for loyalty to their Lord (6:4).

To summarize: During the days of Jeroboam II, from 786–746 B.C., Amos addressed a nation which was still enjoying smooth sailing on calm seas even though, as the prophet warned, the ship of state was headed toward the rocks. By the time of Hosea, the damage had been done. His words were addressed to people on a ship that was already beginning to sink.

Hosea 1:2–9
A Future Without God

The materials in these first three chapters of Hosea should all be understood in the context of the "story" of these chapters, as sketched in the Introduction above.

The encounter between the Lord and Hosea reported here comes from the earliest time in the prophet's work, since verse 4 speaks of the "house of Jehu" of which Jeroboam and his son Zecharaiah, who ruled for only six months, were the last representatives. The movement of 1:2–9 may be traced in connection with the four names it contains.

Gomer. The Lord's word to Hosea is a strange one. Its sense is, "Hosea, go and marry a woman who is a prostitute and raise up a family with her" (1:2). The questions come flooding to mind: Was this woman an ordinary streetwalker, of the sort described in Genesis 38:13–19 or Proverbs 7? Was she one of the prostitutes associated with the worship of Baal (Hos. 4:14)? Was the woman perhaps a former prostitute who promised to quit her profession? How did Hosea feel about all this? Interesting as these questions are, the text answers none of them. The story indicates Hosea's response and names the woman: "So he went and took Gomer the daughter of Diblaim. . . ."

There is something more. The reason for this strange command is given: "for the land commits great harlotry by forsaking the LORD." Hosea would say it time and again: The nation has forsaken the Lord, and that faithless behavior is harlotry.

8

Jezreel. Hosea is told to name their first child "Jezreel." The name itself is a pleasant one meaning "God plants." It refers to a beautiful city and valley between the mountains of Samaria and Galilee, but the beauty of that place had been marred by the events of extreme violence which had happened there. At Jezreel, Jehu had killed the kings of Israel and Judah. There Jezebel had died a cruel death. It was at Jezreel that Jehu displayed the heads of the seven sons of Ahab; he had also engineered the mass extermination of Baal worshipers there (II Kings 9—10). Thus the name of the beautiful city and valley was forever linked with violence and mass murder. To name a child "Jezreel" might be like naming a child today "Auschwitz" or "Hiroshima." An announcement of punishment indicates the ominous significance of the name: "and I will put an end to the kingdom of the house of Israel."

Not pitied. The next child is a daughter whose name has a beautiful ring in Hebrew, "Lo-ruhamah." Used frequently to describe one of God's characteristics, the same root is also translated as "compassion" (Micah 7:19) or "mercy" (Hos. 14:3). Here the negative prefix "Lo" reverses the meaning, and the name conveys doom: The Lord will no longer have compassion on Israel!

Not my people. Since the days of the Exodus and the events at Sinai, the relationship between God and people was often expressed with phrases such as "I will take you for my people, and I will be your God . . ." (Exod. 6:7; cf. Lev. 26:12). Here in the name of the third child is a reversal of that formula. He shall be called "Not my people, for you are not my people and I am not your God" (1:8).

There is a terrifying progression in the sequence of these names. The first announced a future when Israel would have to live without a king, the second a future without God's compassion, and the third a future without God (cf. Jeremias).

For no other prophet were professional calling and personal life so closely linked as for Hosea. He understood the heartache caused by the actions of his young wife as a parallel to the hurting in the heart of God. The three children who grew up in the village and played in its streets also shared in the prophet's task, as walking audio-visual aids in the service of the prophetic message of doom. For Hosea there was no separation between office and home, vocation and family life. No doubt

9

that is why he spoke with such passion. The pain in the heart of the prophet became a parable of the anguish in the heart of God.

Hosea 2:2–23
Can This Marriage Be Saved?

This rather lengthy unit should be understood in the context of the story running through chapters 1—3. The first part of that story announced a future without a king, without God's compassion, and without God (1:2–9). A people hearing such a message would ask, "But why, prophet? Why should all this come upon us?" The sayings in 2:2–13 answer those questions. Verses 14–15, linked to what precedes by "therefore" (cf. vv. 6, 9), tell of a bright future beyond the announced punishment. Because these sayings assume a time when things are still normal in Israel, with the farm economy prospering (vv. 5, 8, 9) and religious institutions flourishing (vv. 11, 13), they fit best into the earliest period of Hosea's ministry, during the last years of Jeroboam's administration. The hopeful picture promised in verses 14 and 15 is amplified in verses 16–23, finally returning to the theme of the children's ominous names.

The background for the language in verses 2–3 is the kind of proceeding which took place at the court in the gate in ancient Israel. The accused in this legal procedure is the wife, or Israel. The one making the charges is the husband, representing the Lord. Here the one with the complaint does not address the accused directly but speaks to the court *about* the accused, calling upon the "children," that is, the faithful portion of the people, to make a complaint against their "mother," that is, Israel as a whole. The charge is stated in verse 2*b*: "she is not my wife, and I am not her husband," which recalls the statement in 1:9. The punishment is announced in verse 3.

What sort of legal process is taking place here? Though one thinks immediately of a divorce procedure as in Deuteronomy 24:1–4, it is clear that the plaintiff's intent is not to bring about a divorce. In fact, he wants his wife to quit her prostitution and adultery so that there can be a reconciliation. The husband still hopes that this marriage can be saved and looks forward to a time when their relationship will be like it was in courting days (2:14–15).

The speech continues to spell out the accusations against the wife/people in verses 4*b* and 5. Israel has been acting like an irresponsible mother and a faithless wife. Worse than an ordinary prostitute who waits for her customers to come to her (Gen. 38:14–19; Jer. 3:2), she has been chasing after her lovers. The literal meaning is clear: Israel has been avidly pushing the worship of Baal and enthusiastically participating in the rites of the Canaanite fertility cults. Throughout her history Israel had known the Lord as the God who *delivered* her from bondage in Egypt, and who had also sustained her in the wilderness and *blessed* her in her new land. The farmer's creed in Deuteronomy 26 brings these two aspects of the action of God together (vv. 5–8, 9–10). The sustaining, blessing activity of God is especially celebrated in the psalms (67; 104; see Claus Westermann, *Elements of Old Testament Theology,* chapter 1). The complaint here is that Israel attributes the "blessings" of a good harvest to "my lovers," that is, to Baal, rather than to the Lord. The essentials of food and clothing (bread and water, wool and flax) as well as life's luxuries (oil and drink) are all credited to the beneficence of the Canaanite fertility god.

The charge against the wife/Israel in verse 8 is, "she did not know!" Once again, Israel thought that she should thank Baal for the grain and wine and oil produced in her land. "But it was I," says the Lord, "who gave her all these gifts." The "she did not know" theme is heard again in the "forgot" of verse 13 and also calls to mind the charge of a general failure in religious instruction, which will be developed in 4:6.

Three "therefores" in this speech introduce important turning points (vv. 6, 9, 14). The first two introduce announcements of punishment. The wayward wife who loves to chase after her lovers will not be able to catch them! Then the ultimate purpose of the punishment is revealed. Instead of saying, "I will go after my lovers" (v. 5), she will say, "I am going back to my first husband—I was better off then than I am now" (v. 7, GNB). Faithless Israel will have to pay the price for infidelity, but the marriage will be saved.

A more extensive announcement of punishment is introduced with the "therefore" of verse 9 (vv. 9–13). There will be no more abundant harvests (vv. 9, 12). The sanctuaries so busy

11

with Baal worship will be shut down (v.11). In these ways the Lord will punish Israel for her faithlessness (v. 13).

The final "therefore" of verse 14 introduces an abrupt modulation into a new and brighter key. A day will come after the tragedy of the immediate future when the Lord will woo Israel like a young lover. There will even be a second honeymoon, and one day Israel's vineyards will be given back to her again. The Valley of Achor (which means "valley of trouble," cf. Josh. 7:24–26) will become a "door of hope." The promise is that things will once again be as they were at the beginning of the relationship, as at the time when the Lord led Israel out of Egypt.

"Why should all this come upon us?" That would be the question of anyone hearing the ominous names of the prophet's children or the announcements of doom with which the Hosea book begins. This speech begins to answer that question. The accusations develop the charge already made in 1:2: "the land commits great harlotry by forsaking the LORD." The citizens of Israel can expect that they will pay a price for their faithlessness, as the announcements of punishment indicate.

Punishment will not be the end, however (2:13). The drive of this speech is toward reconciliation, pleading with Israel to quit her adultery (2:2) and to return to her true lover (2:7). Behind these words one senses a divine love that will not let even a faithless Israel go. The "marriage" between God and people will not end in divorce. This marriage will be saved. Here is a promise that one day there will be a second honeymoon, something like the first one (vv. 14–15). The Lord will show compassion to a people called "not pitied," will address them as "my people," and once again they will say, "Thou art my God" (2:16–23).

When will all of this be? A people who know themselves to be ransomed from the futile ways of their ancestors, "not with perishable things such as silver or gold, but with the precious blood of Christ," a people who have been "called out of darkness into his marvelous light" and who know themselves to be a part of a "chosen race, a royal priesthood, a holy nation, God's own people" will answer that question in terms of the good news about Jesus Christ. They have heard and experienced the good news which the New Testament expresses in terms of a reversal of those ominous names of the children: "Once you were no people but now you are God's people; once you had not received mercy but now you have received mercy" (I Peter 1:18–19; 2:9–10).

Hosea 3:1–5
The Cantus Firmus

Again, this section should be heard in the context of the "story" in chapters 1—3 (see Introduction). This first major portion of the Hosea book now concludes as it began, with a command from the Lord to Hosea. This time the experience is reported in the first person instead of the third, suggesting that this material goes back to the prophet himself.

Once again, the command is a strange one. Hosea is told to "love a woman" who already has another lover (a paramour) and who is living in adultery. Who could this woman be? For those who have been following the story as it has been told so far there can be no doubt: The woman is Gomer, Hosea's wife.

Again, questions come to mind. What had happened to this marriage over the years? Had Gomer returned to her life of prostitution? What about those three children? Did the prophet have to raise them as a single parent? What sort of heartbreak had Hosea—and Gomer and the children—been experiencing?

The text does not answer those questions but is relentless in driving toward another concern. It directs us immediately to the statement which sounds the underlying theme, the *cantus firmus* upon which the remainder of the book plays like a highly developed counterpoint. The happenings between Hosea and his wife are important because they model what is going on between God and people: "even as the LORD loves the people of Israel, though they turn to other gods and love cakes of raisins." "Cakes of raisins" were delicacies apparently distributed at times of celebration (II Sam. 6:19); reference here is to their use in connection with the worship of other gods, perhaps like the cakes for the "queen of heaven" mentioned in Jeremiah 7:18 and 44:15–19.

13

Hosea reports, "So I bought her . . ." (v. 2). The questions arise once more: Was she being sold as a slave? As a prostitute?

Who was selling her? The text is silent about these questions, but the price is recalled, a combination of fifteen shekels of silver and some barley. For comparison: a slave might be worth thirty shekels (Exod. 21:32), and Joseph was sold for twenty (Gen. 37:28; cf. also Lev. 27:1–8).

The repurchased wife is taken home, first for a probationary period (vv. 3–4). Her promiscuity will be curtailed. The couple will refrain from sex for a time. This behavior too models the greater message of which the prophet and his wife are a part: So also Israel will live in isolation for a time, without the support of a monarchy or the devices of religion. The "pillar" was a part of the Baal cult which had come into Israelite religion but which was forbidden (Deut. 16:21–22). The ephod was apparently a vestment (Judg. 8:24–28), and the teraphim were small images (Judg. 17:5); both were pagan equipment which had made their way into Israelite religion. The point is that just as Hosea and Gomer would live in isolation from one another for a time, so Israel would exist in isolation from the king and from the Lord (cf. "Jezreel" and "Not pitied").

The first major section of the book comes to a close on a hopeful note. One day in the future the children of Israel will *return* (v. 5). Here is sounded one of the major themes in Hosea's preaching. The prophet will plead with Israel to return to the Lord (6:1; 12:6; cf. 14:1, part 1). When they refuse to return to their God (5:4; 7:10), he announces that they will return to Egypt, that is to bondage (9:3), because "they have refused to return to me," says the Lord (11:5). Finally one day, Israel will come to her senses and say, "I will go and return to my first husband" (2:7). Just as Gomer had returned to her husband, so will the people one day return to their Lord.

The statements at the beginning and the end of chapters 1—3 which provide the reasons for the commands given to the prophet keep the essentials of this first major section of the book in focus: the faithlessness of the people (1:2) and the faithfulness of God (3:1).

Hosea has often been called the prophet of God's love. The Hebrew word occurs four times in 3:1, translated as "love" or "beloved." Reflection on these four "loves" can help to gain a grasp on the message of the entire book.

14

The love of the paramour ("beloved of a paramour") is an adulterous, illicit affection, the kind of feeling a man has for another man's wife. This sort of love is self-centered and de-

structive because at least one of the parties involved is commit-
ted to another by a vow of marriage.

The people who "love cakes of raisins" have placed their
affections on "other gods." They have fallen in love with the
cults of their day which promise happiness and success. This is
again a self-centered and destructive sort of love, because one
of the parties to the relationship has a previous commitment
which promises having no other gods (Exod. 20:3).

The third love is that of the Lord who loves Israel even
when the people reject this love. This is a love not motivated
by the object; indeed the people "turn to other gods." This kind
of love originates in the heart of God (Deut. 7:6–8), is exempli-
fied on the cross (John 3:16), illustrated in the parable of the
Waiting Father (Luke 15:11–32), and expressed by the New
Testament word *agape* (I John 3:16–18; 4:7–12). This is the kind
of love that keeps on loving no matter what. This is the divine
love that provides the *cantus firmus* for the Book of Hosea.

Finally, it was to this kind of love that the Lord called Hosea
when he said, "Go again, love a woman . . ." and to which God's
people continue to be called: "Beloved, if God so loved us, we
ought also to love one another" (I John 4:11).

Hosea 4:1–3
The Case of the Lord Versus the People

We have seen that the factors governing the arrangement
of chapters 1—3 of Hosea were *thematic,* gathering materials
relating to Hosea and his family so that doom and hope alter-
nate. In chapters 4—11 the doom/hope alteration again is evident. The tone for these chapters is set with the theme of doom
struck in 4:1–3; this mood continues until the concluding hopeful section in chapter 11 (see Introduction).

The background for this saying is a court of law where a
legal procedure is taking place. The plaintiff is the Lord, who
has a complaint against the defendant, Israel:

> Hear the word of the LORD, O people of Israel;
>   for the LORD has a complaint [*rib*]
> against the inhabitants of the land.
>   (author's translation)

(The Hebrew word *rib* here is best translated "complaint" or "charge"; see NEB and James Luther Mays, *Hosea*, p. 62). The form of this saying is a common one in the prophets, with an accusation (vv. 1–2) providing the reason for an announcement of future punishment (v. 3; cf. NEB, GNB; also the sayings in Amos 1 and 2).

1. Crime and Punishment

The complaint begins with three negative charges (v. 1*b*). First, there is no "faithfulness." The fundamental idea behind this word is rock-solid reliability; the word for the huge pillars which supported the doorway of the temple is from the same Hebrew root ("doorposts" in II Kings 18:16). When used in speaking of individuals, the word means people who can be trusted, such as the "able men . . . who are *trustworthy* and who hate a bribe" who assisted Moses (Exod. 18:21, author's italics). The word may also designate the simple truth of a person's word (I Kings 22:16). Such trustworthiness is rare in Hosea's days. In fact, the country is full of lying (v. 2).

Neither is there any "kindness" (Hebrew, *hesed*). When used about God, *hesed* refers to the Lord's *steadfast love* which endures forever (the refrains in Psalm 136). When used to refer to people, it may mean love/loyalty toward God (Hos. 6:4, which speaks of its absence) or love toward another person which expresses itself in concrete good deeds (II Chron. 32:32; Neh. 13:14). In Hosea's Israel, instead of *hesed* one finds killing, stealing, adultery, and murder upon murder. (On this word, see the comments on Hos. 6:6; also Katharine Doob Sakenfeld, *Faithfulness in Action*, especially chapter 5.)

The third negative complaint is a theological one, charging that there is "no knowledge of God in the land." This too is one of Hosea's favorite themes. There is a *cognitive* side to this knowledge, giving it the sense of knowledge *about* God. The duty of priests is to impart such knowledge, and the notion of torah or instruction (RSV, "law") is synonymous with it (4:6). This religious instruction would include teaching about God's saving and blessing acts in Israel's past and present (2:8; 11:3). Additionally there is a dimension of *commitment* in this notion, meaning the *acknowledgment* of God as the only God. This commitment is a sturdy loyalty to God which is synonymous with the notion of steadfast love *(hesed)* toward God (6:6). When the Lord is not acknowledged as God, then Baal takes the

Lord's place (5:4; 11:2–3). When Israel is rightly related to God, she "knows" or acknowledges no other (13:4) and in fact responds as a faithful wife responds to her husband (2:20). This commitment to God is given expression in the *covenant* between God and people. The word "covenant" occurs twice in Hosea, in each case alongside the notion of knowing or having knowledge of God (8:1–3; 6:6–7). In these texts, transgressing the covenant is set in contrast to "knowledge of God"; conversely, to keep the covenant is to know God.

This third complaint stands in the climactic position in the series, suggesting that it is of crucial importance. Israel, says the complaint, does not acknowledge God as Savior and as Giver of good gifts. When this fundamental theological relationship is not in order, then all other relationships in society also break down.

That breakdown is indicated in a series of seven positive charges which follow (v. 2). Each of these has to do with wrongdoing against the neighbor. The first two concern the misuse of words. "Swearing" probably refers to "cursing," that is, calling down evil upon someone in the name of the Lord (cf. I Sam. 14:24). The charge of lying is also made elsewhere in the Hosea book (7:3, RSV, "treachery"; 10:13; 11:12).

The next charges are all violations of the Ten Commandments: the country is full of killing or murder (Exod. 20:13; cf. Hos. 6:9), stealing (Exod. 20:15), and adultery (Exod. 20:14; cf. also Hos. 4:13–14; 7:4). These same crimes are also mentioned by Jeremiah in his temple sermon (Jer. 7:9).

"They break all bounds" apparently refers to acts of violence, and the series is completed by the charge of murder following upon murder. Coupled with the initial three negative complaints, this listing of ten charges constitutes a comprehensive decalogue describing Israel's failure against God and neighbor in both words and actions.

Because this saying fits the typical prophetic pattern of the word of judgment against the nation, the verb in the announcement of punishment should be translated in the future tense:

> Therefore the land shall be dried up,
> and all who live in it shall pine away,
> and with them the wild beasts and the birds of the air;
> even the fish shall be swept from the sea.
>
> (Hosea 4:3, NEB)

17

The charges against the people were failure to acknowledge God and also crimes against humanity. How then should this announced punishment, which threatens an ebbing of the forces of life in all areas of creation, including the animals, be understood? Isaiah 24:4–5 provides a close parallel, linking the drying and withering of the earth to the human breaking of covenant. The same wrongful human attitudes which lead toward covenant breaking, say both of these texts, are ultimately responsible for the withering and the pollution of the earth.

2. Sociology, Ecology, and Theology

The comprehensive nature of the complaint in verses 1 and 2 makes clear the people's total failure in their relationship to God and also to their neighbors. Put in other terms, they are charged with sociological and theological wrong. Themes announced here are picked up in the accusations which run through chapters 4—11. The effect of this comprehensive initial complaint is to charge that "All have turned aside, together they have gone wrong; no one does good, not even one" (Rom. 3:12).

The punishment which is announced in verse 3 is described in terms of an ecological crisis that threatens not only humans but all life on earth. In our own time when one hears of acid rain, the death of the forests, the pollution of the air, the lakes, and the rivers, this announcement has an alarmingly modern ring. The text contains an important insight: The roots of this ecological crisis are to be found in the same attitudes of arrogance, irreverence, selfishness, and greed which expressed themselves in the failure to acknowledge God or to care for the neighbor.

Finally, this chilling opening saying in Hosea 4—11 must be considered in its context in the Hosea book. Preceding it is the account of Hosea and his wife which develops the theme that the Lord keeps on loving his people no matter what (3:1). At the conclusion of chapters 4—11 are Hosea's words about God as parent and the people as rebelling child. Even though "they did not know" (11:3) that it was the Lord who had helped them, the Lord's love will never let them go (11:8).

18

Considered against the background of the total theological and sociological failure of the people, these expressions of the Lord's never failing grace are all the more amazing.

Hosea 4:4–10
The Failure of the Theologians

The complaint in 4:1–3 was comprehensive, addressed to the whole people of Israel. Now the focus narrows with words addressed to one person, a priest (vv. 4–6), followed by words which speak about the priests as a group (vv. 7–10). Since activities at the religious establishments appear to be in full swing, and because there is no mention of political difficulties, the saying is likely located during the last years of Jeroboam II. Its most probable setting would be one of Israel's religious centers, where priests were in the audience.

1. The Neglected Ministry (vv. 4–6)

One could imagine a member of the religious establishment, a priest, who felt himself personally attacked by Hosea's charges, especially concerning the lack of "knowledge of God" in the land, since imparting that knowledge was the priest's responsibility (4:6). The priest began to attack and accuse Hosea much as Amaziah had spoken against Amos (Amos 7:12–13). The prophet then wheeled on the priest, speaking in the Lord's name and saying,

> Yet let no one make a complaint,
>   and let no one reprove,
>   for my complaint is against you, O priest!
>   (author's translation)

Just as announcement of punishment followed complaint against the people in 4:1–3, so the prophet now announces the punishment due the priest: He will "stumble" (cf. 5:5) and the punishment will also extend to his family (mother and children, vv. 5, 6; cf. the punishment on Amaziah's family announced in Amos 7:17). Hosea also mentions "the prophet" here. He can speak in a positive way about the prophet as spokesman for the Lord (6:5; 12:10), as watchman (9:8), or as leader of Israel (12:13). The reference here is to a prophet as derelict in his duties as the priest was in his (cf. Micah 3:5–7).

The charge against the priest is made clear in verse 6. He

19

has neglected the torah (RSV, "law"), that is, instruction about God. In other words, the priest has failed to instruct "my people" as he should have. The "my people" reflects the Lord's concern for Israel, a concern also evident in the use of that expression in 2:23; 4:12; 6:11; and 11:7. This failure is serious enough to be responsible for the people's destruction.

The meaning of the "knowledge of God" has been discussed in connection with 4:1 above. Two points are made here: (1) This knowledge is something that can be taught. Parallel to the charge that "you have rejected knowledge" is "you have forgotten the teaching (torah; RSV, "law") of your God." We would say: You have neglected the religious instruction of those entrusted to your care. (2) Carrying out this instruction is the responsibility of the priest. In a later period, the Book of Malachi describes the priest's responsibility for religious instruction and traces this tradition back to Levi, the ideal priest (Mal. 2:5–7). The priests at that time too were guilty of failing in their teaching responsibilities (Mal. 2:8).

In sum, the priests, the theologians of Hosea's time, have failed in their task of religious instruction. They bear responsibility for the deplorable lack of knowledge about God in the land (4:1), and they must face God's judgment. The punishment is harsh and direct: "Since you have neglected the teaching ministry which goes with your office, I reject you! And since you have 'forgotten' to instruct your people in the faith, I will 'forget' your children," says the Lord.

2. The Disgrace of the Clergy (vv. 7–10)

Still speaking as the Lord's messenger, the prophet now speaks about the priests as a group (vv. 7–10). The group is large enough! The number of clergy needed to staff the multiplying shrines is increasing (8:11; 10:1). However, the more they increase, says the prophet, the more there are to sin against the Lord (4:7)!

This saying alternates between accusations and announcements of punishment. The first accusation: The priests "feed on the sin of my people." Religion, in other words, has become a means of support for a whole cadre of clergy and their families. The people sin and then come to the shrines with sacrifices; the priests feed their families by keeping portions of the animals brought for sacrifice (Lev. 6:24–30; cf. Bel and the Dragon, 10—15). Although the people love this convenient arrangement for dealing with sin (8:13), the Lord would prefer their *hesed,* their love/loyalty (6:6), and the Lord will not respond to this mechanical mockery of religion (5:6). A further accusation is made in verse 10: The priests have forsaken the Lord and have fallen into harlotry, the worship of another God. The punishment is that the clergy will lose the respect of their people and will be publicly disgraced (v. 7). The punishment is announced in the form of futility curses (cf. Deut. 28:30, 38–41): They will eat the meat gained from sacrifices, but will not be satisfied; they will enter into relationships with the prostitutes of Baal (4:14), but the land will not respond with fertility.

3. The Faithful Theologian

This text contains not so much a word for preaching and teaching as words for the preacher and teacher. Few parts of the Bible speak so directly to those entrusted with positions of theological leadership in the community of believers. Here is a call to theologians, to all who speak about God, to carry out their task with faithfulness and effectiveness. This task is described in terms of transmitting the "knowledge of God," which means "knowledge about God" or the "torah" about God. The three dimensions of this knowledge can help to bring into focus the theologian's responsibility:

1. *The covenantal dimension.* For Hosea, failure to "know" the Lord is synonymous with breaking covenant (8:1–2); conversely, knowing the Lord would be equal to living in the right covenant relationship. For preaching and teaching in the church, this covenantal dimension means that such instruction will take place within the context of the worshiping community. Those who have entered into the new covenant with Jesus Christ and who maintain that relationship through worship and participation in the covenant meal (I Cor. 11:23–26) also need to be instructed in the traditions of the people of God.

2. *The cognitive dimension.* This "knowledge about God" can be taught, forgotten, or rejected. There is a content to that knowledge, including information about the God who saves (11:1–3) and who blesses (2:8). For the Christian theologian, the content of this knowledge includes the biblical story of God's acts, culminating in the story of Jesus Christ, and also the story of God's action of creating and blessing. The story is then expanded with the account of the history of that faith in the church and explained with the insights of systematic theology.

21

3. *The commitment dimension.* Such instruction will never be only knowledge *about* God, only head knowledge. We have seen that for Hosea this knowledge can be synonymous with *hesed* or love/loyalty toward God and the neighbor (6:6). Thus all such instruction within the covenant community of believers will tell the old stories of God and his love for "my people," but will tell them in such a way that leads the community toward commitment to the Lord and care for one another.

This text speaks of the failure of the theologians. A model for the faithful theologian is found in the figure of Levi, whose teaching and life harmonized in a beautiful way, so that the Lord said of him:

> He feared me, he stood in awe of my name. True instruction was in his mouth, and no wrong was found on his lips. He walked with me in peace and uprightness, and he turned many from iniquity (Mal. 2:5–6).

Hosea 4:11–14
The Fascination of the Cults

When the Lord is not acknowledged as God (4:1), then some other god will take that place. The theme of this unit is the people's fascination with the fertility cult, specifically the cult of Baal; see also 2:8, 13, 16, 17; 9:10; 11:2; 13:1. The unit is set apart from its context with a proverbial saying at the beginning (v. 11) and at the end ("a people without understanding . . ."). The prosperous activity at the places of worship in Israel again fits well in the earliest period of Hosea's activity, when Jeroboam II was still king.

1. The Fertility Cult

This saying should be understood against the background of Baalism, the Canaanite fertility cult with which the Israelites had become involved. The word "Baal" is a title which means "lord, master," but it came to be used as the name for the most active of the male deities in the Canaanite cult. Various female deities are known from Canaanite sources: Astarte, Anath, Asherah (see the comments by Francis I. Andersen and David Noel Freedman in *Hosea:* THE ANCHOR BIBLE 24, 325). Mentioned most often in the Bible is Asherah; note, for example, I Kings 18:19 which refers to prophets of both Baal and Asherah. "Asherah" may also refer to a hand-made wooden object representing the goddess, which could stand next to Baal's altar (Judg. 6:25; II Kings 23:6) but which was absolutely prohibited in Israel (Deut. 16:21).

According to the mythology of Baalism, the god Baal dies annually, a death which is reflected in the drought of the summer or the frost of the winter, depending on the location. Then for a time Baal descends into the underworld. When he finds his mate there, they enter into a sexual relationship and as a result the rains come, the sun shines, the crops begin to grow, and nature is alive once again. The celebration of the union of Baal and his mate becomes a yearly event.

Worship of Baal took place on hills or mountain tops, the "high places" which are mentioned in Hosea (10:8) and especially in the books of Kings (I Kings 12:31; II Kings 17:9–10; 23:8, 13, 15). Cultic practices were based on the notion of imitative behavior. The participant in the cult entered into a sexual relationship with a cult prostitute, thus imitating the action of Baal and his mate and helping to bring this union about. In this way the action of the participant in the cult is ultimately understood as an aid to restoring fertility in nature (for further discussion of Baalism, see Bright, *History,* p. 118 and the works listed there; also the entries in *The Interpreter's Dictionary of the Bible* such as "Baal," "Fertility Cult," "Asherah," and Wolff's commentary on this passage in *Hosea*).

The Faithless Worship

Reading 4:11–14 against this background we discover three practices associated with the Canaanite fertility cult. Asking questions of a "thing of wood" apparently refers to making inquiries of the wooden Asherah which stood next to the altar (Judg. 6:25). The parallel statement, "and their staff gives them oracles," suggests the same practice, condemned for those who worship Yahweh. Second is the reference to sacrifices "on the tops of the mountains," that is, on the "high places." A portion of the sacrifice would be left for the worshipers to eat. We can imagine a time of socializing, with a group of participants picnicking together in the shade of the oak, poplar, and terebinth trees. The pericope concludes with a reference to cult prostitutes. Details are not provided. Apparently the men would offer

23

sacrifices with these women and then "go aside" to have sexual relations with them.

Because we do not have full information about the Baal cult, a number of details in this text are not clear. The major point, however, is stated without ambiguity in verse 12b. Like a grieving husband or wife who is unwilling to accuse a faithless spouse directly, it is as if the Lord is reluctant to place the blame for what has happened directly on the people. Israel had spoken of leaders who misled "my people" (Isa. 3:12). Micah had placed the blame on both leaders and prophets (Micah 3:1–5). Hosea places the blame on a "spirit of harlotry" which has led God's people to break with their God and pursue a life of infidelity.

3. Fascinating Religion

What was so fascinating about Baalism? Why were people so attracted to this cult? Several things may be inferred from this text. First of all, here was a religion that claimed to provide *immediate answers*. What was involved in "inquiring of a thing of wood" is not entirely clear, but it is clear that here was a mechanism for obtaining what must have been quick and simple answers to questions. Baalism seems also to have had an attractive *social dimension*. Verse 13 hints at people sacrificing and then joining one another for a picnic in the beauty and cool of the woods. One can imagine that this sacrificing, eating, and drinking wine (v. 11) all made for a friendly, welcoming atmosphere. The fertility cult also dealt with *human sexuality*. While we do not know the details of cult prostitution, we do know that here sex was sanctified and incorporated into religion, all of which no doubt added to the mystery and attraction of the Baal cult. Finally, Baalism had an obvious and immediate *relevance to daily life*. The Israelites were a rural farming people. They heard the claim that it was Baal who was responsible for the grain, the wine, the wool, and the flax which provided their food and clothing (Hos. 2:8–9). They must have thought it possible to combine the best of Yahwism with the best of this other fascinating religion which had its focus in the yearly rhythm of planting and harvesting so close to the lives of these people.

It may be precisely these sorts of attractions that make the variety of cults and religious options of today fascinating alternatives to mainstream biblical religion. They may provide ready answers, a welcoming social atmosphere, an approach to sexuality, and an immediate relevance. Hosea's approach to the threat of Baalism in his time can provide an instructive model. In a daring and creative way, Hosea picked up the very claims which Baalism was making and declared that it was actually Yahweh, not Baal, who was responsible for fertility and the products of nature! Israel, said the prophet, had been ignorant of her own religion. The problem was one of education, because "she did not know" (2:8). Hosea's example leads us to look at other resources in the Scriptures which may have been neglected or overlooked. Biblical faith has no "thing of wood" (nor even a super computer) which can provide quick and easy answers to religious questions, but those questions have always been welcome and have always been addressed. One has only to read through the psalms of lament (for example, Pss. 13:1–2; 22:11) to be reminded that the deepest questions may be put to God. The questions may remain questions; even Jesus did not receive an answer to the question raised on the cross (Matt. 27:46). The laments put these hard questions in the context of affirming trust, making requests of God, and even vowing to praise. What of the social attraction of the cults? Again, the church may have forgotten an important dimension of its own tradition. The history of the earliest Christians indicates that they were often together for worship, meals, and mutual support (Acts 2:43–47). It was said of them, "see how they love one another" (Tertullian; note also the greetings at the end of the letters in the N. T.). The warm and welcoming atmosphere of modern day cults can remind us of the biblical tradition of care for the stranger (Exod. 23:9; Deut. 10:19) and of the importance of the ministry of hospitality (Gen. 18; Heb. 13:2). Finally, cults both ancient and modern often deal explicitly with sex. The biblical resources for dealing with sexuality are many, varied, and mostly not used. What of the story of God's interest in matchmaking in Genesis 24? Or wisdom instruction to young people about marriage (Prov. 5:15–19; 19:14; 31:10–31)? Or the erotic love poetry of the Song of Solomon?

4. The Either/Or of Biblical Faith

Hosea declares that the benefits which his people credit to Baal are actually gifts of Yahweh. At the base of the problem was a matter of religious education: Israel did not know (2:8) because her teachers had not taught her (4:6). How was the relationship between the worship of Yahweh and the cult of

25

Baal to be understood? In the Israel which Hosea was addressing, worship of Yahweh was not so much rejected as compro-
mised. The mood was not religious warfare, but what was
considered to be a reasonable tolerance. There was room at the
place of worship, it was thought, for both Yahweh and Baal.

If anything is clear from Hosea and the biblical tradition as
a whole, it is that such a mix of Baalism and worship of Yahweh
is totally unacceptable. The issue is dealt with definitively in the
story of the contest on Mount Carmel, initiated by Elijah when
he had had enough of the Yahweh-Baal compromisers (I Kings
18:20–45). This is the position set forth in the first commandment (Exod. 20:3), in the Shema (Deut. 6:4–5), by Joshua (Josh.
24:15), the Jesus of the Fourth Gospel (John 14:6), and by the
apostles (Acts 4:12).

That which was true for Hosea's time remains a mark of
biblical faith: either the Lord or another god. One is either a
member of the community of believers or an adherent of some
other religion. When it comes to the claims of the Lord and the
claims of a cult or the cults, biblical religion allows no compro-
mises.

Hosea 6:4–6
Religion in Need of Reformation

One of the central themes of Hosea's message is expressed
in the sentence, "For I desire steadfast love and not sacrifice"
(Hos. 6:6; cf. 4:1). According to Matthew 9:13 and 12:7, Jesus
quoted it on two occasions. This saying stands at the pivotal
point of 5:8—7:16 (cf. Jeremias) and should first be heard in that
context.

1. The Context: Hosea 5:8—7:16

The materials in this section are addressed to Israel during the time of the Syro-Ephraimitic war. The broad outlines
of that conflict between Syria-Israel and Judah have been
sketched above (Hos. 1:1, 2; see also Bright, *History* pp. 269–
276). Hosea 5:18—7:16 falls into two parts, with 6:6 as the di-
viding point.

5:8—6:6. The call to sound the trumpet as an alarm in 5:8 signals a new beginning and abruptly changes the theme from clerical and cultic matters (4:4—5:7) to war. The Assyrians, it will be recalled, invaded Israel as a result of the appeal of Ahaz of Judah in 735 B.C. The alarm is to be sounded in Gibeah, Ramah, and Bethaven because the army of Judah is on the march, proceeding northward through these cities into Israelite territory, taking advantage of Israel's preoccupation with Assyria. Verse 9 indicates what will happen to Ephraim/Israel as a result of the invasions of Assyria, then of Judah. "I declare what is sure" provides an ending to this first unit.

The sayings in verses 10–12 and 13–14 both fall into the pattern of the word of judgment against the nation, with accusations (vv. 10a, 13) providing the reasons for announcements of punishment (vv. 10b, 14). Verse 14 found grim fulfillment in the fall of Samaria and deportation of the population in 722 B.C. Verse 15 in chapter 5 provides a transition, announcing that while God is withdrawing for a time, there is still hope for Israel, if they will only repent.

Chapter 6 verses 1–3 contain a song of penitence, picking up the medical imagery of 5:13 and expressing exactly what was called for in 5:15. Rather than going to "Dr. Assyria" for help (Wilhelm Rudolph, *Hosea*; see 5:13), the people of Israel are urged to seek help from the true Physician, the Lord. If they repent, their fortunes will be reversed, just as surely as the dawn comes each morning and the showers come each springtime!

In 6:4–6 we hear the Lord's response to this song. It is not an announcement that "Yes, I will come, as surely as the dawn or the rain," as might be expected. Rather, Hosea tells of the anguish and struggle in the heart of God. Because Israel's love and loyalty has been such a sometime thing, the Lord has had to punish them (6:4–5). Verse 6 then summarizes what the Lord would like from this people.

6:7—7:16. The mid-point of 5:8—7:16 has now been reached. All that went before led up to 6:6; that which follows looks back at it, furnishing the evidence for the charge that Israel's love/loyalty has been only temporary.

The verses in 6:7—7:2 provide a recital of the violence and corruption to be found throughout the land, all of which the Lord describes as dealing faithlessly "with me" (6:7). Chapter 7

27

verses 3–7 recall the series of assassinations after Jeroboam's death in 746 B.C. Hosea 7:8–12 again illustrates the people's lack of loyalty to God, referring to their seeking of security by flitting from one superpower to another, not realizing that their own days are numbered. Finally, the repeated "me" of 7:13–16 reaches back to the "me" of 6:7, again indicating that all of this sin is taken personally by the Lord. Rather than returning to their true God, the people have turned to Baal (v. 16) and are caught up in the rituals of that religion (v. 14).

2. Not "Religion" but Loyalty and Love (6:4–6)

This section at the heart of 5:8—7:16 begins with two questions: "What shall I do with you, O Ephraim? What shall I do with you, O Judah?" Elsewhere in the Old Testament similar questions are raised by a worried father (I Sam. 10:2) and by a weary leader (Exod. 17:4). Here it is the Lord who is worried and wearied. These are questions of one who no longer knows which way to turn. Hosea allows us to understand the frustration and the perplexity in the heart of God as does no other prophet (see also 4:16; 7:13; 11:8; 13:14).

What led to this frustration? The charge is clear: "Your love [*hesed*] is like a morning cloud, like the dew that goes early away" (v. 4). The people were confident that the Lord would come to them just as surely as the coming of the dawn or the spring rain (6:3). Their own love for the Lord, in contrast, is as short-lived as the morning mist or the dew (see also 13:3).

The sense of "love" (v. 4) and "steadfast love" (v. 6), both translations of *hesed,* can be sharpened by attention to the use of the word in a nontheological context: David and Jonathan made a covenant with one another, sealing their friendship (I Sam. 18:1–3). Some time later, Jonathan asked David to remember him and his family, no matter what the future might bring, saying, "If I am still alive, show me the loyal love [*hesed*] of the LORD . . . and do not cut off your loyalty [*hesed*] from my house for ever" (I Sam. 20:14–15). The meaning of the word is thus love, with a strong element of loyalty, between two parties who have made a formal pledge to one another through a covenant (see also I Sam. 20:8). *Hesed* might be called covenant-love. It is also part of the vocabulary for describing the loyal love between two parties in a marriage (Jer. 2:2, "devotion"; and Hos. 2:19, "steadfast love").

In the Book of Hosea, *hesed* may refer to God's love for the people (2:19). It may also refer to the people's love toward the neighbor (4:1). Here in verses 4 and 6 it refers to the people's loyal love to God, or more accurately to the lack of it. Though the people believe that they can fulfill their obligations toward the deity through "religion" which consists of sacrifices and burnt offerings, what the Lord really wants is their love and their loyalty (on *hesed* see Sakenfeld, *Faithfulness*).

Samuel had once said, "Behold, to obey is better than sacrifice, and to hearken than the fat of rams" (I Sam. 15:22; see also Prov. 21:3). Here, with Hosea, it is not a matter of one option being "better than" another. Two completely different ways are set forth: either the one or the other (Jeremias), either the way of sacrifices and offerings or the way of loyalty and love and acknowledgment of God as God.

3. Rediscovering True Religion

The contrast which comes to expression in Hosea 6:6 is between two fundamentally different notions of religion. The one thinks in terms of discharging religious obligations through the machinery of sacrifice and offering; the other speaks of loyal love and of acknowledging God as God.

This must have been an important issue at the time of Hosea, since all four of the prophets of the eighth century address it. Amos spoke in terms of a dichotomy between religion and life, announcing the Lord's rejection of the people's "religious" activities and calling for the establishment of justice and righteousness in everyday living (Amos 5:21–24). Isaiah delivered a similar critique of the religion/life split, concluding with a call to get religion out of the sanctuaries and into the streets by taking up the cause of the powerless (Isa. 1:10–17). The same dichotomy is the concern of Micah 6:6–8, which contrasts a religion eager to bring some *thing* to God with one which calls for the total dedication of some *one* (Mays, *Micah*, p. 136). Hosea expresses the contrast between these two kinds of religion in his own vocabulary, calling for *hesed* and knowledge of God rather than hollow activities in the cult.

It should be noted that none of these prophets ever advocates doing away with sacrifices and offerings. None calls for the abolishment of the cult. Rather, all of them call for a reformation, a rediscovery of a religion which recalls God's acts of blessing and delivering (Hos. 2:8; 11:1; Amos 2:9–11; 3:1; Micah 6:4) and then articulates the response expected from a people who have experienced the gracious acts of God.

We have noted that the New Testament quotes Hosea 6:6 in two contexts, translating *hesed* as "mercy." In the first, the Pharisees are critical of the company Jesus has been keeping. Jesus suggests that his critics have forgotten what religion is all about. Healing the sick is more important than holding to any rules about social associations. Jesus says to his critics, "Those who are well have no need of a physician, but those who are sick. Go and learn what this means. 'I desire mercy, and not sacrifice' " (Matt. 9:12–13). In the second context, the Pharisees are critical when they see Jesus and his followers plucking grain on the sabbath to satisfy their hunger. After citing two Old Testament examples, Jesus says, "And if you had known what this means, 'I desire mercy and not sacrifice,' you would not have condemned the guiltless" (Matt 12:7). Here Jesus says that satisfying the hunger of concrete human beings is of more importance than satisfying regulations about the sabbath.

In the Scriptures, this text thus functions in the context of two misunderstandings of religion. In the one, religion is understood as the carrying out of certain cultic actions. In the other, religion is thought to consist of the fulfillment of legal regulations. The prophets do not advocate doing away with the machinery of the cult, and Jesus does not call for abolishing the law. Instead both the prophets and Jesus call for reform, for getting a derailed religion back on the track.

When religion becomes preoccupied with the niceties of liturgy, the nuances of language, the novelties of music, art, and architecture, but forgets the neighbor, then religion has been reduced to cultic correctness; and the word, "I desire steadfast love and not sacrifice" needs to be heard. Or when religion is conceived only in terms of church attendance, general decency, and doing what is expected, then religion may have become reduced to the satisfying of regulations, and that word from Jesus needs to be heard, "Go and learn what this means. . . ."

True religion has that rich word *hesed* at its center, recalling God's steadfast love (Ps. 136) and mercy (Titus 3:5–7) and then calling for lives which respond to that love with loyal devotion to God and loving service to the neighbor.

Hosea 9:1–9
Watchman or Yes-man?

The imperative of 9:1 signals a new unit which ends with 9:9, set off from its context as words from the prophet in the midst of words from the Lord. This section offers a rare picture of prophetic preaching together with the audience's reaction to that preaching, and also provides an insight into the prophet's understanding of his role as *watchman*. The piece fits well into the time of Hoshea, after the first Assyrian onslaught and the deportation of 733 (9:7 seems to suggest this) but before the final end in 722 (see on Hosea 1:1, part 2).

1. The Cry of the Watchman (9:1–9)

Hosea 9:1–9 falls into two parts. Underlying verses 1–6 are the elements of the prophetic word of judgment with the accusation in verse 1*b* and the announcement of punishment in verses 2–6. Verses 7–9 present the people's reaction to what the prophet has said. The setting is a festival, where there would be rejoicing and exaltation (v. 1). The words about the harvest suggest the fall harvest festival, one of the three major ones in Israel (Deut. 16; II Chron. 8:13).

The feast of *sukkoth* ("booths" or "tabernacles," II Chron. 8:13) was the biggest of ancient Israel's three festivals. Its seven day duration was marked by rejoicing, celebrating the results of the farmer's work during the past year, and anticipating further blessings in the future (Deut. 16:13–15). This festival became known simply as the "feast of the LORD" (Hos. 9:5; Lev. 23:39). It took its name from the custom of camping out in structures called *sukkoth* or "booths" to recall how the Israelites had to live while they were in the wilderness (Neh. 8:13–16). The festival was celebrated in New Testament times (John 7:2) and remains a favorite of Jews today, who will build a *sukkah* out on a New York city fire escape if that is the only available place. Biblical descriptions of the festival tell of joy and dancing (Lev. 23:40; Deut. 16:14–15; Judg. 21:21). We can imagine how families looked forward to the week-long celebra-

31

tion; in anticipation of such events Psalm 122 says, "I was glad when they said to me, 'Let us go to the house of the LORD!'"

The call to "Be glad and rejoice" or to "rejoice and exult" (Joel 2:21, 23; Zeph. 3:14) would have been very much in keeping with the mood of *sukkoth*. Against this background, the opening words of Hosea's speech could hardly be more shocking. He began, "Rejoice not, O Israel! Exult not. . . ."

The prophet has caught the attention of his hearers and makes his charge immediately: "You have played the harlot, forsaking your God. . . ." Once again, Hosea picks up the imagery introduced in chapters 1—3. His accusation is that Israel has been acting like a faithless wife, entering into affairs with other lovers.

The shocking speech continues with a listing of the punishment that will come upon the people. The grain and the wine will fall. The bounty of the harvest will become the booty of the invading enemy (May's, *Hosea,* p. 126). Then comes the harshest word: The people will no longer live in the "land of the LORD" but will "return to Egypt," which may be a figurative return to bondage or a literal flight to Egypt as refugees. The reference to Assyria, however, is not figurative. If this speech was delivered after 733 B.C., the people had already experienced the pains of one deportation. They could look forward to another, says the prophet, and the events of 722 would confirm his words.

The announcements of punishment continue in 9:4–6. When these people have been taken away from their land, there will be no more pilgrimages to the temple. There will be nowhere to go on the festival days. The prophet's speech comes to an end with the chilling announcement that the people can expect to die in a foreign land, while their own land will revert to nothing but thorns and weeds.

Now, in verses 7–9, we hear how these celebrating Israelites received the prophet's words. The prophet quotes what they are saying about him: "The prophet is a fool, the man of the spirit is mad." The Hebrew word is *meshugga,* still used in Yiddish with the sense, "crazy"; Jeremias translates, *Ein Dummkopf.* According to Hosea, elements of the Lord's punishment have already been experienced, probably referring to the Assyrian invasion of 733 (v. 7a). Then he indicates his own understanding of his role: "The prophet is the watchman of Ephraim." A watchman should be appreciated and held in respect by those over whom he keeps watch. These people despise Hosea, though, trying to catch him like one would catch a wild animal (v. 8)! They are as corrupt, says Hosea, as the people were at Gibeah, site of a gang-rape and murder which was long remembered (Judg. 19—21). The watchman's final message from the Lord is unambiguous: "he will remember their iniquity, he will punish their sins."

2. The Watchman

Here for the first time a prophet describes himself as a "watchman." What does this picture tell us about the prophet's role? The task of the watchman was to keep on the lookout for whatever was happening, especially for danger. He might be situated on a high place like the roof over the city gate (II Sam. 18:24–27) or on a special watch tower (II Kings 9:17–20). Watchmen might be posted to keep lookout day and night (Isa. 21:8) and, of course, had to remain alert (cf. Isa. 56:10). The yearning for morning after the long, cold night became proverbial (Ps. 130:6).

Ezekiel 33:1–7 provides a good picture of the prophet as watchman. When danger comes, the task of the watchman is to sound the alarm. If he does not do so, then he has failed in his task. If the alarm is sounded and the people pay no attention, then they themselves are responsible for what happens to them. Ezekiel's task, says the Lord, is to sound the alarm (Ezek. 33:7). The whole succession of prophets can also be called watchmen, rejected by those they tried to warn (Jer. 6:17).

In his book *Night*, Elie Wiesel tells about a man named Moche who tried to warn the Jews in an eastern European village about the death camps operated by the Nazis. The people paid no attention, saying, "Poor fellow. He's gone mad" (p. 16). The reaction was the same as that given to Hosea: "The prophet is a fool, the man of spirit is mad." Yet faithful to his task as the Lord's watchman, Hosea stayed at his post and sounded the alarm.

Another biblical model for the prophet stands in sharp contrast to that of the watchman. This is the prophet as sycophant, as flatterer, aye-sayer, as yes-man. The classic portrayal is the account of Micaiah the son of Imlah versus the four hundred yes-men of Ahab in I Kings 22. Micalah at first poses as such a sycophant (v. 15*b*) but then delivers the authentic message from the Lord. Later on, Micah encountered such "prophets" whose real source of inspiration was the size of their income (Micah 3:5), and Jeremiah tells of his conflict with them (Jer. 23:16–22). Jesus warned his disciples against becoming yes-sayers, seeking to avoid conflict at any cost. He said, "Woe to you, when all men speak well of you, for so their fathers did to the false prophets" (Luke 6:26).

Thus we discover two models for going about the prophetic task: the watchman and the yes-man. This text invites those who preach to ask themselves: Would anyone call me "me-shugga" because of a sermon preached or a position taken? Or have my words become only smooth and soothing words, designed to avoid conflict at any cost and to evoke kind reactions at the doorway? Hosea places before us the figure of the faithful watchman, who sounds the alarm when it needs to be sounded, no matter what.

In his essay, "Costly Grace," Dietrich Bonhoeffer once wrote, "We baptized, confirmed, and absolved a whole nation without asking awkward questions, or insisting on strict conditions. . . . We poured forth unending streams of grace . . ." (*The Cost of Discipleship*, p. 47). Hosea could preach of God's grace like no other, but he also knew that this was not the only task of the one who speaks for God. That person is also a watchman and, when the time is right, a watchman must sound the alarm.

Hosea 10:1–2
Where Is the Heart?
Reflections on Churchbuilding

The natural reaction of those who have experienced the reality of God in a special way is to want to build a place for worship. After his dream in which he saw a ladder reaching to heaven, Jacob set up a stone monument, saying "This stone, which I have set up for a pillar, shall be God's house . . ." (Gen. 28:22). When he had a bit of breathing space after his conquests, a grateful David wanted to build a house for the Lord (II Sam. 7:1–2). When Peter, James, and John witnessed the appearance of Elijah and Moses on the mountain, Peter's reaction was to want to build something (Mark 9:1–8).

34

This desire to build a place for worship is affirmed in the Bible. Solomon's building plans are understood as a fulfillment of the prophetic word to David (I Kings 5:5). After the exile, Haggai proclaimed that the well-being of the community was dependent upon getting a place of worship built (Hag. 1:9).

Hosea 10:1–2 looks back at a time of prosperity in Israel, when a good number of places of worship were built. Now, says the prophet, the Lord will see to it that these buildings are destroyed. Why should this be? The prophet's answer to this question invites reflection on the building of places of worship.

The chapter divides into two parts, with verses 1–8 speaking about the Lord in the third person and 9–15 offering words of the Lord in first-person speech. The piece as a whole seems to reflect the urgency of Israel's final years, under the administration of Hoshea (732–721 B.C.).

1. Building Programs (10:1–8)

"Israel is a luxuriant vine," the saying begins. Once again, the prophet uses an image to describe the people (see on 1:1, part 1). The image refers to Israel in her recent prosperous past, most likely in the years under Jeroboam II; Hosea uses the same imagery to refer to Israel's future in 14:7. The vine picture is also used in Psalm 80:8–16 and in Isaiah 5:1–7 and Jeremiah 2:21.

The altars and pillars were the furniture for worship at the shrines in the Northern Kingdom. In the earliest days of Israel, the altar might be of earth or of field stones which had not been hewn (Exod. 20:24–26). In Solomon's temple the altar was an elaborate structure built of cedar wood and overlaid with gold (I Kings 6:20, 22). The pillar could refer to a monument commemorating a person (II Sam. 18:18) or recalling an event (Gen. 28:18); such a structure could also stand beside the altar. Moses had erected twelve such pillars, symbolic of the twelve tribes (Exod. 24:4).

This saying begins by looking back at the good old days. Those were the times when the line graphing the gross national product was always ascending! The economy was solid, the shekel good. Those professionally involved in religion could draw their graphs too, pointing to the increase in numbers of places of worship and to the renovation and the beautification of existing shrines, no doubt of great historical interest.

The altars and the pillars were not in themselves wrong, at

35

least at this time. A century later, because of their close association with Baalism, pillars were forbidden altogether (Deut.
16:22). Nor was there any wrong in the building of new places
of worship and the renovating of the old; such activity could be
a mark of genuine piety. We have noted above that in good
times believing people have always wanted to express their
gratitude to God by building a suitable place for worship. What
then was the problem?

The prophet's answer comes in verse 2. "Their heart is
false!" The Hebrew word translated as "false" has the basic
sense, "smooth" or "slippery," like a slippery place where one
could easily fall (Ps. 73:18). It also denotes words which are
"slippery," that is, flattering words, in the expression translated "flattering lips" (Ps. 12:3) or tongue (Ps. 5:9) or palate
(Prov. 5:3, RSV footnote). The speech of a harlot trying to en-
tice a young man is "smooth" (Prov. 7:21), as is the talk of a
person betraying his friends (Ps. 55:21). The problem as diagnosed here is deeper than one involving the lips or the tongue
or speech; this slipperiness goes to the core of human con-
sciousness, to the heart.

The Lord, says the prophet, does not wish to have a place
where worship is a mouthing of words and a going through the
motions, where there is an attempt to "smooth-talk" God. The
people of Israel must have believed that religion was an important component in their prosperity. Building more sanctuaries,
therefore, made good sense; this was "simply turning part of the
profit back into the business" (Mays, *Hosea*, p. 139).

Such superficial deception will not work, though, for God
will not be mocked. The Lord will see to it that these newly
built sanctuaries and recently renovated shrines will be destroyed by the armies of the invading Assyrians.

The theme of cultic corruption continues in verses 5 and 6.
The citizens of Samaria are much concerned for the welfare of
the golden calf at Bethel; Hosea announces that the whole thing
will be carried off to Assyria as booty. Verses 3 and 4 are best
understood as words of the people, acknowledging that their
king has been taken away (the capture of Hoshea, II Kings 17:4)
because they do not fear the Lord (cf. II Kings 17:7–41). Verse
4 hints at the failures of kings who talk much but do not honor
the treaties they make. The themes of both king and cult are
picked up in the announcement of punishment which concludes the unit in verses 7 and 8.

36

2. Reflections on Churchbuilding

Amos and Isaiah had denounced the worship offered by a people who had forgotten the powerless in their midst (Amos 5:21–24; Isa. 1:10–17). The Book of Micah declares that the Lord will not be placated by sacrifices in lieu of justice and kindness (6:6–8). Hosea's critique of the building and renovation of places of worship is of a piece with this eighth-century prophetic criticism of religion. At issue is not architecture, but rather the attitude of those assembled in these multiplying places of worship. These impressive projects are rejected because the hearts of those engineering them beat more in rhythm with Baal than with the Lord. To use Hosea's imagery, the worship carried on in these places is similar to a wife making love to her husband, but all the while thinking of another lover to whom she owes her real loyalty. The words are the words of love, but the heart is false. Jesus said it, quoting Isaiah: "This people honors me with their lips, but their heart is far from me" (Matt. 15:8; cf. Isa. 29:13).

The people here are described as a "luxuriant vine." Jesus used the same imagery, and in so doing set forth two essentials for churchbuilding, in the sense of building up the church as the people of God. First, it is essential that church members remain in a living relationship with the Lord: "I am the vine, you are the branches . . . apart from me you can do nothing" (John 15:5). Second, God's people are called to love and care for one another: "By this my Father is glorified, that you bear much fruit, and so prove to be my disciples . . . love one another as I have loved you" (John 15:8, 12). Lives so nourished by the Lord and invigorated by acts of love to the neighbor will be lives filled with joy (John 15:11).

These words of the prophet and the evangelist have something to say about building places of worship. Hosea's words are a reminder that it is possible that God does not endorse our efforts. If the heart of the builders is false, then it may be that all of the bustling business of building is not pleasing to God at all. Luther put the issue with clarity:

> We have been going to St James, to Aachen, to Rome, to Jerusalem, have built churches, paid masses, and withal have forgotten our neighbor; this now is the wrong side up. The Lord, however, here says, Go and take the money with which you were about to build a church and give it to your neighbor. Look

> to your neighbor how you may serve him. It is not a matter of moment to God if you never build Him a church, as long as you are of service to your neighbor.

In another context,

> [God says] "If you want to love and serve me, do it through your neighbor, he needs your help, I don't" (George Forell, *Faith Active in Love,* pp. 110–111).

The words in John 15 provide a guide for keeping priorities straight and a pattern for building the church whose "one foundation is Jesus Christ her Lord." "Abide in me, and I in you. . . . Love one another as I have loved you. . . . These things I have spoken to you, that my joy may be in you, and that your joy may be full."

Hosea 11:1–11
The Loving Parent

With the imagery of the husband and wife, chapters 1—3 of the Hosea book presented an unforgettable picture of God's forgiving love. Now, after a long series of accusations and announcements of punishment in chapters 4—10, this central section of the book concludes by developing an equally memorable picture of God's nurturing love, with the image of God the parent and the people as child and children.

1. The "Story" of Hosea 11:1–11

The central section of the Book of Hosea, which was introduced in 4:1 with the formula, "Hear the word of the LORD . . . ," now concludes with the "says the LORD" formula in verse 11. In the Hebrew Bible, the chapter ends here (see RSV footnote). This chapter declaring the Lord's love for his people brings 4—11 to an end on a positive note, as does chapter 3 for 1—3 and 14:4–9 for 12—14.

The situation addressed assumes that some Israelites are already in Assyria as captives (v. 11), probably referring to the 733 B.C. deportation (II Kings 15:29–31; see on Hosea 1:1, part 2). The cities of Israel have not yet been destroyed but will be shortly (v. 6), and the people will be taken captive (vv. 5–6).

38

Thus the piece fits well into the middle years of Hoshea (732–722), perhaps just after the king had made his ill-fated alliance with Egypt (II Kings 17:4).

Chapter 11 moves through four parts:

The Past: Out of Egypt (vv. 1–4). Here the parent/child imagery is introduced. The emphasis is on all that the parent has done for the child. "I" statements dominate: I loved, I called, I taught to walk, I healed. Yet the child is ungrateful, not acknowledging the parent's care (recall the "she didn't know" of 2:8) and in fact rebelling (v. 2).

Later on, God will be described as the "Holy One" with emphasis on God's otherness or transcendence (v. 9). But here the emphasis is on the Lord's condescension. God is like a parent patiently teaching a child to walk. The Revised Standard Version translation of verse 4 suggests a shift of imagery, to a farmer caring for an animal. With a slight alteration in the text, the parent/child image may be retained: "I was to them like those who lift a baby to their cheeks" (Mays, *Hosea*, p. 150). In any case, this section ends with a picture of the Lord who "bends down" to care for his own.

The Immediate Future: Back to "Egypt" (vv. 5–7). Now the focus shifts from God to the people and "they" verbs dominate. The tone is that of accusation (vv. 5c, 7a) and announcement of punishment (vv. 5ab, 6, 7b). The expression "return to Egypt" appears to have a double meaning here. As a result of the Assyrian conquests of 733 B.C. and the deportation of a portion of the people, some citizens of Israel no doubt did flee to Egypt as refugees. The same thing would happen in 722 B.C. In the context of the whole chapter, however, "Egypt" is also a symbol for bondage. Just as the people had once been in Egypt in the time of Moses (referring to v. 1), so they would experience another captivity, this time in Assyria. Even though the section consists of accusation and announcement of punishment, one can also detect a note of hope: The rebels are still "my people" (cf. 4:6, 12), an indication that while the relationship to God has been strained, it has not been broken.

The Present: The Loving Parent (vv. 8–9). Once again, the "I" of the Lord dominates. The Lord agonizes over the coming punishment, just as a parent agonizes over the rebellion of a beloved child, a rebellion which causes the child to suffer. Admah and Zeboiim were cities destroyed with Sodom and Gomorrah (Gen. 19). The suffering of the child causes the love

39

of the parent to become all the more intense, and the Lord resolves that such a punishment will never take place again. The reason for this promise is in the very nature of God: "for I am God and not man, the Holy One in your midst." This self description of God catches both the dimensions of otherness ("holy") as well as condescension ("in your midst"; cf. the "bent down" of v. 4).

The Distant Future: Home from "Egypt" (vv. 10–11). The story which began by recalling the deliverance of a "son" from Egypt now returns to that theme with the promise that the Lord's "sons" will be delivered from another bondage in the future. Thus the story comes to its end: out of Egypt, back into "Egypt" because of rebellion; then out of "Egypt," back home again because of the Lord's compassion.

2. God the Parent

When Hosea spoke about God and people, he drew upon his own stormy marital experiences with his wife Gomer (Hosea 1—3). Here he uses the imagery of a parent and a child or a parent and children (11:10). What would lead him to use this imagery? We know that Hosea had two sons and a daughter. If the children were born at the earliest part of his prophetic work, and if this material comes from the middle years of King Hoshea or around 727 B.C., this would mean that Hosea's children were just beyond their teen-age years. It would seem reasonable to assume that for a time the prophet functioned as a single parent. In any case, parenting seems to have made an impression on Hosea; 11:3–4 recalls the time when the children were learning to walk. Did Hosea experience rebellion or ingratitude from his children? Would such experiences have suggested the imagery of verses 2 or 3? If Hosea's experience with Gomer provided the ingredients for the husband/wife imagery, it is not unreasonable to suggest that the imagery here is drawn from experiences with the prophet's own children.

The Risks of Parenting: The Beginnings. The piece begins by recalling the earliest days in the history between the Lord and people, the time of the Exodus and the wandering in the wilderness. The prophet had hinted earlier that this was the best time in their relationship (2:15). Now God's dealings with the infant Israel are compared to the experiences of a parent watching a toddler take her first steps. When she falls, her

40

father or mother picks her up and comforts her. So it was at the beginning, when the Lord put the young nation back on its feet time and again. Bringing children into the world and raising them is always a risk. How will that child turn out? And what will become of this nation Israel?

The Pains of Parenting: The Rebellion. We have suggested that Hosea may have experienced the rebellion of a child. Perhaps that child whom he had loved, whom he had taught to walk, whom he had picked up time and again had turned against him! In such terms the prophet describes the behavior of Israel. They rebelled, transferring their loyalties to Baal, and they forgot what the Lord had done for them (vv. 2–3).

God's love is a "tough love" which knows that there is a time in the parent/child relationship for punishment. Thus the prophet announces a new captivity of the kind once experienced in Egypt (vv. 5–7).

Parents are familiar with the saying, "This hurts me more than it hurts you," describing the feelings of a father or mother when a child must be disciplined. This is what God the Parent is saying in verse 8. Here is a rare insight into the suffering heart of God (on this theme see Terence E. Fretheim, *The Suffering of God*). The Lord's compassion expresses itself in the announcement that punishment will not be the final stage in the Lord's dealing with his people.

The declaration, "I am God and not man, the Holy One in your midst," articulates two dimensions of the reality of God. God is the "Holy One." The word "holy" has the sense "separate, other," stressing the "wholly other" or the transcendent dimension of God. This aspect is given dramatic expression in the vision of Isaiah, when the prophet sees the Lord high and lifted up and hears the angels singing "Holy, holy, holy" (Isa. 6). At the same time, the Lord is the Holy One "in your midst." The transcendent God is also the God who condescends to be with God's people.

The theme of God's condescension also comes to expression in the statement about the Lord's "bending down" in verse 4. The same vocabulary occurs often in the psalms, in the form of a prayer to God to "incline thy ear" (Pss. 17:6; 31:2; 71:2; 86:1; 88:2; 102:2) or in a report that the Lord has responded to prayer by "inclining" to the one who has prayed (Pss. 40:1; 116:2). In Psalm 113, God's transcendence (vv. 1–5) and condescension

41

(vv. 6–9) provide the reasons for praising God. The condescending of the Holy One receives its final expression in the coming of God in Jesus Christ (for example, Phil. 2:1–11).

The Joys of Parenting: The Homecoming. The final section of Hosea 11 and of this major segment of the book describes a homecoming, when God's children will come home from all over the world (vv. 10–11).

Finally, the movement of this chapter as a whole suggests comparison with the parable of the Prodigal Son or, as Helmut Thielicke has named it, the Waiting Father. That father knew the risks of parenting, as he allowed his son to take what he had coming to him and set off on his own. He must have known the pain of parenting as well; we can imagine him hearing reports about his son who was squandering his inheritance and wasting his time and money with prostitutes (Luke 15). But that father's love would not let the rebelling son go. When he saw him in the distance one day, he ran down the road to meet him, embraced him, and threw a homecoming party. So it is with God, says the parable, when God's rebelling children come home.

3. A Note on God as Parent

While Israel is clearly identified as the "son" here (11:1), God may be understood either as Father or as Mother. Thus we have referred to the imagery here as parent/child or parent/son.

When the Bible speaks of God as parent, the image used most often is that of God as Father. Explicit naming of God as Father is somewhat rare in the Old Testament, occurring nine times (Deut. 32:6; Jer. 3:4, 19; 31:9; Isa. 63:16 twice; 64:8; Mal. 1:6; 2:10). In passages like Exodus 4:22 or Isaiah 1:2–3 the parent/child imagery is present, though God is not named "Father." The Apocrypha calls God "Father" in Sirach 23:1, 4 and Tobit 13:4 (all prayers) as well as in the Wisdom of Solomon 14:3 and III Maccabees 5:7. The "Father" picture in the New Testament is a frequent one, including the Lord's Prayer (Matt. 6:9 and parallels), references in the Sermon on the Mount (Matt. 5:45; 6:1, 6, 14, 15, 26, 32; 7:11), Paul's letters (Rom. 8:14–17; Gal. 4:6), plus many more.

The Bible uses feminine images for God as well. In Psalm 131, God is compared to a mother quieting a child at her breast. The same image is found in Isaiah 49:15 and in Isaiah 66:13. Psalm 123 pictures the people as a maid, God as a mistress. The

42

New Testament can picture God as a woman searching for a lost coin (Luke 15:8–10); Jesus compares himself to a hen trying to gather her chicks (Matt. 23:37).

Masculine imagery for God dominates in the Bible, reflecting the culture out of which the biblical writings have come. The important thing to remember is that God is neither male nor female, but a living Person who transcends such categories. The fact that both masculine and feminine images are found in the Bible suggests that we ought to be imaginative in developing our own theological language in both directions. In so doing, we shall be following in the creative tradition of Hosea himself (see on Hos. 1:1, part 1).

Hosea 12:2–6
God Is Not Finished Yet!

The third major part of the Hosea book runs from 11:12 through chapter 14. This final section is again arranged according to the doom-hope pattern, with chapters 12 and 13 charging Israel with deceit and announcing the nation's death and 14 sounding a hopeful note (see Introduction). Chronologically, all of these materials reflect the situation of Hoshea, Israel's last king.

The sentence in 11:12 sounds the theme for 11:12—12:14: "Ephraim has encompassed me with lies, and the house of Israel with deceit." The theme is developed in four parts: 12:1 makes the charge against Israel/Ephraim, first in metaphorical terms (v. 1*a*) and then with a literal reference to Hoshea's futile foreign policy (II Kings 17:3–4). Since the formulation, "The Lord has an indictment [*rib*] against Judah," (12:2) is an exact parallel to 4:1, the editor is introducing the third major part of the book in a manner which matches the second. Hosea 12:2–6 retells the old story of Jacob and applies it to the new time of Hosea. Verses 7–8 support the theme of the chapter with an accusation grounding an announcement of punishment in verse 9. The final saying concludes with an accusation (v. 14*a*) and announcement of punishment (v. 14*b*).

There are hints that this chapter was updated to address an audience in Judah after Israel had fallen in 722 B.C. The state-

43

ment about Judah in 11:12b sounds like a comment made with a later Judean audience in mind. Since Hosea spoke only to Israel, so far as we know, it also seems reasonable to suggest that "Judah" of 12:2 replaces what was originally "Israel."

1. An Old Story for a New Time

Once again, a major section of the book begins with the announcement that the Lord has a legal complaint against his people (cf. 4:1). Verses 3–6 spell out the charge by recalling three incidents from the life of Jacob, the ancestor of the people of both Northern and Southern Kingdoms. In retelling these stories, the prophet is saying to his contemporaries, "Jacob's story is your story too. You are chips off the old block" (cf. Mays, *Hosea*, p. 162).

The first incident (v. 3) is recalled in the statement, "In the womb he took his brother by the heel. . . ." The reference is to Genesis 25:19–26, which tells about Rebekah giving birth to twins. Esau was the first to emerge, but as he came forth his brother Jacob was holding onto Esau's heel. The prophet uses a bit of homiletic imagination to suggest that even while he was still in the womb Jacob was trying to gain advantage over another. He was fighting with his brother, trying to be the first born and thus to gain the firstborn's privileges. The prophet makes the first charge with this old story: From the earliest beginnings, this people Jacob/Israel has been self-centered and contentious.

The second incident, reported in more length (vv. 3b–4a), recalls what happened to Jacob on the banks of the Jabbok river as recorded in Genesis 32. The stranger with whom Jacob wrestled turned out to be a messenger from God, an angel. As Hosea recalls the wrestling match and Jacob's request for a blessing, he declares that Jacob sought the angel's favor. The reference to weeping is absent in Genesis and appears to be a homiletical embellishment. The charge is once again clear: In his maturity, Jacob went so far as to get into a fight with an angel!

The third incident, recalling Genesis 28:10–17, is related at greatest length (vv. 4b–6). Chronologically, Jacob's dream at Bethel about the ladder took place earlier than the bout with the angel. As Hosea recalls this incident, he names no specific charges against Jacob. However, Jacob was a fugitive at this time, on the run from Esau. The prophet is making the point that this ancestor of the people whom he was addressing had a

44

history of getting into trouble with those around him and in this instance even had to run for his life.

Then Hosea reports what God said to Jacob at Bethel, and in paraphrasing these words, tailors the story to his own audience. Genesis says that the Lord promised Jacob, "Behold, I am with you and will keep you wherever you go, and will bring you back to this land . . . " (Gen. 28:15). Hosea says that at this point the Lord said to Jacob, "As for you, by the help of your God, you will return" (author's translation, the Hebrew is a future tense here, not an imperative as the RSV translates). The exhortations made to Jacob are now addressed to Hosea's audience: "Hold fast to love and justice, and wait continually for your God."

In this way the prophet uses this old story as the "text" for the sermon which he addresses to his own contemporaries. Hosea applies the Jacob story with considerable freedom, rearranging the order of events to suit his homiletical purposes. The incident at Bethel comes last because Bethel was a central holy place for the people in Hosea's day, and the prophet wanted these words of the Lord to be at the sermon's climax. He uses all three incidents to illustrate Jacob's deceit and sinfulness, even though in Genesis, Jacob is never criticized for what he has done. When Jacob betters Esau, it is understood as the fulfillment of a word from the Lord (Gen. 25:23). His tenacity in seeking a blessing from the angel was affirmed when the name "Israel," understood as "the one who wrestled with God," was given to the whole people (Gen. 32:28). Additionally, at Bethel the Lord restated to Jacob the great covenant promises originally made to his grandfather Abraham.

The prophet is engaging in what we might call revisionist history, or perhaps even homiletical history. He is saying to his people, "Even though you are about to leave your homeland, just as Jacob was, this is not the end. God is not through with you yet. With God's help and because of his love for you, you will one day return. In the meantime, hold on to love for God and your neighbor, maintain justice in your society so that the powerless are cared for, and be patient. The God in whom you place your hopes still has some surprises for you."

2. Love, Justice, and Patience

The progression of this prophetic sermon follows the basic pattern of a Christian service of worship. After a confession of sin (at the Jabbok), there is a word of good news from the Lord (at Bethel) and finally a charge to lead a life marked by loyalty to God, service to the neighbor, and hope for the future (v. 6).

Verses 2–4 take the hearers to the banks of the Jabbok and lead to a confession of sin. Hosea pulled no punches. He told his hearers that God had judged them and found them guilty. He produced the evidence for the charge by running back through their history, demonstrating that they had been a self-centered and contentious people from the beginning, seeking advantage over others and even contending with God's angel. The first part of the sermon leaves Jacob weeping on the banks of the Jabbok, asking the Lord for help.

This is just where Hosea's hearers were. They were about to leave the promised land, and they knew it. They also knew that they deserved whatever punishment came their way. They knew that "we have sinned against thee in thought, word, and deed, by what we have done and by what we have left undone." While there was a positive story of Jacob in Genesis, Hosea's version laid bare the people's sinfulness. All could only come before the Lord weeping like Jacob and saying, "I am sorry."

After the struggle and sorrow at Jabbok comes the word of good news at Bethel, the house of God. There is no mistaking who pronounces this word: It is "the LORD the God of hosts, the LORD is his name." The word given is pure gospel: "As for you, by the help of your God, you will return" (v. 6a). The prophet is saying: God is still *your* God (twice, for emphasis). He is not through with you yet! Though you are struggling and sorrowing, he will bring you home again and will make things right once more.

This is the promise heard at Beth-el, the House of God. For the Christian, that good news comes in a fresh way, but still from the God of Jacob. Hosea had told his hearers that God had found them guilty in his court. Paul asserts that *all* human beings are so judged (Rom. 3:12), then the apostle begins to tell the good news (Rom. 3:24). For those who know Christ, the verdict of God's court has been changed from guilty to innocent (Rom. 8:1). This is the gospel at the heart of the New Testament (John 3:16).

The sermon thus moves from the struggles at the Jabbok to the good news at Bethel, but it does not end there. After the promise, "God will bring you home," comes some direction on how to live in the meantime, restating the familiar themes of Hosea and of his contemporaries Amos and Micah. "Hang on to love," says the prophet. This is the word *hesed* (see on 6:4–6), first defined by God's love for his people and then continuing with the passing of that love on to the neighbor. "Then," continues the prophet, "be concerned for justice." This is the justice for which Amos had called, a justice which that prophet hoped would roll through the land like a mighty stream (Amos 5:24). Finally, says Hosea, "Be patient, living each day in hope with your God." The whole saying recalls Micah's charge to "do justice, and to love kindness [*hesed*], and to walk humbly with your God" (Micah 6:8).

Paul's letter to the Christians at Rome also follows this pattern. It also proceeds from the Jabbok to Bethel, from struggles with sin to the good news about Christ. However, Paul's letter does not end at Bethel either. Paul calls a new people of God to come out of the house of God and go into the streets and the cities: "Let love be genuine; hate what is evil, hold fast to what is good; love one another with brotherly affection (Rom. 12:9–10).

Hosea 13
No Kind and Gentle Death

This next-to-the-last chapter of Hosea collects four of the prophet's sayings delivered just before the death of the nation in 722 B.C. No other chapter in the Hosea book provides a better example of the imaginative power of the prophet, who can deliver a chilling message either in literal terms (vv. 9–11, 16) or with images (vv. 3, 7–8, 13, 15). All four of these sayings are permeated with the stench of death. Nevertheless, when Paul writes about the hope for resurrection life in the first letter to the church at Corinth, he picks up a quotation from this chapter of Hosea.

1. The Stench of Death

The first saying consists of an accusation in verses 1 and 2 providing the reason for an announcement of punishment in verse 3. The accusation charges Israel with Baal worship in the past (v. 1) and also in the present; the people even kiss the calf image used in the Baal cult (v. 2; cf. I Kings 19:18)! The an-

47

nouncement of punishment describes what the nation will be like on the day after the destruction. The description is impersonal, with no mention of the Lord. The images are quiet and gentle ones, all four conveying the same message: Nothing will be left of Israel. Where is the morning mist or the glistening dew in the heat of the day? Where is the chaff that blew away from the threshing floor or the smoke that has gone up from the chimney? They are all gone forever. So also will Israel be, the day after the coming disaster.

The second saying again follows the pattern of an accusation (vv. 4–6) giving the reason for an announcement of punishment (vv. 7–8). This time the accusation begins by recalling God's mighty acts (vv. 4–5). The charge is focused in the last words of verse 6: "they forgot me" (cf. 2:8; 11:3). In this second saying, though, the death imagery is in sharp contrast to that of the first. This time the Lord's involvement is announced clearly: The Lord who once delivered Israel will now destroy them. The first saying described the day after the destruction; this description is of the day before the end of the nation. In the first saying the imagery was gentle; here it is violent. The Lord will attack with the ferocity of a lion (cf. Amos 3:12). The Lord will lie in ambush, waiting like a leopard. The images become even more graphic and violent, comparing the Lord to a bear robbed of her cubs who will tear and rip her victim (cf. Prov. 17:12). The nation's death will be no kind and gentle one, but an end marked by gasping, struggling, and suffering.

The target of the first two sayings has been the worship life of the people. In the third saying, verses 9–11, the charge has to do with the institution of the monarchy. The punishment is announced straightaway, "I will destroy you, O Israel." The implied accusation in verse 10 is that Israel has trusted in her kings rather than in her God. Verse 11 suggests that the last of the kings is gone, thus dating the piece during the final three-year siege of Samaria after Hoshea had been taken captive (II Kings 17:4–5).

The final saying, verses 12–16, like the first, speaks of Ephraim's sin (v. 12) and guilt (v. 16). Accusations appear in verses 12–13 and 16a. The announcement of the nation's death is first made figuratively (v. 15) and then literally (v. 16). Now the prophet projects onto the screen picture after picture of death. Israel is like a child in the womb which never had the chance to realize the potential given it by its Creator (v. 13).

48

Then comes the wind again (cf. v. 3*b*), this time the searing "wind of the LORD" which parches away all life (v. 15). The final scene is of a battlefield, with a dead soldier, a battered child, and a young woman who will never live to mother the baby in her womb (v. 16). At one point it seems as if the Lord may come to the rescue before the end comes. "Shall I ransom them?" the Lord asks. "Shall I redeem them?" The language is that of the Exodus, and the Lord seems to be considering delivering Israel once again. In answer, this time there will be no deliverance and no compassion. The final questions of verse 14 are commands to "Death" to get on with its work: "O Death, where are your plagues?" (Bring them on!) "O Sheol, where is your destruction?" (Let it come!)

A final observation about this litany of death. The question most asked at the time of a death is "Why?" In most cases, that question must go unanswered. Here the answer is clear and frames the chapter. The cause of death is written plainly on Israel's death certificate: sin and guilt and rebellion (vv. 1–2, 16).

2. The Trumpet Shall Sound (I Cor. 15)

When Paul wrote to the Christians at Corinth about death and resurrection, he quoted from this thirteenth chapter of Hosea. He cited the lines freely, perhaps from memory, and prefaced them with a quotation from Isaiah 25:8 (I Cor. 15:54–55). The two questions from Hosea 13:14 are placed at the climax of Paul's discussion of death and resurrection. In this new context they are not commands, but victory cries: "O death, where is thy victory?" (Nowhere! Death itself has been defeated.) "O death, where is thy sting?" (Nowhere! It has been taken away.) After the quotation comes a word of praise, "Thanks be to God, who gives us the victory through our Lord Jesus Christ."

Although both Hosea 13 and I Corinthians 15 deal with the theme of death and are linked to one another with this quotation, it would be difficult to find two more contrasting presentations. The imagery of Hosea 13 is ferocious, naming nature's fiercest animals: a bear robbed of her cubs, a leopard waiting along a path, a lion on the attack. In Paul's letter we find quiet metaphors taken from the world of the farmer: the harvesting of the first fruits (v. 20), the sowing and the growth of the grain (vv. 36–37). The God of Hosea 13 is angry (vv. 7, 8, 11) and will shortly bring about his people's defeat (vv. 15–16); Paul speaks

49

of the God of grace (v.10, twice), the Father (v. 24) who gives new life (v. 38), and victory through Jesus Christ (v. 57). The next-to-the-last chapter of Hosea ends with the sounds of defeat and dying, a mother weeping for an unborn child; the next-to-the-last chapter of First Corinthians concludes with the sound of the trumpet, announcing victory and resurrection through Jesus Christ.

What accounts for this total change from defeat to victory, from disaster to good news? The answer is what God has done through Christ. The problem of the sins of the people has been dealt with: Christ has died for their sins and has won the victory over sin's power (I Cor. 15:3, 56–57). Even death has been defeated. The resurrection of Jesus Christ is the "first fruits" that guarantee that there will be more resurrections to come (I Cor. 15:20–23). The new life will be both like and unlike the present one, just as there is both sameness and difference when comparing the seed with the full grown plant (I Cor. 15:35–50). Then the trumpet will sound. At that sound, says Paul, all will be raised and the final victory over death will be achieved.

The sayings of the prophet in Hosea 13 reek with the stench of death. The sermon of the apostle rings with the sound of the trumpet, calling all who hear to give thanks to the God who has given the victory through Jesus Christ.

Hosea 14
The Way to Wellness

The first major part of the Hosea book concluded with a declaration of the Lord's forgiving love (3:1). The second part climaxed with a picture of the Lord's nurturing love (11:1, 4). At the center of this final part of the book (chapters 12—14) is a word about God's healing love. To a people who have stumbled and fallen the Lord says, "I will heal their faithlessness; I will love them freely" (14:4).

The announcement of punishment in 5:5 had declared, "Ephraim shall stumble in his guilt" (Hebrew, *'ewon*). This concluding chapter begins by declaring that the nation has stumbled because of its iniquity (again, *'ewon*). The saying in 5:5 predicted that the nation would stumble and fall; this one says that the fall has already taken place. Thus the piece is to be dated in the very last days of Israel, at the time of its fall to Assyria in 722 B.C.

The imperative "return" of verse 1 signals a new beginning, introducing this final three-part chapter (vv. 1–3; 4–8; 9).

1. From Wounded to Well (14:1–8)

This concluding section of the Hosea book is especially rich in imagery. The picture in the first part is that of a wounded person lying along a roadside in pain (vv. 1–3). This person has "stumbled" and is hurting; the word about healing in verse 4 assumes such a hurting. The wounded one, a picture of Israel, has been ill for a long time, and in fact had attempted to find healing by going to see "Dr. Assyria" (5:13), but that physician was not able to provide any help. The prophet makes a clear diagnosis of the cause of the sickness and the stumbling: It was "your iniquity" (v. 1). Hosea had warned that Israel would stumble (5:5); now it has happened. Verses 2–3 tell the people what they ought to do next and even provide the script telling them what they should say. They should return to the Lord, not with sacrifices but with words. The words should be a request for forgiveness, "Take away all iniquity," thus implying an acknowledgment of wrongdoing (v. 2). Israel should also confess their faith in the Lord in the form of a denial of trust in other nations or in Israel's military machinery or in other gods (v. 3).

How would God react to such a confession of sin and request for forgiveness? Verses 4–8 answer that question, first with the Lord speaking *about* Israel (vv. 4–7) and then *to* them in the second person (v. 8). In response to the people's confession and request, the Lord announces that his anger has passed and that he will heal Israel. Here is expressed the good news about God's healing love which comes at the climax of this final part of the Hosea book: "I will heal their faithlessness; I will love them freely."

The book now comes to a close with three pictures of the healthy life, describing an Israel that has experienced the Lord's healing love. In the first, the Lord says, "I will be as the dew to Israel . . ." (v. 5). Hosea has used the image of dew as a negative figure for the transitory nature of the people's love for God (6:4; 13:3). Here the image is used in a positive sense. In Israel's dry climate, the dew is that which gives life to grass and plants. Thus it is a figure for the happiness of a people living in harmony (Ps. 133:3), for the Lord's quiet watching over his people (Isa. 18:4), or for the words of a teacher (Deut. 32:2). It would be difficult to find images more contrasting than those used for the Lord in chapter 13 (a lion, a leopard, a bear robbed of her cubs) and this picture of the Lord as gentle dew. The same contrast is expressed in Proverbs 19:12, "A king's wrath is like the growling of a lion, but his favor is like dew upon the grass." The Lord will be like dew for Israel, enabling the people to flourish like the lily, the olive, and the fragrant gardens of Lebanon.

The second image of the well life with the Lord is that of an existence sheltered from the burning sun by the Lord's shade. The basic notion here is of protection; thus shade can be a picture of protection given by a nation (Isa. 30:2) or by political leaders (Isa. 32:2). It is especially used for the Lord's protection, a "shelter from the storm and a shade from the heat (Isa. 25:4; cf. 4:6) and the one who protects the traveler with his shade (Ps. 121:5). The image of shade also conveys delight, as a lover who delights in sitting in the shadow of her beloved (Sol. 2:3). Once before, Hosea had spoken of an unfaithful people who liked to spend their time at the Baal shrines, sitting under the trees there "because their shade is good" (4:13). Here it is the Lord who provides the protecting and delighting shade.

In verse 8, the Lord addresses the people in the second person. In the form of rhetorical questions he asserts that he alone is their God and then declares that he is the one who cares for this people (v. 8a). God is in fact the source of life for Israel, "I am like an evergreen cypress, from me comes your fruit." The chapter had begun with a picture of Israel as wounded, lying in pain along a roadside. It ends with an image of Israel as healed and healthy, cared for by the Lord.

2. A Word to the Wise (14:9 and chapter 14)

The editor's comment in verse 9 indicates that those who collected and arranged the words of Hosea were convinced that they provided a guide for leading a good and godly life. Those who choose to walk in the way of transgressors will "stumble," just as Israel had stumbled (14:1); those who are wise will walk in the Lord's way. This final chapter provides a summary of Hosea's message, outlining the prophet's prescription for those who wish to walk in that way.

This prescription is addressed to those who are wounded

and who have stumbled because of their sin (v. 1). These words are not for those who have it all together, but for those for whom it is all coming apart. Hosea himself knew plenty of the brokenness of human life. He had experienced divorce, probably had to manage as a single parent, may have known the rebellion of a child, and surely was sensitive to the breakdown of morality in his own land. Yet Hosea also knew of God's love, which kept on loving a people who were unfaithful and rebellious. Hosea would have understood why Jesus associated with the tax collectors and the outcasts of society. The ministry of Jesus was the embodiment of that promise from God which Hosea related, "I will heal their faithlessness, I will love them freely" (14:4). Hosea would have understood what Jesus meant when he said, "Those who are well have no need of a physician, but those who are sick. . . . For I came not to call the righteous, but sinners" (Matt. 9:12–13). Like the good news which Jesus announced, Hosea's words are not addressed to the well but to those who are wounded.

The prophet's prescription for a return to wellness directs his hearers to return to the Lord, to ask for forgiveness, and to affirm trust in the Lord alone (vv. 2–3). A people wishing to find their way back to a healthy relationship with God are invited to acknowledge that they are at the end of their rope, that they have not been able to find help from others nor within their own resources nor with quasi-religious systems of self-help designed by human minds and hands (v. 3). Those wishing to find their way back to the Lord should identify themselves as orphans, helpless children in need of parents, claiming God's promise to act as parent for the parentless (v. 3; cf. Exod. 22:22–23).

Any hope that the wounded have is based on the healing love of God (v. 4). We have seen that this promise of the Lord's healing love stands at the climax of this chapter and of this third part of the prophetic book. Taken together with the statements about God's forgiving love (3:1) and nurturing love (11:1–3), the promise of Hosea 14:4 is the basis for the hope of those who are wounded and broken.

The prophet Hosea gave expression to God's forgiving love with the picture of the husband and the wife; the New Testament uses the same imagery in describing Christ as the husband and the church as the bride (Eph. 5:21–33). Hosea expressed God's nurturing love in the picture of the parent and the child

53

(Hos. 11); Jesus gave this kind of love unforgettable expression in the picture of a father who had been watching for a son's return, and who ran down the road to welcome him home (Luke 15:20). The healing love of God received its ultimate expression on the cross, where the one who told that parable gave his life to take away the sin of the world (John 3:16).

Finally, in Hosea 14:5–8, the prophet pulls out all of his imaginative stops to describe the blessed life of those who have experienced God's healing. Image after image tumbles forth: They will be like a blossoming lily, a deep-rooted tree, a fragrant garden, a beautiful olive tree, a productive vineyard sustained by the Lord's dew and protected with the Lord's shade. The Lord will be to his people like an evergreen tree which nourishes them with its fruit. He is their God who promises, I will "look after you."

To such a blessed life the prophet calls a people who are broken and wounded, but who know that because of God's healing love there is a way to wellness.

THE BOOK OF
Joel

Introduction

"Tell your children of it, and let your children tell their children, and their children another generation" (Joel 1:3). The Book of Joel begins by referring to a story that is worthy of being told and retold. The community has experienced a rural crisis of such magnitude that nothing like it has ever happened in the memory of the oldest of the present generation nor of their parents. In addition, the people have experienced a deliverance so memorable that the prophet wants his hearers to tell their children, so the story can be passed from generation to generation.

What was the nature of this crisis? And how did the deliverance come about? Just what is it that should be told to the children and to their children? We begin by looking at the book as a whole and noting the "story" it tells.

1:1–4: The book begins with a four-part introduction. The title identifies that which follows as a word from God, through Joel (v. 1). Next is a call for the attention of the entire community (v. 2a) and a rhetorical question asserting that something has happened that has not happened in the memory of anyone present (v. 2b). Following this is a command to tell the children about all of this, and to keep that telling going throughout posterity (v. 3). The hearer or reader asks: What is it that has happened that is worthy of such telling and retelling?

The fourth part of the introduction begins to answer that question by telling of the rural crisis. A plague of locusts, commonly called grasshoppers, came and totally destroyed all the crops (v. 4).

1:5—2:17: This section of the book is concerned with the locust plague. Its arrangement is broadly chiastic, beginning with a call to "gather the people for fasting and prayer" (1:5–14) followed by a reason for this activity, "For the day of the LORD is near" (1:15–20). Then follows a restatement of the reason for gathering, describing the coming Day of the Lord (2:1–11), and a concluding call to gather the people for fasting and prayer (2:12–17).

2:18–32: With 2:18, the "storyline" is picked up again. We may assume that the service of fasting and prayer has taken place. Here we are told that the Lord has heard the prayers of his people, has brought the plague to an end, and is promising a full harvest (2:18–27). The "afterward" of verse 28 signals more promises for the distant future. All members of the community will receive the gift of the spirit (2:28–29), and when the Day of the Lord finally does come, those who call on the Lord's name will be rescued (2:30–32).

3:1–21: This last section of the book continues to speak of the distant future, which will mean punishment for the nations (3:1–12) but rescue for God's people on the Day of the Lord (3:13–17). Finally, the blessings of prosperity and peace are promised for the people of God (3:18–21).

Behind the Book of Joel is a story about a crisis and a deliverance from that crisis. That story has been shaped into something of a liturgy so that future generations can hear the story once again and also discover what to do in their own times of crisis. The individual texts selected for exposition in what follows should be heard in the larger context of the "story" of the book as a whole.

Joel 1:1
The Prophet Joel

In contrast to the books of Hosea, Amos, Micah, Zephaniah, Haggai, and Zechariah among the Book of the Twelve, the title for this book does not locate the prophet in the time of any ruling king. It simply points to that which follows as word of the Lord, and identifies Joel in reference to his father (cf. Jonah).

56

1. Joel, the Son of Pethuel

The name Joel means "Yahweh is God" and is a fairly common one in the Old Testament (I Sam. 8:2; I Chron. 5:4, 8; 15:7, 11; Ezra 10:43; Neh. 11:9). A careful reading of the book allows us to draw some conclusions about the prophet. It appears that he lived in or near Jerusalem, since his entire orientation is around the temple (1:9, 13–14, 16; 2:17), Mount Zion (2:1, 15, 32; 3:17, 19–21), Judah, and Jerusalem (2:32; 3:1, 6, 8, 17, 19). Joel identifies himself solidly with the people whom he addresses. "My God," he says, is "your God" and indeed "our God" (1:13, 16). The suffering the people are experiencing is "our" suffering (1:16). He speaks the language of the farmers whom he addresses and uses a variety of technical agricultural terms (1:4, 7, 12; 2:25).

Joel seems to have studied the words of the prophets who had worked before him. He quotes their sayings: 1:15 cites Isaiah 13:6; 3:16 quotes Amos 1:2; 2:1–2 uses material from Zephaniah 1:14–15. He sometimes paraphrases earlier prophetic sayings (2:3 and Isa. 51:3). The relationship between Joel 3:10 and Isaiah 2:4 and Micah 4:3 is discussed in the comments on that Micah passage. (For a full list of allusions to earlier prophets in Joel, see Hans Walter Wolff, *Joel and Amos,* pp. 10–12).

Joel also has poetic and rhetorical gifts of his own. His figures of speech are striking: The swarming locusts are described as an attacking nation or as a ferocious lion (1:6). The people are called to lament like a young bride who has lost her husband (1:8). The redness of the moon is like the color of blood (2:31). The Lord is pictured as a fortress or a stronghold (3:16). The prophet links chains of words together to achieve dramatic effect (1:4; 2:2), and his description of the Day of the Lord builds to a terrifying climax (2:1–11).

In reading the Book of Joel, one gets the impression of a man of great sensitivity. He has been impressed by the sound of a bride's weeping (1:8). He has heard the groans of starving cattle and describes them as perplexed, dismayed, even crying to the Lord (1:18, 20). He has noticed the suffering of boys and girls in times of warfare (3:3).

Joel is aware of the entire community of believers. He addresses his words to the aged (1:2) and is concerned about the children (1:3). He invites the children, even nursing babies, to come to worship (2:16). The gift of the spirit will be inclusive,

57

poured out on young and old, male and female, even the servants (2:28–29).

2. The Setting

The immediate occasion for the prophet's work is clear. The land has just experienced a plague of locusts (1:4), the like of which has never been seen (1:2). These creatures have devastated vineyards and orchards (1:7, 12). Pasture lands have been ruined as if by fire (1:19–20), and the animals are suffering (1:18, 20). There is no harvest and the granaries stand empty (1:5, 10, 11, 17). The community is suffering a food shortage (1:16), and no produce is available for offerings at the temple (1:9, 13).

When did this terrible plague take place? There are a few clues to dating in the book itself. The references to Israel being scattered among the nations and the promise to restore the fortunes of Judah and Jerusalem assume the destruction of Jerusalem in 587 B.C. and the dispersion of its citizens (3:1–2). The temple has been rebuilt (1:9, 13, 14), therefore the date would have to be after 515 B.C. If 2:7 and 9 assume the existence of a wall around Jerusalem, the date would have to be after the work of Nehemiah in about 440 B.C. Mention of Sidon in 3:4 points to a date before the destruction of that city in 343 B.C. (Wolff, *Joel and Amos,* p.4). In sum, a date for Joel's activity around 400 B.C. seems reasonable, though the matter is by no means certain.

We return to the fact that no kings are mentioned in the title of the book. The editors of the Book of the Twelve could provide chronological information when they wanted to, as they did in Hosea, Amos, and Micah. It is possible that such information was intentionally omitted from Joel so that this word from the Lord could continue to address each new generation as a word especially for them, as the story of what happened in the days of Joel was told to "your children" and to the succeeding generations of children.

Joel 1:2–4
What Shall We Tell the Children?

After the opening call for attention and the declaration that something unprecedented has occurred, the first sentence in

the Book of Joel is a command: "Tell your children of it. . . ."
This is a crucial statement for understanding the book and directs its subsequent appropriation in preaching and teaching.

1. Telling the Story: The Old Testament

"Telling the children" has a long tradition in the Old Testament. In Psalm 78, for example, the worshiping congregation is invited to hear "things that we have heard and known, that our fathers have told us." Then a resolution is made that the telling of these things will go on through the generations:

> We will not hide them from their children,
>   but tell to the coming generation
> the glorious deeds of the LORD, and his might,
>   and the wonders which he has wrought . . .
> that the next generation might know them,
>   the children yet unborn,
> and arise and tell them to their children,
>   so that they should set their hope in God,
> and not forget the works of God. . . .
>   (Ps. 78:3–7)

Three things are clear from this psalm: (1) The people resolve to keep the process of telling going from generation to generation; (2) The content of the telling is the "glorious deeds of the LORD" and the "wonders" which God has done; (3) The purpose of the telling is for the good of the next generations, so that they "should set their hope in God, and not forget the works of God, but keep his commandments" (v. 7; cf. also Exod. 12; 13:8, 14; Deut. 6:20–25; Judg. 6:12–13; Ps. 44:1–2).

Thus one generation passed the faith to the next by telling the story of the mighty acts of God. These acts might include the Exodus, the leading in the wilderness, and the conquest. Such a telling took place in the circle of the family and also, as these psalms indicate, in the gathering of the community for worship.

2. The Deliverance

Seen in this context, the command to "tell" in Joel is not an unusual one. What is to be told, though, in this instance? This time it is not the familiar canonical story of exodus-wilderness-conquest. Now a new "mighty act" has been added to the series. The story to be told concerns a deliverance from a plague of locusts.

We can trace the outline of the story in the book. First, the severity of the attack is reported: "What the cutting locust left, the swarming locust has eaten. . . ." Then we hear the people called to gather for fasting and prayer; in such a dire situation, this was all that could be done. No one knew in advance how God would respond to such a gathering (2:14). Then we are told how God responded to the gathering: God had pity on his people and answered their prayers. The locust plague came to an end. The story does not end at that point, however. The people had heard about the "Day of the Lord," which was to come in the future, and had considerable anxiety about the events of that day. The prophet addresses that anxiety, telling them that "the LORD is a refuge to his people, a stronghold to the people of Israel" (3:16).

3. Telling the Story: The New Testament and Beyond

The tradition of telling the mighty acts of God continues into the New Testament. At Pentecost, Jews from all over the world heard the disciples of Jesus "telling in our own tongues the mighty works of God" (Acts 2:11). Samples of how that telling was done may be found in the sermons of Acts (Acts 13) as well as the letters (I Cor. 15:3–4). In such ways the faith is passed from generation to generation, as witnesses tell of the mighty acts of God.

This word from Joel raises the question: What shall we tell our children? Considering that question on the basis of the whole Bible, the first answer will be: Tell them about the mighty acts of God, culminating in the story about what God did through the life, death, and resurrection of Jesus. The Book of Joel suggests that the children also be told about other things God has done in the history of our own people and our own family. We are encouraged to look for our own stories to tell: What events have occurred in our own histories which correspond to the deliverance from the locust plague in Joel?

"I Love to Tell the Story" has been one of the favorite hymns of the church. I recall a teacher who once borrowed from a bank a sign which said, "teller." He hung it around his neck and then walked into the classroom, to dramatize that such was the calling of each of God's people.

60

This text invites God's people to be "tellers," to continue in the task of telling the story and the stories of the faith in ever new and imaginative ways. In so doing they will carry on a tradition as old as the people of God itself.

Joel 1:5—2:17
The Rural Crisis

This segment of the Book of Joel consists of two parallel sections arranged in chiastic order as follows:

A	B
Gather the people for fasting and prayer (1:5–14)	because the Day of the Lord is near! (1:15–20)
B'	**A'**
The Day of the Lord is near (2:1–11)	so gather the people for fasting and prayer! (2:12–17)

The movement of the whole may be summarized: The plague which we have experienced is of such magnitude that it must be a sign that the day of the Lord's punishment is near. In the face of this, let us all gather for fasting and prayer. Who knows (v. 14)? The Lord may deliver us!

1. When the Grasshoppers Came

The statement about the plague at the beginning of the book indicates that some sense of this crisis is essential for understanding the prophet's message:

> What the cutting locust left,
>   the swarming locust has eaten.
> What the swarming locust left,
>   the hopping locust has eaten,
> and what the hopping locust left,
>   the destroying locust has eaten (1:4).

Commentators debate whether the reference is various stages in the development of the locust (Wolff, *Joel and Amos,* p. 27) or whether the prophet is piling up a series of terms for rhetori-

61

cal effect (Leslie C. Allen, *The Books of Joel, Obadiah, Jonah, and Micah,* pp. 49–50). In any case, the meaning of 1:4 is clear: A terrible crisis has struck the land.

The Israelites had experienced plagues of locusts throughout their history. Most notable among these was the eighth of the plagues in Egypt (Exod. 10:1–20; cf. Pss. 78:46; 105:34). Other such plagues were experienced in their own land (I Kings 8:37; II Chron. 6:28; Amos 7:1–3).

The plague to which Joel refers was so severe that nothing like it had happened in the past, and it was worthy of being remembered to all generations of the future (1:3). What might it have been like for an Israelite farmer to experience such a plague? Commentators frequently refer to descriptions of plagues of locusts in modern Palestine (see George Adam Smith, *The Book of the Twelve Prophets,* Vol. II, 398–408; Wolff, *Joel and Amos,* pp. 27–28; Peter Craigie, *Twelve Prophets,* p. 86; Allen, *Joel, Obadiah, Jonah, and Micah,* p. 50). I know of no description of a plague of grasshoppers, however, which matches that of O.E. Rolvaag in *Giants in the Earth,* a story about Norwegian immigrants who settled on the prairies of South Dakota. Three farmers, Syvert Tonseten, Hans Olsa, and Per Hansa, have been talking about the good weather, and the good crops they are expecting. The narrative continues:

> Tonseten turned in his seat, to face a sight such as he had never seen or heard before. From out of the west layers of clouds came rolling—thin layers that rose and sank on the breeze; they had none of the look or manner of ordinary clouds; they came in waves, like the surges of the sea, and cast a glittering sheen before them as they came; they seemed to be made of some solid murky substance that threw out small sparks along its face.
>
> The three men stood spellbound, watching the oncoming terror; their voices died in their throats; their minds were blank. The horses snorted as they, too, caught sight of it, and became very restless. . . . Down by the creek the grazing cows had hoisted their tails straight in the air and run for the nearest shelter; and no sooner had the horses been turned loose, than they followed suit; man and beast alike were overcome by a nameless fear.
>
> And now from out of the sky gushed down with cruel force a living, pulsating stream, striking the backs of the helpless folk like pebbles thrown by an unseen hand; but that which fell out of the heavens was not pebbles, nor raindrops, nor hail, for then it would have lain inanimate where it fell; this substance had no sooner fallen than it popped up again, crackling and snapping—rose up and disappeared in the twinkling of an eye; it

flared and flittered around them like light gone mad; it chirped and buzzed through the air; it snapped and hopped along the ground; the whole place was a weltering turmoil of raging little demons; if one looked for a moment into the wind, one saw nothing but glittering, lightninglike flashes—flashes that came and went, in the heart of a cloud made up of innumerable dark-brown clicking bodies! All the while the roaring sound continued. . . .

They whizzed by in the air; they literally covered the ground; they lit on the heads of grain, on the stubble, on every-thing in sight—popping and glittering, millions on millions of them. . . . The people watched it, stricken with fear and awe. Here was *Another One* speaking! . . .

Kjersti was crying bitterly; Sorine's kind face was deathly pale as she glanced at the men, trying to bolster up her courage; but the big frame of her husband was bent in fright and dismay. He spoke slowly and solemnly: "This must be one of the plagues mentioned in the Bible!"

"Yes! and the devil take it!" muttered Per Hansa, dark-ly. . . ." But it can't last forever."

To Tonseten the words of Per Hansa, in a hour like this, sounded like the sheerest blasphemy; they would surely call down upon them a still darker wrath! He turned to reprove his neighbor: "Now the Lord is taking back what he has given," he said, impressively. "I might have guessed that I would never be permitted to harvest such wheat. That was asking too much!"

Then more plagues of locusts began to come. The descrip-tion echoes that of Joel 1:4:

... they would swoop down, dashing and spreading out like an angry flood, slicing and shearing, cutting with greedy teeth, laying waste every foot of the field they lighted in (pp. 331–333, 341).

2. The Day of the Lord (1:15—2:11)

To the prophet, the terrible plague of locusts was a sign that the "day of the Lord" was near (1:15; 2:1). He does not explain what he means with this expression, but assumes that his hear-ers are familiar with it. The "day of the Lord," which means a time or occasion when the Lord will intervene decisively in history, had been spoken about in two ways in the time before Joel.

1. *The Day of the Lord will be a time of salvation for Israel.* Amos 5:18–20 indicates that those whom Amos addressed at mid-eighth century in the Northern Kingdom had such an idea of the Day of the Lord. It would be, they assumed, a time of

63

happiness, brightness, and joy. Along with the notion that the Day of the Lord means salvation for Israel goes the idea of doom for Israel's enemies. Thus Isaiah 13 announces concerning Babylon, "the day of the LORD is near; as destruction from the Almighty it will come!" Ezekiel proclaims that "the day is near, the day of the LORD is near," which will be "a time of doom for the nations" (Ezek. 30:1–3). Obadiah announces the Lord's day against Edom and the nations (Obad. 1:8, 15) which will be a time of deliverance for God's people (17–20).

2. *The Day of the Lord will be a time of doom for Israel.* It was Amos who first announced this, reversing the popular notion and declaring that the day coming was a day of "darkness, and not light . . . gloom with no brightness in it" (Amos 5:18–20). A century later Zephaniah declared that the Day of the Lord was at hand (1:7, 14), naming it an occasion when the Lord would turn against the people of Judah and Jerusalem (1:4).

Joel speaks of the coming Day of the Lord in both ways. In 2:31 and 3:14 it is an occasion of doom for Israel's enemies, but of salvation for Israel. In 1:15; 2:1; and 2:11, however, the prophet says that the day is near at hand (1:15; 2:1) and that it will be a time of doom and destruction for Israel (1:15), of darkness, gloom, clouds, and thick darkness (2:2), a day which none will be able to endure (2:11).

Will this fearsome day coming in the near future bring another plague of locusts? The description in 2:1–11 is of a terrible invasion by those whose appearance is "like the appearance of horses" and who attack "like a powerful army." Does this means locusts, or does it mean an "army" of another, supernatural kind? The matter is not entirely clear. What is clear is that this will be a day so terrible that none will be able to endure it.

What could the people do, having experienced such a plague in the past and now being faced with even more peril in their immediate future? Where could they turn? The prophet tells them that there is only one thing to do. They should gather for prayer and fasting and return to the Lord.

3. When You Don't Know Where to Turn (Joel 2:12–14)

64

The words in this section were first addressed to a péople who had just experienced a devastating crisis in their community. Like the Norwegian-American farmers cited in *Giants in the Earth,* they must have been certain that the plague of locusts was a punishment from God. Now, as they look to the future, they fear an even more terrifying event: the Day of the Lord.

These words were addressed to a people who, like the animals that lived among them (1:18), were perplexed, dismayed, and did not know where to turn. Therefore the text will be especially applicable in such a situation. This is a text for the difficult times, for the time when a community or an individual has experienced a crisis and may be anticipating another in the future. This is a word addressed to a people who are at the end of their rope and who do not know where to turn.

The message of this text, certified as a word from God with the "says the Lord" formula, is: When you do not know where to turn, return to the Lord! The text then invites reflection on the how and the why of returning, and finally on what to expect from the Lord in the future:

How to return. How should a people return to the Lord? The Israelites knew the traditional practices of fasting and prayer, and in both 1:14 and 2:15 there is a call to "sanctify a fast, call a solemn assembly." A few words about fasting in the Old Testament will help to understand this call for such a gathering.

The fast in the Old Testament could either apply to an individual (II Sam. 12:16) or the whole community (II Chron. 20). The occasion for calling a fast was an emergency situation, such as the time David's child was deathly ill (II Sam. 12:16) or when the community is experiencing a military threat (II Chron. 20). By the time of the post-exilic period, fasts were still called on special occasions (Jonah 3:5; Esther 4:16; Joel), but there were also set days for fasting (Zech. 7:3, 5; 8:19). The entire community was invited to participate, including the children (II Chron. 20:13). In Jonah, even the animals are included in the fast (Jonah 3:7–8; cf. Judith 4:9–11). In longer accounts, the actual words to be used might be given, consisting of confession (I Sam. 7:6) or praise and request (II Chron. 20:6–12). Actions associated with fasting have the aim of bringing about humility or demonstrating humility by taking away beauty; thus we hear of wearing sackcloth and putting dirt on the head or sitting in ashes (Jonah 3:6–9; Jer. 4:8; Neh. 9:1). The outcome of the fast must be left in the hands of God. Note the attitude

65

expressed in the prayer of Jehoshaphat faced with a military crisis, and of the king of Nineveh in response to Jonah's preaching (Jonah 3:9).

Seen against this background, the fast called for in Joel contains much that is typical for such occasions. The entire community is invited, including the aged, babies, and even the newly married (Joel 2:16; cf. Deut. 24:5). The fast was occasioned by the emergency of the locust plague in the immediate past and the anticipated Day of the Lord in the future. Actions include fasting as well as wearing sackcloth (1:13) and taking away beauty by tearing clothing (2:12–13). As for the words, the prophet advises his people to cry to the Lord (1:14) as he himself does (1:19) and as even the beasts do (1:20). Specific words for the people's prayers are given, requesting God's help and giving a reason for the request (2:17). Finally, the outcome of the fast is not certain. Not even the Lord's prophet can predict what God will do (2:14). The best that can be done is to pray and fast, and then leave matters in the hands of God. Who knows? It may be that God will call an end to the plague and even call off the approaching Day of the Lord which looms like a storm on the horizon.

How should a people return to the Lord? This saying from the Lord in 2:12–13 frames the traditional practices of fasting with the assertion that a true return to the Lord is a matter of the heart. With this, that which is most essential about the practice of fasting has been identified. The outward practices are not condemned here; what is said is that an appropriate inward attitude should accompany them.

Isaiah 58 provides some instructive comments on fasting. Here the prophet addresses a people who have been going through the typical practices associated with fasting, including wearing sackcloth and sitting in ashes (Isa. 58:5), yet the Lord seems not to respond. Why? The prophet says, "In the day of your fast you seek your own pleasure, and oppress all your workers" (Isa. 58:3). Then he indicates the kind of fasting the Lord does want:

> The kind of fasting I want is this: Remove the chains of oppression and the yoke of injustice, and let the oppressed go free. Share your food with the hungry and open your homes to the homeless poor. Give clothes to those who have nothing to wear, and do not refuse to help your own relatives (Isa. 58:6–7, GNB).

Here is a somewhat surprising approach to the matter of fasting. It says that fasting coupled with social injustice is not acceptable to God; like the religion which Jeremiah denounced, it is only skin deep (Jer. 4:4)! Where true fasting is found, the heart will be touched, and a heart rightly oriented cannot neglect and oppress the poor.

Why return? After the word from the Lord calling for a return in verses 12–13, the prophet seconds that call, telling the people *why* they should return. "Return to the LORD," he says, because of what God is like: "gracious and merciful, slow to anger, and abounding in steadfast love, and repent(ing) of evil." This is well-worn, traditional language that would be familiar to Joel's hearers (cf. Exod. 34:6; Jonah 4:2). "Gracious and merciful" is a frequent pairing in the Psalms (111:4; 112:4; 145:8). The Hebrew root behind "merciful" is related to the word for womb; the sense seems to be "motherly love" (see the comments on "compassion" in Micah 7:19). "Slow to anger" is a human virtue (Prov. 14:29; 15:18; 16:32), but is most often used of the Lord (Neh. 9:17; Pss. 86:15; 103:8; 145:8). "Steadfast love" is the Hebrew *hesed;* see the comments on Hosea 6:6.

Two biblical pictures can make concrete these words which describe God. First is the picture of Hosea who welcomed back his erring wife when she returned to him. When he discovered that he still loved her despite what she had done, he gained an insight into the forgiving and loving heart of God (Hosea 1—3; cf. the "return" and "turn" of Hosea 14:1, 2, 4, 7). The second picture is that of the rebellious son who finally decided to return home. He went home because he remembered what his father was like. He returned to find his father running down the road to embrace him. So it is with a God who welcomes returning sinners, said Jesus (Luke 15:11–32).

The prophetic call to return was later taken up by John the Baptist. "Repent," he said, which meant "reorient your priorities, reaim the direction of your life, return to the path you once followed." The reason he gave was, "for the kingdom of heaven is at hand," which referred to what God was doing through the life, death, and resurrection of Jesus Christ. Thus the reason is the same: Return, because of what God is like. He is a God who so loved the world that he gave his only Son for the sake of that world.

67

What to expect. Having returned to a loving God, what then can be expected from the future? The prophet offers no guarantees that God will come to the rescue. David returned to the Lord with prayer and fasting, but his child died (II Sam. 12:15–23).

We can be instructed by the example of Jehoshaphat, whose prayer concluded, "We do not know what to do, but our eyes are upon thee" (II Chron. 20:12), or by the King of Nineveh, who said, "Who knows, God may yet repent and turn from his fierce anger, so that we perish not" (Jonah 4:9).

What do we do when there is no place to turn? These texts provide some models for attitude and action in such times. The Lord calls for a reorientation that is more than skin deep. The prophet reminds us what God is like. Then, with the King of Judah, we shall have to say, "We do not know what to do, but our eyes are upon thee." The matter will have to be left, then, in God's hands. As Joel put it, "Who knows whether God might leave us with a blessing?"

Joel 2:18–32
An Answer to Prayer and a Promise

A return to the narrative style introduced in 1:2–4 signals the beginning of this new section of the book. It is framed by the expression, "the LORD answered and said" (2:19) and "as the LORD has said" (2:32).

1. The Plague Is Ended (2:18–27)

The story told in the Book of Joel began with 1:4, where the locusts were the subjects of the action: "What the cutting locust left, the swarming locust has eaten. . . ." The first major section of the book (1:5—2:17) was dominated by verbs in the imperative, with the people the subject of the desired action: "Sanctify a fast . . . and cry to the LORD" (1:14). We are to assume that the people did gather for prayer and fasting. Now, with 2:18, the subject of the verbs is the Lord, as we hear of the divine response to the prayers of the people. The story begins, "Then the LORD became jealous for his land, and had pity on his people" (2:18).

68

Verses 19 and 20 offer divine sayings. The people's prayers have been answered. The agricultural crisis will end. There had been no grain, wine, or oil (1:10, 16a); now the Lord promises to send them. The people had feared mockery from the neighbors (2:17), but the Lord will take away Judah's reproach (2:19). Finally, the Lord will deal with the locusts. Just as the Lord once drove the locusts into the Red Sea at the time when Israel was in Egypt (Exod. 10:19), so now they will be driven into the Dead ("eastern") and the Mediterranean ("western") seas.

The section in verses 21–23 stands apart from what precedes it because it no longer presents words of the Lord but rather three sayings which speak about the Lord. The first two are linked with the repeated "fear not"; the first and last tie the section together with the repeated "be glad and rejoice." Each saying consists of an imperative followed by a "for" clause which provides a reason for the imperative. The sayings are arranged climactically, with the reason progressively increasing in length. The first saying is addressed to the land. Once the ground had mourned (1:10); now it is told to "be glad and rejoice" because of what the Lord has done (v. 21). The second saying addresses the beasts. Once groaning, perplexed, and dismayed (1:18), they are now told not to fear because they will again be fed (2:22). Finally, the people themselves are told to rejoice. They had experienced parched and barren fields (1:19–20); now there will be rain, the triple mention of it indicating that it will come in abundance (v. 23).

The promises that are the answer to the people's prayers continue in verses 24–27. There will be wine and grain in abundance, again in contrast to the description in 1:10. In the "I" saying in verse 25, the Lord promises to restore all that was lost during the years of the locust plagues; compare verse 25 with 1:4. The first three clauses in verse 26 continue with promises. Then verse 26*d* introduces a refrain which is repeated at the end of verse 27, "and my people shall never again be put to shame." This refrain frames three important statements from the Lord, which bring 2:18–27 to a climax. The Lord says: (1) I am in the midst of Israel; (2) I, the Lord, am your God; (3) There is no other God.

With this, the portion of the book that deals with the locust plague comes to an end. The prayers of the people have been answered.

2. Earth, Wind, and Fire (2:28–32)

The important word in verses 28–29 is "afterward," which indicates that the prophet is now speaking about what the Lord

will do in the far distant future. This short section is framed with
the thematic statements, "I will pour out my spirit." The first
of these adds "on all flesh," and the material in between the
framing statements spells out what is meant by "all flesh," naming six classes of people and telling the effects of their receiving
the gift of the spirit. The theme of the Day of the Lord reap-
pears in verses 30–32. The immediate coming of that day has
been postponed in response to the fasting and prayers of the
people, but that day will yet come, in the distant future, and will
be heralded with cosmic signs (vv. 30–31). Verse 32 is framed
with a reference to "calling," those who call on the Lord, and
those upon whom the Lord calls. The understanding of the Day
of the Lord here is a shift from that in 1:15; 2:1; and 2:11; this
day in the distant future will be one of salvation for "all who call
upon the name of the LORD."

The Spirit. We have seen that the theme of verses 28–29
is, "I will pour out my spirit." The Hebrew word for spirit is
ruach. In its most literal sense it can mean wind, as in the wind
of a storm (Jonah 1:4) or the wind with which the Lord blows
the sea back (Exod. 15:8). Associated with the coming of the
ruach is *power.*

The common element in reports about the receiving of the
spirit in the Old Testament is the reception of power, which
may manifest itself in extraordinary acts. When the spirit of the
Lord comes upon Samson, he is empowered to tear a lion apart
with his bare hands (Judg. 14:6) or to kill thirty men of Ashkelon
(Judg. 14:19) or to burst the ropes which bind him (Judg. 15:14).
This spirit-given power can also manifest itself in acts of in-
spired leadership. Gideon receives the spirit of the Lord, sounds
a trumpet, and rallies the clans to lead them into battle (Judg.
6:34). The power of the spirit can even bring life out of death.
In Ezekiel's vision, when the Lord's spirit enters the dried out
bones in the valley, the bones connect once again and come
alive (Ezek. 37:1–14).

The power which is received with the spirit may also manifest itself in words, such as words of prophecy. Saul meets a
band of prophets at Gibeah and begins to prophesy with them
(I Sam. 10:10). Micah describes his own experience, testifying to
the power of speech given him by the spirit:

70

> But as for me, I am filled with power.
> with the Spirit of the LORD,
> and with justice and might,

> to declare to Jacob his transgression
>> and to Israel his sin.
>>> (Micah 3:8)

To receive the spirit is to receive power, which can manifest itself both in acts (mighty deeds) and words (prophecy).

The spirit poured out. Viewed against the background of these texts about receiving the spirit, two aspects of Joel 2:28–29 stand out: (1) The giving of the spirit as promised here will be an *inclusive* gift. "All flesh" means just that: male and female, young and old, slave and free. Since these are identified as "your" people, all within the community of Israel are included. (2) The reception of the spirit will mean the experience of a *direct relationship with God.* Prophecy, dreams, and visions are all biblical means of God's revelation. God may communicate through dreams (Gen. 28; 37). This is one of the standard means by which the prophets receive communication from God (Num. 12:6; Deut. 13:1, 3, 5; cf. Jer. 23:27, 28, 32). "Seeing visions" is also a normal way for receiving communication from God (II Sam. 7:17; cf. Ezek. 13:7; Amos 1:1; Isa. 1:1).

The point of the saying in Joel is that one day a time will come when all individuals among God's people will have the kind of direct relationship to the Lord which previously was possible only for prophets and selected individuals. This future gift of the spirit will be the fulfillment of the wish of Moses (Num. 11:29) and the prophecies of Ezekiel (Ezek. 39:29) and of Jeremiah (Jer. 31:34).

The first Christian sermon. Joel 2:28–32 has been given a unique honor in the history of the Christian church because it was the text for the first apostolic sermon, preached at Pentecost by Peter (Acts 2).

The theme for the Book of Acts is sounded in 1:8, where Jesus promises the apostles:

> But you shall receive power when the Holy Spirit has come upon you; and you shall be my witnesses in Jerusalem and in all Judea and Samaria and to the end of the earth.

Once again, to receive the Spirit is to receive *power* (the Greek is *dynamis,* cf. dynamite). In this case the power will enable the apostles to witness effectively to the ends of the earth. This spirit-powered witness will be accomplished through words, "And with great *power* the apostles gave their testimony . . .

71

(Acts 4:33), as well as through acts; after healing the lame man, the apostles say that the *power* to heal came from God (Acts 3:12). The ministry of Jesus is described in terms of the Holy Spirit and *power,* which enabled Jesus to do good works and to heal (Acts 10:38). Stephen is described as doing great wonders and signs, "full of grace and *power* (Acts 6:8, author's italics). Thus in Acts, to receive the Holy Spirit means to receive power, which manifests itself in actions (signs and wonders) and in words (witnessing and preaching).

The account in Acts 2 associates the coming of the Holy Spirit with the rush of a mighty wind (cf. Jonah 1:4 and Exod. 15:8) and with flames of fire. The Spirit then empowers those present to speak, this time in the languages of Jews gathered from all over the world. Peter declares that all of this is the fulfillment of the promises made by the prophet Joel (Acts 2:14–21). The interpretation of Acts 2:19–20 is debated. Has the promise of "wonders and signs" been fulfilled in the miracles of Jesus (note the same words in Acts 2:22)? Does that promise continue to be fulfilled in the signs and wonders done by the apostles (Acts 2:43)? Does the speaker understand the darkening of the sun and the reddening of the moon to have been fulfilled on Good Friday (Mark 15:33)? Or are these promises still outstanding, to be fulfilled immediately before the final Day of the Lord (Luke 21:25; cf. Rev. 6:12)?

One thing is clear from this first apostolic sermon: The age of the fulfillment of prophecy has begun. This theme is restated throughout the sermons in Acts (cf. 2:16; 3:18, 24; 10:43; 13:32–33).

The declaration that "whoever calls on the name of the Lord shall be saved" taken from Joel 2:32 becomes an important saying which circulates in the early church. To "call on the name of the Lord" means to announce allegiance to the Lord, specifically to be a follower of Jesus Christ (Acts 9:14, 21; 22:16). Paul uses this saying from Joel, putting the accent on the *all,* to emphasize that the good news is also for the Gentiles (Rom. 10:13).

Pentecost preaching. Joel 2:28–32, the text for the first Christian sermon recorded in the New Testament, remains an appropriate text for Christian preaching, most obviously on Pentecost Sunday. Preaching on that day would center on such themes as: (1) *Earth, wind, and fire.* The receiving of the Spirit at Pentecost was associated with the roaring of a mighty wind and with flames of fire, both symbols of power. The empowered apostles then tell the good news through both words and acts to the ends of the earth. Such telling and doing remains the task of the church (Matt. 28:16–20), a church which is driven by the wind and ignited by the fire of the Holy Spirit. (2) *Reorientation.* This first Christian sermon announced the fulfillment of prophecy (2:17–21) and told about the life, death, and resurrection of Jesus (2:22–36). This is the good news, the core of the Christian message. Instead of ending with a proclamation, the sermon also issued an invitation, to become reoriented, to be baptized, to receive forgiveness and the gift of the Holy Spirit (2:38–39). Preaching modeled after this sermon will then consist of both proclamation of what God has done through Jesus and also imaginative invitation to claim the gifts offered. A people so gifted with the Spirit will live lives marked by those gifts (patterns are provided in Gal. 5:22–26 and I Cor. 13). (3) *We've only just begun.* Peter's sermon indicates an ending of sorts; the promises have been fulfilled. It also signals a beginning: Empowered by the Spirit, these earliest Christians began to take the story of God's mighty deeds to the ends of the earth. They might well have said, "We've only just begun." The text invites those who hear the good news to continue in the task, driven and fired by the Spirit, of taking that good news to the ends of the earth.

Joel 3:1–21
Tell the Children:
A Mighty Fortress Is Our God

This final chapter of the Book of Joel divides into three parts, each of which contains a central biblical theme:

1. The Day of Judgment (3:1–12)

This section is marked as a unit by the expressions which frame it at beginning and end: "valley of Jehoshaphat" (vv. 2, 12), "gather all the nations" and "gather . . . all the nations" (vv. 2, 11–12), "judgment" (v. 2), and "judge" (v. 12). The theme of the section is: Gather the nations for judgment!

INTERPRETATION

The expressions "in those days" and "at that time" (v. 1) throw that which follows into the same distant future as was introduced by the "afterward" of 2:28. In that time, the Lord will restore the fortunes of Jerusalem and there will be a great judgment for all the nations in the "valley of Jehoshaphat." The word "Jehoshaphat" means "the Lord judges" and is apparently a symbolic term, rather than an actual place name. The language of verses 2–3 indicates that the Lord is strongly on the side of his people: my people, my heritage, my land, my people. The Lord has four charges against the nations: they have scattered Israel, they have divided Israel's land, they have given the people over into slavery, and they have sold even the young children into slavery.

Verses 4–8 announce that on this day of judgment the Lord will punish Tyre, Sidon, and Philistia. The punishment will fit the crime: Because they have sold the Lord's people into slavery (v. 6), their own children will be sold (vv. 7–8).

The "gather the nations" theme of verse 2 is taken up again in verses 9–12. The Lord will tell the angels at his command to summon the nations for a great battle, using the typical language of the call to battle (vv. 9–10; for calls to battle, cf. Isa. 21:5*b*; Jer. 46:3–4; 51:11*a*). Then the purpose of the gathering is announced: "for there I will sit to judge all nations."

This theme of the Lord as Judge runs through the Bible, from Genesis 18:25 where the Lord is named "Judge of all the earth" through portrayals of judgment in the psalms (96:13; 98:9) and promises of judgment in the prophets (Isa. 2:4; Micah 4:3; Ezek. 34:17–22) and in apocalyptic texts (Dan. 7:9–14). The scene in Matthew 25:31–46 is especially well known; as in Joel (3:3), the basis for the judgment is the manner in which those judged have treated the weakest members of society. The New Testament can speak of this activity of judging as the responsibility of God (Acts 17:31) or of the risen Christ (II Cor. 5:10). In all three of the ecumenical creeds, judgment is the responsibility of the risen Christ.

2. A Mighty Fortress Is Our God (3:13–17)

Central to this section is the "Day of the Lord" theme, now sounded for the final time in the book (cf. 1:15; 2:1, 11, 31). The sequence here is chronological. Before the Day of the Lord comes, the Lord's army is commanded to execute its task: The nations are like a field ready for harvest, cut them

74

down! They are like ripe grapes packed into a wine press, crush them (3:13)!

Verses 15–16 describe the actual Day of the Lord, which is accompanied by signs in the heavens (cf. 2:10, 31). The "cutting down" and "crushing" of the nations is not described; we hear only the roaring of the Lord's voice from Zion (cf. Amos 1:2), and we feel the shaking of the heavens and the earth. In the midst of such terror is a word of comfort: "The LORD is a refuge to his people, a stronghold to the people of Israel" (16*b*).

Verse 17 describes the situation after the Day of the Lord has come. The language in Hebrew is identical to that of the climactic statement in 2:27: "you shall know that I am the LORD your God," with the additional statement, "who dwell in Zion" (cf. 2:32).

Of central importance to this part of the Book of Joel is that statement, "But the LORD is a refuge to his people, a stronghold to the people of Israel." If we translate the Hebrew literally, "to the children of Israel," then we are reminded of the charge at the beginning of the book: "Tell your children of it, and let your children tell their children, and their children another generation" (1:3). Reflection on that charge and on the assertion in 3:16*b* can help to get a grasp on the message of the Book of Joel as a whole.

What did the prophet want the children of the next generations to be told? (1) Tell the children to *remember* how God delivered us from the locusts. This was the concern of 1:5—2:27. We have seen that the charge to remember the mighty acts of God is one which runs throughout the Old Testament. The Book of Joel suggests: Tell the children also about the minor acts of God, the deliverances and the blessings experienced by a family or a clan or a town in the ordinary working out of their lives. Tell them so that they will have some basis for hope when they face similar crises. (2) When the children do encounter such crises and when they do not know where to turn, tell them to *return* to the Lord. This return is motivated by the kind of God the Lord is and is to be a complete reorientation of priorities, from the inside out (2:12–14). (3) When the next generation or the one after them lives in fear of whatever cataclysmic event threatens in the future, be it named "Day of the Lord" or "nuclear holocaust," what should they be told? Joel has a word for such people. It is, "the LORD is a refuge to his people, a stronghold to the children of Israel" (3:16*b*). In the words of

75

the Reformation hymn: Tell them that *our God is a mighty fortress.* Some comments on this important assertion in 3:16 follow.

In contrast to the prophet Hosea, Joel is sparing in his use of metaphors to speak of God. His theological vocabulary includes "Yahweh" (RSV, LORD), "God," and "Almighty" (1:15). One finds pictures of the Lord as leader of an army (2:11, 25) or as judge (3:2, 12) or as a roaring lion (3:16).

Only in 3:16 does Joel use nouns as metaphors in a direct theological statement. The Lord is a *refuge.* In a literal sense, the Hebrew word means a shelter from the storm or rain (Isa. 4:6; 25:4 "shelter"; Job 24:8 "shelter"). The word is used for a place of refuge in the rocks for badgers (Ps. 104:18). It is a favorite metaphor for God in the psalms. "God is our *refuge* and strength, a very present help in trouble" (Ps. 46:1, author's italics; cf. also 14:6; 61:3; 62:7–8; 71:7; 73:28; 91:2, 9; 94:22; 142:5). The meaning is clear: In the Lord is to be found safety and security.

The word translated *stronghold* is used in its literal sense in military settings. The place where the king goes for safety is the "fortress" (Dan. 11:7, 10, 19). This word is also frequently used metaphorically for the safety and security found in God (II Sam. 22:33 "refuge"; especially the Psalms, as 27:1; 31:4 "refuge"; 37:39 "refuge"; cf. also Jer. 16:19; Prov. 10:29).

Both words occur together in one other Old Testament context, again describing the security to be found with God: "For thou hast been a stronghold to the poor, a stronghold to the needy in distress, a shelter [translated "refuge" in Joel 3:16] from the storm, and a shade from the heat" (Isa. 25:4).

In the New Testament, this kind of language is used of Christ, who is the sure foundation (I Cor. 3:11) and the solid rock upon which one can build a life (Matt. 7:24–27). These metaphors have been popular in the hymnody of the church: "Rock of ages, cleft for me. Let me hide myself in thee"; "Built on a rock the church shall stand . . ."; "A mighty fortress is our God"; and "You were their rock, their fortress and their guide . . ." (from "For All the Saints").

3. The Lord Among Us (3:18–21)

The expression, "in that day," throws this final section of the Joel book into the distant future again (cf. 3:1 and the "afterward" of 2:28). That future will bring the reversal of the plagues which occasioned the prophecy of Joel. First, prosperity will be restored to nature. The "sweet wine" had been cut off (1:5); in the future, the mountains will drip with it (3:18). The cattle had groaned with neither pasture nor water (1:18, 20); in the future, the hills will flow with their milk (3:18). The streams had been dried up (1:20); in the future they will flow with water (3:18). The temple had been a place of sadness, devoid of offerings or the sound of joy (1:13, 16); in the future it will be the source from which blessings flow (3:18).

Then the future prosperity of the people is described, a prosperity which necessitates the destruction of their enemies (3:19). The final sentence picks up the theme of the climactic declarations in 2:27 ("I am in the midst of Israel") and 3:17 ("I am the LORD your God, who dwell in Zion") with the announcement that "the LORD dwells in Zion."

This theme of *the Lord among us* as articulated in the last sentence of Joel and also in 2:27 and 3:17 is an important one in the Bible, from the time of the wilderness wandering (Num. 5:3) and the settlement in the land (Num. 35:34) to the monarchy, when the psalms speak of God dwelling with his people on Mount Zion (Pss. 74:2; 68:17) or in Jerusalem (Pss. 46; 135: 21). The New Testament transposes this notion into a new key with the declaration that "the Word became flesh and dwelt among us" (John 1:14) and with the promise that "where two or three are gathered in my name, there am I in the midst of them" (Matt. 18:20).

The Book of Joel began by raising the question, "What shall we tell the children?" It comes to a conclusion with this statement: "Tell them that the Lord is a mighty fortress, a refuge, and a stronghold, and that the Lord dwells in their midst." Here is something worth passing on to the next generation and the next.

THE BOOK OF
Amos

Introduction

On the outside wall of a synagogue in St. Paul, facing the Mississippi River, is a saying from the prophet Amos: "Let justice well up as waters, and righteousness as a mighty stream." Whoever chose these words to be put in that place had an instinct for what is central to the prophet's preaching. Those who drive or walk along Mississippi River Boulevard can hardly miss the point: May justice and righteousness roll through the land like the mighty Mississippi!

What is the original context for this saying on that synagogue wall? What called forth these words? Who was Amos, and what does the biblical book bearing his name have to say? That book divides into seven parts:

1:1–2: These verses locate the prophet in space (Tekoa) and time (the days of Uzziah and Jeroboam) and introduce his message. Amos has heard the voice of the Lord and compares that experience to hearing the roaring of a lion, a roaring that causes pastures to dry up and forests to wither. The sayings in the remainder of the book should be heard with that roaring in the background. Amos seems obsessed with it, describing his call experience in terms of meeting a lion (3:4, 8) and speaking of Israel's encounter with the Lord in lion imagery (3:12; 5:19). We wonder: What could have set off that divine roaring?

1:3—2:16: The first and longest prophetic speech in the book announces seven times that the Lord will send fire to destroy the sophisticated defense systems of the nations who are Israel's neighbors. The speech comes to a shocking climax: The Lord's most severe accusations are directed against Israel.

These accusations have to do with the way the people of Israel have been treating the poor and the powerless in their midst. Now we get a hint at the reason for the Lord's roaring, and we begin to understand what is behind those words of the prophet written on the synagogue wall.

3:1—6:14: The initial focus was on the nations. Here the lens zooms in on Israel, with three collections of sayings which begin, "Hear this word . . ." (3:1; 4:1; 5:1). First, the people are reminded who they are and the prophet sets forth his own credentials (3:1–8). Next are sayings directed against a people who feel secure with their strategic defense systems (3:9–11), who revel in the perks which accompany affluence (3:15; 6:1–6), who busy themselves with religion (4:4–5; 5:21–23), but who are not heartbroken over what is happening to their nation (6:6). In Israel there is affluence and power, but there is also indifference to the poor. This is why the Lord has roared, and this is why the prophet calls for justice and for righteousness (5:24).

7:1—8:3: The kind of preaching reported in the book to this point has gotten Amos banished from the royal chapel at Bethel and earned him a one-way ticket back to Judah (7:10–17). The words in chapters 1—6 are strong medicine for anyone hearing them. As a reminder of where the prescription originated, this section reports four visionary encounters between God and the prophet. Israel, the prophet learned, did not measure up to the Lord's standards (7:7–9). The Lord has spoken, and the prophet calls for justice and righteousness.

8:4—9:15: The book concludes with another collection beginning with "Hear this. . . ." These sayings pick up themes introduced at the beginning of the book. The first prophetic speech considered Israel in the context of other nations (1:3—2:16); 9:7 does the same. The prophet's first accusation against Israel charged them with oppressing the poor (2:6–7); the last accusation makes the same charge (8:4–8). The book began with a picture of a powerful God (1:2); it concludes with a section rich in theological insight and imagery (8:11—9:15, with 9:5–7 as the centerpiece): God has acted and continues to act in the history of Israel and all nations (9:7), God acts in nature (9:5–6), and this mighty God is also *your* God (9:15). The beginning of the book reports that when the Lord speaks, the fields and forests wither (1:2); at the end of the book the Lord's voice promises that one day the mountains and hills will drip with sweet wine (9:13).

80

A careful reading indicates that considerable thought has gone into the collecting, selecting, and editing of the "words of Amos" (1:1) as they are gathered here. Some of the prophet's sayings were no doubt eliminated. Others were supplemented, to make them more suitable for the new audiences they would address. At certain points we hear remarks such as a modern teacher or commentator might make (3:7; 5:13). At others, the editor has inserted fragments of hymnic material (4:13; 5:8–9; 9:5–6).

All of this editorial work was done with the aim of making the words of the prophet from Tekoa more accessible to those who would hear them as they were read before the gathered community of believers. The fact that 1:1 mentions the king of Judah before the king of Israel suggests that this editing was done in Judah, after the fall of Israel in 722 B.C. had validated such prophetic words as 7:17.

The texts chosen for the expositions which follow are those which are central to the prophet's message and which have special potential for teaching and preaching. The editor of the Amos book intended that those who encounter these materials first hear what is said in 1:1–2; it will be important to begin by considering these sentences carefully.

Amos 1:1
The Prophet Amos

The opening sentence in the Amos book introduces the prophet by vocation, hometown, and historical setting.

1. Amos of Tekoa

The name "Amos" is derived from the Hebrew verb which means "to load" or "to carry a load." Martin Luther associated the prophet's name with his message: "He can well be called Amos, that is 'a burden,' one who is hard to get along with and irritating . . ." ("Word and Sacrament," *Luther's Works* 35, 320).

The introductory sentence indicates the prophet's voca-   **81**
tion. People are frequently introduced this way, as a carpenter (Mark 6:3) or a salesperson (Acts 16:14) or a plumber or a com-

puter programmer. The word translated "shepherd" is also used of Mesha, the king of Moab, who dealt in livestock by the hundreds of thousands (II Kings 3:4). This would suggest that we ought not think of Amos as a lonely rustic, wandering from pasture to pasture with a few sheep under his care. As a "sheep breeder" (the translation in II Kings 3:4) he was no doubt a man of substance and influence. We might compare him to a modern-day rancher or a large-scale farmer; 7:14 indicates that he was also involved in horticulture. Amos himself makes clear that he was a layman, called to be a prophet while going about his ordinary work (7:14–15).

Amos is from the town of Tekoa. Again, this is a common way to introduce someone; a person may be from Moresheth (Micah 1:1) or Nazareth (John 1:45) or Thyatira (Acts 16:14) or Cincinnati or St. Louis. What would it mean to be from Tekoa? The town was small, located a few miles to the south of Jerusalem. It appears that Tekoa was noted for its cultivation of a kind of rural common sense, a folk wisdom of the type found in the Book of Proverbs and coming to expression in the words and acts of people such as the professional "wise woman" from Tekoa (II Sam. 14; see Hans Walter Wolff, *Amos the Prophet*). We say, "You can take the man out of the country, but you can't take the country out of the man." As we listen to Amos, we shall not be surprised to hear echoes of the folk wisdom which was part of the small-town climate in which he lived.

A careful reading of the remainder of the book tells more about Amos. Though from a small town, he is interested in international affairs (1:3—2:5; 9:7). He has considerable skill as a speaker, making effective use of such techniques as similes and metaphors (see below), repetition, and building to a climax (1:3—2:16; 4:6–12). His announcements of judgment against both the individual and the nation fall into the typical pattern of accusation plus announcement of punishment, often joined with a messenger formula (7:16–17; the sayings in chapters 1 and 2; 4:1–3; 8:4–8; see Claus Westermann, *Basic Forms of Prophetic Speech*). One of his techniques is to accuse his hearers by quoting their own words (2:12; 4:1; 5:14; 6:2, 13; 7:16; 8:5–6, 14). Amos is courageous, addressing the wealthy women (4:1–3), the powerful priest (7:10–17), and the downtown businessmen (8:4–8) with words which did not gain him any favor and in fact earned his deportation from the country (7:12–13).

This shepherd-farmer has the eye and ear of a poet, and his language reflects the world in which he lives. He has seen a wagon straining under a heavy load from the field (2:13) and has watched the well-fed cattle grazing on the hills of Bashan (4:1). The oaks and cedars have impressed him with their towering strength (2:9) and the streams with their surging power (5:24). He knows what a lion can do to a lamb (3:12) and what locusts can do to a crop (7:1).

The sayings in the book indicate an acquaintance with life beyond that of the shepherd. Amos knew something of warfare: the sound of the alarm (3:6), the sight of fires set by invading armies (1:4, 7), and the stench of death rising from the camp (4:10). He was acquainted with construction practices (7:7–8) and the work of the surveyor (7:17). Amos had observed the lifestyle of the rich, with their expensive homes (3:15) and luxurious tastes (4:1; 6:4–6). In the places of worship he had heard both the hymns of praise (5:23) and the cries of lament (5:1, 16). He was acquainted with grief (8:10). His ear had caught what went on behind the counters in the shops of the merchants (8:5) and his eye had seen what happened to the poor in the courts (5:12).

Amos's experiences and observations furnish the linguistic vessels which transport his message. When he tells of his encounter with the Lord he compares it to being terrified by the roar of a lion (3:8). A misplaced confidence in a "day of the Lord" is compared to escaping from a lion but then meeting a bear (5:19). The nation Israel, nearing the end of her days, is like a young virgin who dies before her time (5:1–2). The courts have turned justice into poison (5:7; 6:12). Amos looks for the day when justice will roll through the land like a cleansing stream (5:24). On the day of judgment, Israel will no more escape than a rock can pass through the fine mesh of a sieve (9:9).

This is Amos of Tekoa: informed, able, courageous, imaginative. He is also something else. What could impel such an intelligent and sensitive person to say what he did in the places he said them? Why would he conduct himself so that he would be remembered as "a burden . . . hard to get along with and irritating"? Amos answers the question simply: He was called

83

and commanded by the Lord and could not have responded in any other way (3:8; 7:15).

2. The Days of Jeroboam

The initial sentence in the Amos book dates the prophet's activity in the time of Uzziah king of Judah and Jeroboam king of Israel, suggesting that if we are going to hear these prophetic words rightly we need first to hear them addressed to that particular time and place.

The days of Uzziah (king from 783–742) and Jeroboam (786–746) were days of calm, peace, and prosperity for both Israel and Judah. Jeroboam had restored Israel's borders to the dimensions of the kingdom during the glorious days of Solomon (II Kings 14:23–29; cf. I Kings 8:65). Neither Egypt nor Syria was interfering in Israelite affairs. Assyria was under the leadership of three weak rulers who were occupied with domestic affairs and did not campaign into the west.

Amos looks back upon Jeroboam's military successes, which suggests dating the prophet's activity at a time well into that king's administration (Amos 6:13–14; cf. II Kings 14:25). The earthquake of 1:1 is also mentioned in Zechariah 14:5 and has been dated by archaeologists as around 760 B.C. (see Wolff, *Joel and Amos,* p. 124, and James Luther Mays, *Amos,* p. 20). Thus the prophet's work may be located in the years after 760 B.C. (see Bright, *History,* pp. 253–266, for more detail on this historical situation).

The most useful information for understanding the situation which Amos addressed comes from a reading of the book itself. The prophet spoke to a people enjoying affluence, eating their meat (a luxury) and drinking their wines to the accompaniment of novel music (6:4–6). The women are preoccupied with drink, putting demands on their husbands to keep their liquor cabinets well stocked (4:1). New houses with expensive ivory decorations are being built, some people having separate residences for summer and winter (5:11; 3:15). Business downtown is booming (8:5). Attendance at places of worship is good (5:21–23). Sacrifices are being offered and the tithes are rolling in, all with appropriate publicity (4:4–5).

The people feel secure in Samaria, their capital city. They have a "We're number one" view of themselves among the nations of the world (6:1) and look to the future with optimism,

84

confident that the "Day of the Lord" will bring even greater things (5:18–20).

In sum, the time of Uziah and Jeroboam was a time of calm, but it was the calm before a storm. In a few years Israel's security would all be over. Storm clouds were gathering on the horizon, and soon a succession of great empires would dominate Israel's part of the world; Assyria would be the first, then Babylon, Persia, Greece, and Rome. It was the task of Amos to announce that the storm was about to strike, and to tell why.

Amos 1:2
No Still Small Voice

Amos 1:1 introduced the prophet and placed him in his historical setting. Amos 1:2 introduces the prophet's message with a saying that sets the tone for the entire book.

The sentence begins, "The LORD roars from Zion, and utters his voice from Jerusalem." The verb "roar" means the roaring of a lion, as it does in Amos 3:4 and in Judges 14:5; Psalm 104:21; and Hosea 11:10. The shepherd Amos mentions lions several times. He has heard the lion's roar when it has caught its prey and he has seen what a lion can do to its victim (3:4, 12). The automatic response upon hearing a lion's roar is terror (3:8). The only proper reaction to an encounter with a lion is to seek immediate safety (5:19).

Such a concern for lions would not be unusual in the place where Amos lived. I Kings 13 preserves a story about a prophet devoured by a lion as he was traveling on the road from Bethel to Judah, just the road Amos may have taken. I Kings 20:36 tells of another prophet killed by a lion. The presence of lions in eighth-century Samaria is indicated by II Kings 17:25.

The lion captured the imagination of a number of biblical writers. Named "the mightiest among beasts" (Prov. 30:30), it is used in apocalyptic literature as a symbol for terrifying power (Dan. 7:1–4; Rev. 13:2). It may function as an image for the devil (I Peter 5:8). In the messianic age to come, lions will be tame (Isa. 11:6–7) or absent (Isa. 35:9).

85

Amos had heard the voice of the Lord. It was no "still small voice" such as Elijah reported (I Kings 19). The only thing to which he could compare the word of the Lord was the roar of a lion. Upon hearing that roar, who would not be terrified? Upon being addressed by that voice, who could but prophesy?

The roaring came from Mount Zion in Judah. Amos prophesied in Israel, the Northern Kingdom, but both this reference at the beginning of the book and also the mention of David at the end (9:11) are reminders that Amos was a southerner who lived not far from Jerusalem and the temple on Mount Zion. The effects of the Lord's roaring are described in language drawn from Amos's world:

> "The pastures dry up,
> and the grass on Mount Carmel turns brown" (GNB).

The placing of the statement about the terrifying roaring of the Lord's voice at the beginning of the book indicates that all the sayings of Amos should be heard against the background of that roaring. Abraham Heschel once wrote:

> Most of us who care for the world bewail God's dreadful silence, while Amos appears smitten by God's mighty voice. He did not hear a whisper, "a still small voice," but a voice like a lion's roaring that drives shepherd and flock into a panic (*The Prophets,* I, 29).

In the preaching and teaching of the church today, most of us tend to favor those biblical pictures of God that are comforting and secure: the caring shepherd (Ps. 23), the nursing mother (Ps. 131), and the waiting father (Luke 15). In contrast we open the Book of Amos and discover on the first page that encountering the Lord is like meeting a lion. We find that the first announced acts of this God are the sending of fires and an earthquake. This picture of God as a roaring lion conveys the ferocity and the wrath of a God whom we have tried to domesticate and tame.

What could have set off such a divine roaring? What could have unleashed such fury against a people whom the Lord still calls "my people" (7:15; 8:2)? If there remains within us, alongside a certainty of God's comforting love, any sense of God's terrifying wrath, then we shall do well to listen to how the prophet from Tekoa, who had heard the roaring of lions and of the Lord, answers these questions.

86

Amos 1:3—2:16
The Earthquake and the Fire

A message may be found in that lion's roaring heard in the beginning of the Book of Amos. One could imagine a powerful stereophonic receiver switched on but not tuned to any station. All that can be heard is a hissing, a crackling, a roaring. When the receiver is tuned in, the signal becomes intelligible.

In the remainder of the Amos book the signal will be tuned in, and the message hidden in the roaring of the lion will be unscrambled. The transmitting of the message is the task of the prophet.

1. The Prophet as Messenger

"Thus says the LORD." So the first speech in the book begins, and these words are repeated throughout that speech (1:3, 6, 9, 11, 13; 2:1, 4, 6) as well as elsewhere in the Amos book (3:11, 12; 5:3, 4, 16; 7:17). Consideration of this expression as it occurs in the Old Testament provides a model for helping to understand the figure of the prophet.

The expression has its origin in the practice of sending messages in the ancient world. When Jacob wishes to communicate with his brother Esau, he sends messengers who introduce their message with, "Thus says your servant Jacob" (Gen. 32:4). When Jephthah is involved in negotiations with the Ammonite king, his representatives begin their speaking with "Thus says Jephthah" (Judg. 11:15). When the Assyrian emperor has a message for the king of Judah, his messenger introduces that message with "Thus says the great king, the king of Assyria" (II Kings 18:19; cf. v. 29). In considering these accounts of message sending, we observe that: (1) The origin of the message is with the sender. The messenger is in the communications business, relaying a message from one person to another. (2) The authority behind the message lies with the sender. The messengers sent by Jephthah and by the Assyrian empire were not killed but were granted diplomatic immunity because of whom they represented. (3) The "I" of the messenger's speech is the "I" of the message sender; (4) the

87

messenger has a degree of freedom in the formulation of the message, as is clear in the last two examples. The messenger could be described as an international diplomat, an ambassador rather than a postman.

The expression "Thus says the LORD" is drawn from this world of international diplomacy. The prophet may be understood as an "ambassador from the Lord," after the model of the messengers in the texts considered above. The origin of the prophetic message was not with the prophet but with the Lord (Amos 7:15). The authority for the message lay with the Lord who sent the prophet; this alone explains how a prophet could address a king in sharply critical terms and not be executed (II Sam. 12). The "I" in the prophet's speeches is the "I" of the Lord, and we may assume that the prophet had some freedom in the formulation of the message he brought. Amos sounds very different from Hosea; this is because the personality of the prophet was involved in the formulation of the message. The prophets too were ambassadors, not postmen.

2. God of All Nations (1:3—2:5)

This first major speech in the Amos book can be read aloud in Hebrew in less than ten minutes. Allowing for interruptions, the actual delivery of such a speech would not take more than about twelve minutes. Like a master rhetorician at a political rally, the prophet makes use of repetition, audience participation (the question in 2:11), and shocking surprise to give his speech maximum impact. The first seven parts of the speech are short, each following the same basic pattern. The *messenger formula*, "Thus says the LORD," identifies the prophet as the Lord's messenger. Next comes a *general accusation* in the form "For three transgressions of . . . and for four. . . ." First to be accused are two of Israel's longtime enemies, the Syrians and the Philistines. These two are also linked at the end of the book in 9:7, the prophet naming them as the most unlikely candidates, in the opinion of his hearers, to have benefited from the Lord's action in their histories. The last nation in the series of seven is Judah, with whom Israel shared a common history and a common faith. The fourth, fifth, and sixth nations are Edom, Ammon, and Moab, nations that have a kinship relationship with Israel. The Edomites were considered descendants of Esau, Jacob's brother (Gen. 36:1). Ammon and Moab, ancestors of the nations bearing their names, were sons of Lot, Abraham's nephew (Gen. 19:36–38). The saying about Tyre follows after the first two and before the series of kinship nations. Thus there seems to be a progression from traditional enemies through nations sharing kinship to the people most closely related to Israel.

The listing of Israel's neighbors indicates that the God of Amos is concerned with international politics. The first thing the prophet says about God in this speech is that God is active in the histories of other nations, even in the histories of Israel's worst enemies! God has worked for the good of those nations (9:7) but will also punish them for their crimes. The Lord is not the private deity of Israel. The Lord cares when the Moabites commit crimes against Edom and will punish them for such (2:1–3). The tendency of any grouping of the people of God, both past and present, is to inscribe "God with us" (Amos 5:14) on its weaponry, "In God We Trust" on its coinage, and then begin to claim God as its own private possession and to identify its own purposes with those of God. These first oracles in the Book of Amos help to keep things in theological perspective. To be sure, God has entered into a special relationship with those whom God brought out of Egypt and with those who have become God's people through Jesus Christ (I Peter 2:9–10). God is also concerned about the other peoples of the world, though, even those who have been enemies of God's people (Nineveh, in the Book of Jonah; see also Matt. 8:11; 28:16–20; and Acts 1:8).

The *specific accusations* in the first six sayings all have to do with crimes in war. Damascus has treated the people of Gilead with extreme cruelty, grinding them as grain is ground on a threshing floor. The Philistines and the people of Tyre have been involved in large-scale programs of deportation. Tyre has violated an international treaty, the "covenant of brother-hood." The Edomites are accused of pitiless and ongoing cruelty against a "brother" people. The atrocity of the Ammonites is especially reprehensible: Innocent civilians, pregnant women, are killed by the sword, taking two lives at one blow. If the Ammonites exterminated life before birth, the Moabites are accused of extending their atrocities beyond death, burning human bones to make consumer products, in this case for whitewashing walls (the same word is translated "plaster" in Deut. 27:2, 4).

Judah's wrongdoing is described in different terms. They have "rejected the law of the LORD, and have not kept his

89

statutes" (2:4). Judah is judged differently because it is differently related to the Judge. Judah is part of that "whole family" which the Lord brought out of Egypt (3:1). Israelites hearing this accusation of their relatives would be well aware that they too had a special relationship to the Judge.

Seven times the *announcement of punishment* involves the Lord sending fire. The reference seems to be to the fires set by invading armies as part of the technique of warfare; the battle cry and the sound of the bugle are also part of that technique (1:14; 2:2). At the end of the Amos book, the Lord promises a day when the vineyards will be heavy with grapes and the mountains will drip with sweet wine. As the book begins, however, the prophet speaks only of the roaring lion and the ravaging fire.

The pattern often concludes with a final *messenger formula* (1:5, 8, 15; 2:3, 16).

What would have been the effect of this speech upon the audience to this point? We can almost hear them cheering and applauding after each neighboring nation was condemned. We can imagine the prophet playing the audience, drawing out those repeated phrases, extending the pauses, waiting for the cheers to come. The speech is building to a climax as three, four, five nations are placed under divine judgment. With the mention of Judah the number reaches seven. Now the congregation might assume that the sermon was finished, since seven in the Bible so often signals completeness (for example, Gen. 1:1—2:3; 4:15, 24; Lev. 26:18, 21, 24; Matt. 18:21-22; Luke 17:4; see "Seven, Seventh, Seventy," *Interpreter's Dictionary,* pp. 294-295). A listener might now be ready to comment agreeably on the speaker's style and skill, chat amiably about the affairs of the week, and then go home. Now comes the surprise. The prophet who spoke of God in terms of the roaring lion and the ravaging fire was not finished yet.

3. God and the Powerless (2:6–8, 12–16)

The last saying in the series begins like all the rest with "Thus says the LORD." It continues with the familiar "For three transgressions . . . ," but then Israel is named, and the pattern is shattered.

90

The *specific accusation* against those hearing the prophet's words is expanded to seven crimes: (1) The "righteous," that is ordinary honest citizens, are being sold as slaves. The decent person who had come upon hard times was sold "for silver." (2) The needy are sold into slavery when they owe only a small amount, such as the cost of a pair of sandals (this expression means "a very little"; see Gen. 14:23 and Sirach 46:19). (3) The poor are oppressed, "trampled," in this image. (4) The "afflicted" or poverty-stricken do not get fair treatment in the courts; this is the sense of "turn aside the way" (2:7; cf. 5:12). (5) A young woman hired as domestic help is sexually abused not only by one of the young men in the family but also by the father. (6) A debtor might be required to give a creditor a coat for security. The legal system protected the debtor by requiring that such a garment be returned before the cold of night (Exod. 22:26–27). Here the wealthy creditors are charged with using these garments as blankets while picnicking in the temple area. (7) In the case of certain crimes, fines were charged to make restitution for injuries (Exod. 21:22 and Deut. 22:19 provide examples). Apparently a poor farmer could pay a fine with the wine he had produced. Now, that wine was being indiscriminately consumed by those who had plenty in their own wine cellars.

The seven sayings directed against other nations tell of a God who is concerned about the happenings on the international scene. In the saying against Israel, we hear that this same God is also concerned when legal aid is denied the poor, when a young woman is sexually abused, or when the machinery designed to protect the dignity of the powerless in a society is quietly disregarded. These "polite" sins, which take place in an outwardly orderly and civil society, are denounced in the same speech as the war crimes and atrocities that the prophet's hearers rightly deplore among their neighbors!

If the first seven sayings demonstrate God's interest in international politics, the Israel saying indicates God's concern for the individual powerless. This bipolar way of speaking about God, describing God's majesty and might in working on the international scene on the one hand and God's care and mercy in dealing with the individual on the other, is typical of the Bible. Psalm 113, for example, praises the power and might of God (1–4) but also praises God because of the Lord's concern for the poor and the childless (6–9). The same combination may be observed in the Song of Hannah (I Sam. 2) and the Magnificat of Mary (Luke 1). The scene of the great judgment in Matthew 25 portrays the Lord as presiding over the judgment of all

91

nations, but also as present in the stranger, the naked, and the hungry.

The Lord's concern for the poor and needy was not a theme unique to Amos. In considering this topic note first of all Isaiah 10:1–4, which directs a woe-saying against those who oppress three groups: widows, orphans, and the poor. These three have in common a lack of power in society. The widow has no husband, the orphan no parent, the poor no money to give them power in public life. These we may call the *powerless*. To them may be added the stranger or sojourner, who has no friend (Exod. 22:21; 23:9; Deut. 14:29; 26:12), and the aged, who may be without spouse, money, friends, or strength (Lev. 19:32).

The theme of the Lord's concern for these powerless runs through the Bible: It is found in legal materials: from the book of the covenant, Exodus 22:21–24; 22:25; 23:3, 6, 9, 10–11; from Deuteronomy, 14:28–29; 15:7–11; 26:12–15; from the Holiness Code, Leviticus 19:9–10; 19:15, 32; 25:35–38.

The theme is a frequent one in the psalms (72:2–4, 12–14; 82:3–4; 107:41; 113:7; 132:15; 146:7) and in Proverbs (14:21, 31; 19:17; 21:13; 22:9, 22–23; 23:10–11; 29:7, 14; 31:9, 20).

It is also heard from other prophets. Note Amos's contemporaries from Judah: Isaiah 1:10–17, 21–26; 5:1–7; 10:1–4; Micah 3:1–4, 9–12; 6:6–8. We have called attention to Matthew 25:31–46; see also James 1:26–27, where true religion is defined in terms of visiting the orphan and widow, with the poor discussed in James 2. (See also the commentary on Amos 5:21–24 and Micah 6:6–8.)

The *announcement of punishment* against Israel is found in 2:13–16. The Hebrew is emphatic: "Behold, I [*myself*] will press you down..." (author's italics). The picture is of a farmer's wagon, heavily loaded at harvest time, digging deep ruts into the ground and destroying that over which it rolls. The reference is apparently to an earthquake, likely the one mentioned in 1:1. How will the people react to this punishment? Not even the strongest, the swiftest, or the bravest will be able to escape (vv. 14–16). The final "says the LORD" is a messenger formula, certifying the authenticity of the message.

4. Telling the Story (2:9–12)

The saying against Israel contains a new element not found in the pattern of the sayings against other nations. Speaking as the Lord's messenger, the prophet reminds his audience of God's mighty acts in their past, recalling the Exodus, the guiding through the wilderness, the conquest of the land, and the sending of prophets. The audience is invited to respond to this retelling of the story: "Is it not indeed so, O people of Israel?"

The prophetic task has been described as concerned with the future (foretelling), addressing the present (forthtelling), and recalling the past (retelling). Telling the story of God's mighty acts remains an aspect of the tasks of both preaching and teaching. In hearing this story and discovering it as their own story, a people of God can rediscover who they are. They will be reminded of what God has done for them and will be motivated to respond in acts of love.

The new element in the preaching of Amos is the chilling announcement that God is about to punish a whole people, God's own people. There is no automatic relationship between God and people. The God of the Bible does not have one attribute only! It is true that this God is the good Shepherd, the nursing Mother, the waiting Father, but the God of Amos is also the roaring Lion, who can send the earthquake and the fire.

Amos 3:1–8
Who Do You Think You Are?

The "Hear this . . ." of Amos 3:1 introduces the first of four collections beginning with such a call for the attention of the hearers (also 4:1; 5:1; 8:4). Since the themes of the last three sayings (vv. 9–11, 12, 13–15) occur in later sections of the book, the focus here will be on 3:1–8.

The long speech in chapters 1 and 2 had ended with the announcement of an earth-shaking punishment which was to come upon Israel. Those who originally heard that speech, and those who would subsequently hear it as it was read to the community from the Amos book, would have two questions in mind: (1) Could all this really happen to us? After all, are we not God's chosen people? (2) Who does this person think he is? Where does he get the authority to speak to us in this way? Verses 1–2 deal with the first of these questions and verses 3–8 with the second.

93

Amos 3:1–8 also has a function in regard to the sayings directed against Israel which follow, making clear the identity of Israel as a chosen people and the identity of Amos as a prophet called by the Lord.

The sayings in verses 1–2 and 3–8 may originally have been spoken on different occasions. As they are now placed in the book, however, they are framed by the sentence "the LORD (God) has spoken" (vv. 1, 8) and carefully fitted between the long speech which precedes them and the shorter sayings which follow.

1. Chosen People (3:1–2)

At issue in this short saying is the identity of the people Israel. The preceding long speech (chaps. 1 and 2) had climaxed with the announcement of a terrible catastrophe which was to come upon Israel. We have suggested that the hearers of this speech would be asking: Could all this really happen to us? After all, are we not God's chosen people? This saying deals with that issue.

First of all, it gives expression to the *relationship* which exists between God and people with its strong I/you language: "against *you* . . . *I* brought up . . . *You* only have *I* known . . . *I* will punish *you*" (author's italics).

Second, it *reminds* the prophet's hearers in three ways who they are: (1) These citizens of the Northern Kingdom are a part of the whole people of God, God's "whole family." The saying is thus addressed not just to political Israel, Jeroboam's Northern Kingdom, but to theological Israel, the whole people of God. In this way it remains relevant to the people of God who survive the fall of the Northern Kingdom in 722 B.C. (2) As a part of that "whole family" these hearers are a rescued people, "brought up out of the land of Egypt." (3) Finally, they are also a chosen people. Speaking as the Lord's messenger the prophet says, "You only have I known of all the families of the earth" (one is reminded of the listing of those "families" in the preceding speech). The Hebrew word here translated as "known" was used in a variety of contexts in the biblical world, ranging from the use of cognates in Near Eastern treaties ("know" means "recognize as treaty partner") to its use in Genesis 4:1 to denote the sexual relationship. Especially instructive is the use of the word in Genesis 18, where the Lord is speaking about Abraham:

94

... I have *chosen* [the same Hebrew word as that translated "known" in Amos 3:2; see RSV footnote] him, that he may charge his children and his household after him to keep the way of the LORD by doing righteousness and justice (v. 19; author's italics).

This verse refers to the choice of Abraham reported in Genesis 12:1–3. This choosing is for a task, described in terms of lives marked by righteousness and justice.

Finally, this saying also assumes that a *response* is expected of this people who have been reminded of their unique relationship to the Lord. The response, like that called for in Genesis 18:19, should take the form of justice and righteousness; note the same words in Amos 5:24 as well as 5:7 and 6:12. Amos's hearers have responded only with "iniquities," and for this even the chosen people—*especially* the chosen people—can expect punishment.

The language here is reminiscent of the covenant made on Mount Sinai: "out of the land of Egypt" (Exod. 20:2), "iniquities" (Exod. 20:5 and Deut. 5:9; see also Exod. 34:7 and Num. 14:18). The relationship-reminder-response themes also recall the structure of that covenant. The giving of the commandments is preceded by a declaration of the relationship between God and people ("I am the LORD your God"), a reminder of what God has done ("who brought you out of the land of Egypt ..."), and then a spelling out of the expected response in the Decalogue. Thus Amos is saying nothing new to his hearers. He is calling them to remember who they are, what God has done for them, and how they are expected to live.

2. Called Prophet (3:3–8)

The second question from those who heard the long speech reported in chapters 1 and 2 might have been, "Who are you to say these things to us? By what authority do you speak this way?"

A number of indications in the Amos book point to the opposition the prophet encountered. The first mention of prophets and prophecy is in 2:11–12; here we get a hint of the reception prophets received, with Amos quoting the words of those who said, "You shall not prophesy!" Amos 7:10–17 reports the words and acts of the priest Amaziah at Bethel, who sent Amos on his way home and banned him from a return engagement (vv. 12–13). This section assumes a hostile context, with

95

people asking questions like those given above. The prophet begins by firing a volley of seven rhetorical questions at his hearers. We could imagine him pausing after each one, waiting for the "No" response. After these seven questions, the climax of this short speech follows in verse 8.

Each of the first seven questions is designed to evoke from the audience an acknowledgment of the inevitability of a reaction to an action, a result to a cause. The first question is the most difficult to understand with certainty. Apparently what is meant is that when two people are seen walking along a road together (the result) one can assume that this is so because of a prior decision to travel together (the cause). The other questions are more clear. Why would a lion make such a roaring (the result)? Because the lion had just made a catch (the cause). Why would a bird suddenly fall to the ground? Because it has been caught in a snare! Why does a trap spring up? Because the trigger has been tripped!

With the question in verse 6 the order "result/cause" is reversed. When the alarm is sounded in a city, the people are afraid! The word is literally "tremble"; it is used to describe the reaction to the trumpet-alarm in I Kings 1:49. Next, the prophet makes a theological assertion: When evil comes upon a city (the result), you can be sure that the Lord has caused it! With this, we are reminded of the punishments announced in chapters 1 and 2.

The point of all seven of these questions is the instantaneous, automatic reaction to a particular action. When the alarm sounds, when the siren goes off, when one hears the roar of a lion, one does not debate, "Shall I be afraid or not?" Not at all, says Amos. Your heart races, your blood pressure leaps up, and you are scared to death! After a parenthetical comment about prophecy (v. 7) comes the climax (v. 8). First, the lion theme again: "The lion has roared!" "Who will not fear?" asks the prophet, and we can imagine the audience responding, "No one!" Then finally, "The LORD GOD has spoken, who can but prophesy?" Again the audience could only respond, "No one!"

The prophet plays his audience with admirable rhetorical skill. As in the speech in chapters 1 and 2, he gets them to respond seven times in just the way he wants. Now he has gained some momentum. He has his rhythm going. Following these seven responses comes the climax. Amos has spoken as he has because the Lord spoke to him! He has been called. He could not do otherwise, any more than one could do other than respond in terror upon hearing the shriek of an alarm or the roar of a lion.

Where does this person get his authority to speak this way? His critics have their answer.

3. Identity Crisis

We speak of a person suffering from an "identity crisis" when that person has forgotten who he or she is. This prophetic saying indicates that it is also possible for a whole people to suffer from an identity crisis. "Who do you think you are?" Amos might well have asked his hearers. He answered the question himself by reminding them who they were: a part of the family of God, the people with whom God had entered into a special relationship, for whom God had done much and of whom God expected a response.

Amos 3:1–2 puts us in touch with the biblical theme of election or the chosen people. The beginnings of this theme can be traced to the call of Abraham in Genesis 12:1–3. The theme is sounded with variations in Exodus 19:3–6 and Deuteronomy 7:7–11 and continues into the New Testament. Paul began his sermon in the Antioch synagogue with a reference to the choosing of Abraham and continued by telling what God had done for his people up through the story of the life and death of Jesus Christ (Acts 13:16–41). He used "chosen" language when writing to that troublesome congregation in Corinth (I Cor. 1:26–31). One of the great descriptions of the church uses this "chosen" language, reminding Christian hearers that to be a chosen people means to be chosen for a task (I Peter 2:9). Other expressions of this theme are found in John 15:15–16; I Thessalonians 1:4; II Timothy 2:10; Titus 1:1; 2:14 ("a people of his own" echoing Exod. 19:5); James 2:5; II John 1:1.

These "chosen" texts agree that the act of choosing always originates from the side of God and is rooted in God's amazing grace (especially Deut. 7:7–8; cf. John 15:16). They also stress the unique and intimate relationship between God and the chosen which may be expressed in such terms as covenant (Exod. 19:3–6) or a vine and branches (John 15). These texts also indicate that a response is expected from those chosen, described in the language of justice and righteousness (Gen. 18), obedience and covenant keeping (Exod. 19), keeping com-

97

mandments (Deut. 7), bearing fruit (John 15), or telling the mighty acts of God (I Peter 2).

These other biblical "chosen" texts thus evidence the same "reminder-relationship-response" themes as were heard in Amos 3:1–2. If the first two themes are sounded with clarity and with imagination, the hearers will be motivated to respond in words and works of love.

The prophet's own answer to the question of his identity is characteristically straightforward. We imagined the audience asking, "Who do you think you are?" Amos answered that he had been called by the Lord and could not do other than speak for that Lord. Other prophets and apostles give expression to that same sense of call and that compulsion to speak (Isa. 6; Jer. 1; 20:9; Gal. 1:15–16).

Amos 3:3–8 contains no word from God through the prophet to the people but it does help the reader to understand the person of the prophet. In a similar way these words are not so much words for preaching as they are for the preacher. The modern-day preacher may be haunted by the question of identity: Who am I, anyway? What right do I have to stand before my people week by week, day by day, and speak to them about God and the meaning of life?

This text locates the source and the authority which animates and certifies all that the preacher says and does: That authority comes from the Lord, whose speaking is like the roaring of a lion, who has spoken through the prophets and more recently through his Son (Heb. 1:1–2), and who continues to address the Lord's people through preaching (Rom. 10:14–17; I Cor. 1:21).

Amos 4:1–3
Women's Work

The setting for this prophetic saying is a public place where women are gathered, such as at the market place. We can imagine the prophet observing the women for a time, watching them go about their ordinary affairs, picking up a snatch of conversation from here or there. Then Amos calls for the attention of the crowd, "Hear this word!"

1. The Shocking Metaphor

At this point there would be a pause, then a hush, as these citizens of Samaria turned to look at the stranger. Amos observed his audience for a moment. What came to his mind was the image of sleek, well-fed cattle moving about in their pastures with contentment. He connected that image with the scene before him and spoke, "You cows of Bashan who are in the mountain of Samaria." Bashan was to the east of the Sea of Galilee, an area noted for its timber (Isa. 2:13; Ezek. 27:6), pasture land, and fine cattle (Deut. 32:14; Ezek. 39:18; Ps. 22:12).

What would this label have meant to this audience? It is true that the Bible uses images in manners which have quite a different sound in our own context. The young lover in the Song of Solomon, for example, compares his beloved's hair to a flock of goats and her teeth to a flock of shorn ewes (4:1–4). One expects such extravagant and inflated language in love poetry. The words of Amos, however, were spoken in public, in the context of confrontation. It is difficult to imagine that those who heard them would take them as a compliment! Amos has called for the attention of his audience, and now he has it!

This prophetic saying falls into the familiar pattern of the accusation (v. 1) grounding an announcement of punishment (vv. 2–3; see on 1:1, part 1). The prophet makes three charges against the women before him. First, they "oppress the poor." The same language is used in wisdom literature: "He who oppresses a poor man insults his Maker," declares Proverbs 14:31; see also Proverbs 22:16; 28:3; and Ecclesiastes 4:1–3. The second charge "who crush the needy" uses a metaphor. Just as a bowl is crushed and broken (Eccles. 12:6) so the needy are destroyed. These first two charges are familiar ones, similar to those made in 2:6–7. The third is more subtle. Amos had learned something about his audience and had picked up bits of what they were saying. Now he quotes their own words, accusing them of a self-centered lifestyle. These women may not directly cheat the poor in the marketplace (8:5–6) nor do they deny them justice in the courts (5:11–12), but they are held responsible for the condition of their society nonetheless. Their part in the oppression of the powerless consists of putting demands on their husbands to maintain a highly expensive style

99

of life. Their liquor cabinets must be kept full, so that they can while away their leisure hours to the accompaniment of the proper wines.

The announcement of punishment is introduced with a particularly solemn oath formula, "The LORD GOD has sworn . . ." (cf. also 6:8; 8:7). Then the prophet returns to the cattle image, "They'll lead you out of here with cattle prods," the prophet is saying, "and push you along the way with harpoons" (the RSV, "fishhooks" must refer to some harpoon-like instrument normally used for fishing, but which could also be used for driving cattle).

Lined up in single file like so many cattle, these women of Samaria will be led, pushed, shoved through the breaches the invaders will make in the city walls. They will begin the long trek toward the northeast, toward Mount Hermon (apparently the sense of "Hermon" here) and the pasture lands of Bashan from where they came. Speaking without metaphor, these women could expect to be deported to exile in Assyria.

2. Who Is Responsible?

This prophetic saying makes clear that the conditions in Israelite society are the responsibility of all citizens, both the women and the men. This is especially apparent when one compares this saying with the one addressed to the businessmen in 8:4–8. Both sayings consist of an accusation and an announcement of punishment. Both begin with a "Hear" formula. In each, the accusation concerns mistreatment of the poor and needy and the prophet quotes the words of the accused against them. Each introduces the announcement of punishment with the oath formula.

Thus we have two sayings which are remarkably parallel in theme and structure, the one addressed to women, the other to men. These sayings develop the theme sounded in 2:6–7. There the prophet accuses Israel of trampling upon the poor. Here the audiences are more restricted but the charge is no less comprehensive: the women crush the poor, the men cheat them. Both are guilty and both can expect punishment.

We have noted how concern for the poor and powerless is a theme which runs through the entire Bible (see on 2:6–7). This saying declares without ambiguity that responsibility for what happens to the widows, the orphans, and the poor in a society

100

does not lie with the male segment of the population only. Exercising such responsibility is women's work too.

Amos 4:4–5
Busy Religion

> O come, let us worship and bow down,
>   let us kneel before the LORD, our Maker!
> For he is our God,
>   and we are the people of his pasture,
>   and the sheep of his hand.
>
> (Ps. 95:6–7)

Using the words of an ancient psalm, this call to worship is still used in services today. Its structure is simple: (1) the invitation, using imperative verbs; (2) the reason, expressed in the sentence beginning with "for." A pilgrim who had traveled a long distance and who had finally arrived at a holy place like Bethel would be cheered to hear such an invitation and would anticipate an experience of communion with the God once revealed at that place. This call to worship provides the background for understanding the saying in Amos 4:4–5.

1. The Busy-ness of Religion

"Come to Bethel," Amos began. We are to imagine him standing outside the place of worship, watching as the crowd made its way to the sanctuary. This was Bethel, buzzing with chatter, bustling with cattle, busy with religion. Bethel. The name itself reeks of an ancient holiness. It means "House of El," El being the old Canaanite name for the deity. Bethel had been a holy place long before the God of the Israelites was worshiped there. It was already a place of worship when Jacob stopped there and had his dream about the ladder reaching from heaven to earth (Gen. 28:10–22). It remained an important religious center in the time of the judges (Judg. 20:18), and when King Solomon died and the kingdom split, one of the places chosen as an official center for worship was Bethel (I Kings 12:28–32).

Bethel had a distinguished past, but it also had a unique distinction in the present, in that Bethel was the place where

101

the royal family worshiped. It was called "the king's sanctuary . . . a temple of the kingdom" (7:13).

"Come to Bethel," the prophet began. Then comes the shock. Instead of familiar words about worship, about kneeling and bowing down, comes a harsh word, ". . . and transgress!" The effect is more jarring, more jagged, than the translation "transgress" (RSV) suggests. The Hebrew word is used to denote what happens when an ungrateful child steals from aging parents (Prov. 28:24) or when a grown child turns against loving parents, rejecting them and their values (Isa. 1:2). When eleven brothers plot to kill a twelfth, the same word is used (Gen. 50:17). On the national level, the word describes the action of a part of a nation deciding to tear itself away from the other part ("rebellion," I Kings 12:19).

"Come to worship and rebel against God! Come to services and sin!" That is what the people heard the prophet saying. Although worship should be a time when the bond between God and people is strengthened, in Israel precisely the opposite was happening. Worship had become revolt, rejection, rebellion, a ripping and tearing of the ties between a people and their God.

Here for the first time in the Amos book we hear the prophet using religious language. The sacrifices of which he speaks involved killing animals, eating the meat in a meal together, leaving choice portions for the priests and other parts on the altar for God. The tithes were the tenth part of the farmers' crops, to be given for the support of religion (Deut. 14:22–29; Gen. 28:22). The "sacrifice of thanksgiving" was an offering burned on the altar, the "freewill offering" a voluntary contribution.

All of this may seem to us quite primitive: the sight of smoke, blood, and slaughter, the smell of burning flesh, but Amos was only describing the religious practices of the day. In language unmatched for irony in the Bible, he invited his hearers to participate in these activities, declaring that in so doing they would only increase their rebellion against the Lord all the more!

The final imperatives, "proclaim freewill offerings, publish them," help to diagnose the religious illness. The real concern of the prople was to enhance their own reputations by being recognized for their generosity.

102

After seven imperatives comes the climax of this saying. The call to worship in Psalm 95 had followed the imperatives with a reason, giving worship a solid theological grounding: "For he is our God, and we are the people of his pasture and the sheep of his hand" (Ps. 95:6–7). The kind of worship which Amos criticizes here was not grounded in God but in a human fondness for going about the busy-ness of religion: "For so you love to do!" The motivation for worship was the desire to receive the praise of others, to be recognized in the community, and to achieve a feeling of self-satisfaction.

2. The Religion of Busy-ness

Until this point in the book the preaching of Amos has had to do with the horizontal dimension: the oppression of the powerless. In this saying the prophet goes for the vertical, naming what takes place at the most important sanctuary in the land as rebellion.

The prophet makes clear that the problem does not have to do with the adequacy of the worship services, but rather with the attitude of the worshipers. Despite their harsh words about the practice of religion (I Sam. 15:22; Isa. 1:10–17; Amos 5:21–24), the prophets never called for doing away with the existing forms of religion. It was not a matter of the liturgy being antiquated or the order of service being out of date. The problem was a deeper one.

When the motivation for worship is recognition by others and satisfaction for self, then that religion is rebellion, says the prophet. When the place of worship is a whirlwind of activity but the poor in the neighborhood are being crushed and cheated, then that religion is a mockery. All of the busy-ness of religion may lead to making a religion out of busy-ness.

Others would pick up on these same themes, pronouncing a woe upon those who loved religion but neglected justice, mercy, and faith (Matt. 23:23–28), or even defining religion in totally nonreligious terms (James 1:26–27). We shall hear more from Amos on this theme in 5:21–24.

The pattern given in Psalm 95 can help to keep things straight. God's people know themselves to be "the people of his pasture, the sheep of his hand." They look to the Lord as Creator (vv. 3–5), as Savior (v. 1), and as Good Shepherd (v. 7). Realizing all of this, they respond to the call to worship with acts of worship (v. 6) and with songs of thanksgiving and praise (v. 2). Then they leave the place of worship with a new dedication to what is right and to justice.

Amos 5:21–24
A Roaring, Rolling Stream

This saying, which climaxes in the call for justice and righteousness to roll through the land, stands as the centerpiece for 5:1—6:14 and is central to the preaching of the prophet. While there is no indication of the setting, these words were probably delivered at a place of worship, most likely Bethel.

1. Communion or Commotion?

Speaking as the Lord's messenger, the prophet interrupts the busy activity at the shrine by announcing the Lord's reaction to all that is going on. He begins with two verbs, "I hate, I despise," and then continues with four more negated verbs. "I take no delight in" is, literally, "I don't like the smell of"; the same verb is used with a positive sense to indicate the Lord's delight with the offering that Noah made after the flood (Gen. 8:21). After "I will not accept," the next two verbs express the divine reaction in terms of other senses: "I will not look upon . . . I will not listen." Taken together, these statements make clear that the Lord's rejection of the people's worship is total. The Lord does not like the smell, the sight, or the sound of what is happening in Israel's sanctuary.

After this general announcement of rejection, the prophet lists seven aspects of Israel's worship, all of which are rejected. The "feasts" are the three great yearly festivals: passover, pentecost, and booths or *sukkoth* (Deut. 16:16). The "solemn assemblies" are worship gatherings; see II Kings 10:20 where Jehu called for such a gathering. The "burnt offerings" (literally "goings up") are those in which the entire animal is consumed in flames and thus ascends to heaven. "Cereal offerings" are gifts of grain. The "peace offering" was accompanied by a sacred meal in which parts of the animal offered were eaten. The "noise" and "melody" refers to the singing, the instrumental music, all the sounds emanating from a place so busy with activity.

104

If the verbs made clear that the Lord had totally rejected the worship of the people, the listing of seven aspects of worship indicates that the Lord rejects the totality of all that was going on at the shrine, since seven is the biblical number for totality (see on 1:3—2:16, part 2).

After the listing of seven things the Lord does not want comes the climax, telling what the Lord *does* want; that is for justice and righteousness to roll through the land like a surging, churning, cleansing stream.

How should these sharply negative words against worship be understood? Why was this worship not acceptable? The saying in 5:4–5 helps to answer this question. The Lord says, "Seek me and live, but do not seek Bethel, and do not enter into Gilgal or cross over to Beer-sheba. . . ." The same idea is expressed in 5:6, "Seek the LORD and live." These sayings indicate that participation in worship at these places had become an end in itself. Those attending the services there were interested in enhancing their own reputations or inflating their own self-esteem (4:4–5), when, says the Lord, they should be seeking "the Holy One, not the holy place" (Mays, *Amos,* p. 86). Religion had become a matter of solemn gatherings, sumptuous feasts, sacrifices, and singing, nothing more. The soul had gone out of it. There was no communion with the Holy One, only a commotion at the holy place.

2. The Other Six Days

There was another reason for the Lord's rejection of the people's worship. This did not have to do with what went on inside the sanctuary but with what took place outside of it. It did not have to do with what happened on the day of worship but with what happened—or did not happen—on the other six days.

Amos 5:21–24 climaxes with a call for justice and righteousness. Two other sayings in this complex report that the pure, clear waters of justice have been polluted and turned to wormwood, that is, to poison (5:7; 6:12). What would this pollution of justice have meant in the days of Amos?

The other sayings about justice in 5:1—6:4 fill in the picture. In 5:14–15 we hear a call to "establish justice in the gate." Cities in ancient Israel were surrounded by rectangular walls. At the point where the walls met there would be an overlap of perhaps forty feet, with the walls roughly that same distance

105

apart, thus leaving a square between an outer and an inner gate. This was the place where court was held. When one person had a complaint against another, that person would summon ten citizens and assemble an impromptu jury (Ruth 4; for pictures of benches in city gates, see Edward F. Campbell, Jr., *Ruth:* THE ANCHOR BIBLE 7, 101). This was the "court in the gate" and in Amos's time something was wrong with that court system.

Chapter 5 verse 11 indicates that the small farmer was being charged an exhorbitant percentage for the rental of land, and the wealthy landlords were taking more than a fair share of the crop. This was yet another example of trampling upon the poor. When the poor went to court to complain, their words were hated and abhorred, even though they were true! (Just so, says 6:8, the Lord "hates" and "abhors" the pride of the powerful and wealthy, and in the same way the Lord "hates" their worship, 5:21.) After the accusation in 5:11 comes the expected announcement of punishment. The form is that of the "futility curse," where an activity is announced in the first half of a statement and its frustration in the second half (see, e.g., Deut. 28:30, 38–41). These landowners have invested much time and energy in the building of houses, but they will never live in them. They have worked hard at planting and caring for their vineyards, but they will never enjoy their wine.

More of what was happening at the court in the gate is reported in 5:12. Those making judgments were accepting bribes, again favoring the wealthy and the powerful. The poor person who could not pay for a favorable decision was not given a hearing. This charge becomes the grounds for the coming disaster announced in verses 16–17.

What does it mean for justice to be turned to poison? These sayings answer the question. The poor and powerless are oppressed by an unfair economic system. When they try to get their complaints heard in court, they are turned away. Court decisions are not based on the truth (v. 10) but on the size of the bribe (v. 12).

3. Doing Justice, Prophetic Style

What would it mean for justice to "roll down like waters?" What might it be like if justice were established in the gate? Consideration of the vocabulary for justice in Amos and the eighth-century prophets suggests three dimensions to the prophetic notion of doing justice:

First of all, the fundamental biblical expression is to "do justice." Justice is a *dynamic* notion. When the question is asked, "With what shall I come before the Lord," the answer is that the Lord wants the worshiper "to do justice, and to love kindness, and to walk humbly with your God" (Micah 6:8; see the commentary on that passage).

The picture that the word "justice" brings to mind in our western tradition is that of a woman, blindfolded, holding a set of balances before her. Thus "justice" is a static concept, a noun, describing the achievement of fairness and equality and symbolized in the state of balance where all is at rest. The image Amos calls to mind is entirely different. Justice is like a surging, churning, cleansing stream. All is in motion and commotion. Nothing is at rest. The same language is used in Judges 5:21 to describe the "torrent" of the Kishon River. This is the prophetic picture of justice; it is more like an onrushing torrent than a balanced scale.

Secondly, justice is the expected *response* of God's people to what God has done for them. The prophet Isaiah once put his message in the form of a folk song (Isa. 5:1–7). He sang about a friend who carefully tended a vineyard, digging it, clearing it of stones, building a watchtower in it, and hewing out a wine vat; but the vineyard produced only wild and worthless grapes! This, said the prophet, was a picture of Israel. Although God had done much for this nation, when the Lord looked for the fruits of justice and righteousness they were not there, and the vineyard had to be destroyed.

God's people doing justice is like a farmer's vineyard producing grapes. Doing justice is the people of God responding to what God has done for them. This pattern of divine indicative followed by expected human response runs through the Bible. The story of what God did in the exodus (Exod. 1—15) is placed before the account of what God expects, as those expectations are spelled out in the commandments (Exod. 20). The structure of the Decalogue itself consists of a reminder of what God has done (Exod. 20:2) followed by an outline of the expected response (Exod. 20:3–7). Paul's letter to the Romans begins with an exposition of the gospel (chapters 1—11) followed by suggestions for the expected response to that good news (chaps. 12—16). The letter to the Ephesians consists of

107

an exposition of teachings (1—3) followed by expectations expressed with imperatives (4—6). In Colossians, the meaning of the Christ event is explained in 1:1—3:4 and the imperatives follow in the remainder of the letter. The first letter of John puts the matter most simply: "We love, because he first loved us" (I John 4:19).

Finally, to do justice means to act as *advocate* for the powerless. When we investigate texts where the Hebrew vocabulary for justice appears, we keep running into three categories of people: the poor and those who have been widowed or orphaned.

Isaiah 10:1–4 is a woe-saying directed against those who are making laws which deny justice (v. 2) to these three: the widow, the orphan, and the poor. These are the powerless.

The prophet Isaiah once denounced the dichotomy between worship and life in Judah in much the same way as Amos did in Israel (Isa. 1:10–17). Isaiah sketched the sort of response the Lord expected from his people. They should:

> "cease to do evil,
>   learn to do good;
> seek justice,
>   correct oppression;
> defend [literally, "do justice for"] the fatherless,
>   plead for the widow."
>
> (Isa. 1:17)

To "seek justice" here means to take up the cause of the widow and the orphan, to act as advocate for the powerless.

Precisely this same idea comes to expression in Isaiah 1:21–26. The word "justice" in verse 21 describes what was once the situation in Jerusalem. The cognate verb comes up in verse 23, where the accusation against the princes declares, "They do not defend (literally, "do justice for") the fatherless, and the widow's cause does not come to them." Again, to "do justice" means to act as advocate for the powerless. To this trio of widow, orphan, and poor the Bible adds the stranger or sojourner (Deut. 16:11; 24:19–22) and the aged (Lev. 19:32). We have seen that the theme of concern for the powerless runs through the entire Bible (see on 1:3—2:16;3).

Thus when the prophets speak of justice, they do not enter into the realm of the theoretical or speak of philosophical or legal notions like "justitia" at all. Rather, they lead us through those quarters of the city where the poor live and they invite us to look into the eyes of the lonely widow, the hurting orphan, and the hungry beggar. Or they take us through the country-side and introduce us to a young couple about to lose the family farm. Or we may be led through a home for the aged, where a lonely hand reaches out to be touched.

When the people of God expend their imagination and their energy in advocacy, in working to remove the discrimination built into the economic and legal systems, in finding ever new and more effective ways to take up the cause of the power-less, then justice will begin to roll through the land like waters, and righteousness like an everflowing stream.

Amos 6:1–7
For Whom the Bell Tolls

Woe-sayings have been placed on either side of 5:21–24, the centerpiece of Amos 5:1—6:14. It is appropriate that the first of these sayings (5:18–20) is preceded by a portrayal of national mourning, because the customs and words associated with funerals and mourning provide the clue to understanding the prophetic pronouncements of woe.

1. Funerals, Mourning, and Woe-sayings

The first saying in the Amos book speaks of mourning, describing the pastures as mourning at hearing the roaring voice of the Lord (Amos 1:2). In addition, the unit 5:1—6:14 is introduced with an account of mourning; Israel is personified as a young virgin who has died and Amos calls his audience to join in in lamenting this tragic, premature death (5:1–3). The end of the book also speaks of the mourning of all the inhabitants of the earth (9:5).

In the Old Testament world, professional mourners were engaged to aid the grieving process by encouraging those who were hurting to work out their grief through weeping. Most of the professional mourners were women (Jer. 9:17, 20; Ezek. 32:16), but men could also sing the laments (II Sam. 1:17; II Chron. 35:25). Customs associated with mourning included shaving the head, cutting the beard, wearing sackcloth, and singing sad songs (Jer. 48:37–38; Amos 8:10).

Central to the sounds of mourning was the Hebrew cry *hoy* or *ho*, translated as "woe," "ah," or "alas" in the Revised Standard Version. When one heard that cry, the question would come to mind, "Who has died?" We could compare this to church bells in a small town tolling to announce a funeral, reminding all who hear of the transitory nature of human life and also raising the question, "Whose funeral is it? For whom does the bell toll?" Several examples occur in the Old Testament: I Kings 13 reports the death of a "man of God" who had been killed by a lion; the people mourn, saying "Alas [Hebrew, *hoy*] my brother!" (v. 30). Jeremiah once announced that no one would lament the death of Jehoiakim, saying "Ah [Hebrew, *hoy*] my brother" or "Ah lord" or "Ah his majesty!" (Jer. 22:18).

When the prophet pronounced a "woe," the effect on those addressed would be chilling, comparable to hearing one's own death announced on a news broadcast or reading one's own name in the obituary column of the daily paper.

2. "We're Number One!"

The woe-saying in 6:1–7 is framed by the word "first": The notable men of the "first" of the nations will be the "first" of those to go into exile. The saying divides into two parts: Verses 1–3 switch to second-person plural verbs in 2 and 3 and are concerned with national arrogance; verses 4–7 continue the woe-saying in the third person, focusing on indifference. The piece as a whole fits the pattern of the judgment against the nation saying (see on 1:1, part 1), with 1–3 and 4–6 furnishing the reasons for the punishment announced in verse 7.

The first part of the saying indicates that the prophet is addressing the leadership of Samaria. He also refers to those in Jerusalem, on Mount Zion. Such a double concern is not unusual in view of the mention of Zion at the beginning of the book (1:2), the reference to "these kingdoms" (Israel and Judah) in 6:2, and the concern for the Davidic kingdom as a whole at the book's conclusion (9:11–15) The leaders whom Amos addresses seem to have a "We're number one" attitude, considering theirs to be the "first" among the nations.

In verse 2, Amos appears to be quoting his hearers, just as

110

he does in 2:12; 4:1; 5:14; 6:13; 7:16; 8:5–6, 14; and 9:10 (Mays, *Amos,* p.115). The arrogant leaders of Israel ask their people to look at the cities of Calneh, Hamath, and Gath. None of these, they say, is greater than "these kingdoms," that is, than Judah and Israel. "Their territory is not larger than your own," the leaders say. The quotation ends with verse 2, then verse 3 accuses the leaders who try to push the "evil day" (cf. 5:18–20) into the future.

The second part of this woe-saying portrays the luxurious lifestyle of Israel's rich and perhaps famous. The use of ivory for decorative purposes is also mentioned in 3:15. The sense of "stretch themselves" (v. 4) is to "hang over" as a blanket hangs over a bed (Exod. 26:12–13, which describes the curtains that "hang over" the back of the tabernacle). This is how Amos pictures those who sprawl about in indolence, draping themselves across their expensive beds.

The description of the affluent society continues. These are the people who can afford to eat meat at their meals. Their banqueting and lounging is accompanied by music; the sense of "sing idle songs" appears to be "improvise," painting the picture of persons idly picking out ditties on stringed instruments. Wine would normally be drunk from goblets, but here it is consumed by the bowl full. "Oils" refers to expensive perfumed body lotions (Sol. 1:3; 4:10; Esther 2:12; cf. Prov. 21:17).

After a sequence of seven verbs (lie, stretch, eat, sing, invent, drink, anoint) comes the climax: "but are not grieved over the ruin of Joseph." The problem with these leaders is that they do not care. To translate more literally, they are "not sick" about what has happened to their nation.

The announcement of punishment which concludes the saying in verse 7 is terse and direct. These notables of the "first" of the nations, these affluent who can afford the "first" of the expensive perfumes (v. 6), will continue to be "first"— the first to be taken captive! Those who drape themselves across their beds in exhaustion will be driven out of their land into exile.

3. Arrogance, Affluence, and Indifference

The first theme in this saying is a *prophetic critique of arrogance.* More precisely, the prophet denounces an egocentric arrogance which comes to expression in words of boasting.

111

Amos spoke of those who placed all their trust in the "mountain of Samaria." Their security was based upon the city and the strongholds they themselves had built, and of which they were proud. But the Lord abhors and hates this pride (6:8)! The Lord will destroy the "strongholds" of the nations surrounding Israel by sending enemies against them (1:4, 7, 10). On another occasion, the prophet announced that Samaria's elaborate defense systems in which the people take such pride will be destroyed by "an adversary" who will surround, invade, and plunder the city (3:9–11). This self-confident arrogance which bases the security of a people wholly on their own achievements is expressed in the "We're number one" attitude of their leadership, leaders who take special pride in the territorial extent of the combined kingdoms of Israel and Judah (vv. 1–2).

Amos's contemporary Isaiah also had sharp words to say about arrogance and pride (Isa. 2:12 and context; 9:8–21; 37:22–29). In a woe-saying that has similarities to Amos 6:1–7, Isaiah announces the death of those in Judah who spend their time partying, but who have no sense of gratitude for what the Lord has done for them (Isa. 5:11–14).

The other theme in this saying is a *denouncement of individual affluence coupled with social indifference.* The prophet addresses those who enjoy a life of luxury and ease, but who are indifferent to the sociological and political problems which are about to bring the roof down upon their heads.

Jesus once told a story about an affluent individual, one of the "notables" of his own day, who wore only the best clothing and consumed only the finest food. Outside the door of his home lay a man named Lazarus, who was hungry and poor. The rich man did not persecute Lazarus, nor did he drive him away. He was simply indifferent to him (Luke 16:19–31).

This text has something to say to those who enjoy a relatively high standard of living and especially to those in positions of leadership. This word of Amos calls a prosperous church to be aware of Lazarus who lies at the gate. This is not a call to mouth pious words about poverty (James 2:16), but to heal, to feed, and to clothe. This word from the prophet would jar an affluent people of God out of arrogance into an awareness of dependence upon God. It would rouse them out of indifference into action aimed at healing the brokenness of the communities and the world of which we are all a part.

112

Amos 7:1–9; 8:1–3
The Advocate

The biblical prophets claim to have experiences which are unique. These may be classified as visions and auditory experiences; most often, the encounter with the Lord which they report contains both visual and auditory elements.

1. Four Visions

The texts provide no clue as to when these visions and auditory experiences which Amos reports took place. The most likely time would be at the very beginning of his prophetic activity. These powerful personal experiences would then explain what motivated Amos to leave his work in Judah and travel north to Israel to speak as he did.

Other prophets also report visionary experiences. Micaiah the son of Imlah tells of his vision of "the LORD sitting on his throne and all the host of heaven standing beside him on his right hand and on his left" (I Kings 22:19). Isaiah reports the visionary and auditory experiences which impelled him to prophesy (Isa. 6). The same is true for Jeremiah (Jer. 1) and Ezekiel (Ezek. 1—3). These prophetic vision reports are characteristically in the first person, presumably going back to the prophets themselves. They are preserved to explain why these individuals embarked on a prophetic career and to exhibit their credentials.

The structure of the first pair of visions is identical. First, says Amos, he saw the Lord forming locusts. The Book of Joel tells of a terrible grasshopper plague (Joel 1—2); what Amos sees is a cloud of grasshoppers destroying the work of a whole season (note the description in Joel 1:4). The meaning of the vision was clear: Just as the locusts had destroyed the crop, so the Lord planned to destroy Israel! Here Amos intercedes, asking the Lord to forgive, because Jacob (Israel) "is so small."

The prophet's intercessions are successful. The Lord "who forgives all your iniquity" (Ps. 103:3) and who does change his mind (Joel 2:13) calls off the destruction with the announcement, "It shall not be."

113

Then the prophet reports his second visionary experience. This time he sees a fire which devours the "great deep," that is, the waters under the earth (Gen. 7:11; Ps. 36:6) and then begins to burn up the land. The image of fire here is likely to be associated with the fires announced in the speeches of chapters 1 and 2 (1:4, 7, 10), which apparently refer to the fires set by invading armies.

The meaning of the vision is once again obvious and the prophet once again intercedes, asking the Lord to call it off! Once again the reason for the prophet's prayers is the weakness of the people, "He is so small." Again, the Lord does call off the disaster with the word, "This also shall not be."

The pattern changes with the third vision report. This time Amos sees the Lord standing by a wall with a plumb line, like a construction foreman checking to see if the work measures up to acceptable standards. Now the meaning of the vision is not so obvious. When the Lord asks Amos what he sees, the prophet answers, "A plumb line." The Lord is checking "my people Israel" to see whether they "measure up." The obvious answer is that they do not.

If a wall is out of plumb, it cannot do the job for which it was designed. Just as a foreman must give the order to destroy such a structure, so the Lord now announces the destruction of Israel (see also II Kings 21:10–15). The places of worship (high places, sanctuaries) will no longer be busy with activity (cf. 4:4–5; 5:21–24) but will be desolate. The punishment will even reach the royal family.

Now instead of interceding, Amos is silent. This time a reason has been given for the announced punishment: Israel does not measure up! The prophet's silence here is a preview of the terrible silence, the silence of death, with which the final vision report concludes.

The structure of the fourth vision report, after the biographical section in 7:10–17, is like that of the third. This time Amos sees an object, a basket of summer fruit, in Hebrew, *qayits* (cf. Jer. 40:10, 12). When the Lord asks what he sees, Amos answers, "a basket of *qayits.*" The Lord constructs a pun on that word, announcing that "the end [Hebrew, *qets*] has come upon my people Israel." Then comes the same statement heard in the third vision, "I will never again pass by them."

114

This last vision report and this section of the book concludes by calling attention to sounds. The series of visions had begun with the sound of the whirring wings of the locusts and the crackling and roaring of the fires. Now it ends with the sounds of wailing and lament replacing the songs of praise and partying (5:23; 6:5). Finally there is the stench of death and then only the silence.

2. Advocate for the Powerless

These vision reports have something to say to those interested in carrying out ministry in the tradition of the prophets and the apostles.

First, such vision reports have been included in the prophetic books to exhibit the credentials of the prophet. Amos was not just an angry reformer nor was Ezekiel a dreamy visionary. Each of the prophets spoke because they had been spoken to. More often than not, they delivered messages which were not popular and which said precisely the opposite of that which the cadre of religious professionals of their day were saying (cf. I Kings 22; Jer. 23; Micah 3:5–8).

These vision reports indicate that the prophet spoke as he did because he had heard a word from the Lord. They suggest that if contemporary preaching and teaching is to have about it the ring of prophetic authority, it will have to be rooted in that same word from the Lord, now available in the collected Scripture of the Lord's people.

Second, the first two reports say something about the Lord's responsiveness to the weak and the apparently insignificant. Twice Israel's punishment was called off because Amos reminded the Lord that Israel was "so small." The theme of God's care for the "small" or weak runs through Scripture. Israel was chosen as "the fewest of all peoples" (Deut. 7:7–8). In response to their cry in a time of national weakness, the Lord delivered them (Exod. 3:7–9). The cries of widows and orphans are heard in heaven (Exod. 22:21–24); we have seen how the theme of concern for the powerless runs through the Bible (see on Amos 2:6–8).

Finally, these reports set forth an important aspect of the prophetic task. The prophet was a messenger, responsible for bringing a word from God to the people, but the work of the prophet also moved in the other direction. The prophet was also an advocate, bringing a word *to* God on behalf of the people.

115

We have seen that the call to "do justice" is the call to act as advocate for the powerless (see on Amos 5:21–24). In these vision reports we discover that the prophet practices what he has preached. We hear Amos speaking on behalf of Israel, whom he names Jacob, calling on God to forgive them because they are "so small." The nation's leaders would never have thought of themselves that way (Amos 6:1), but so Amos saw them before God. Twice he prayed for them, and twice the Lord called off the scheduled punishment.

The figure of Amos, praying for the people, acting as their advocate, stands as a model not only for prophetic ministry but also for pastoral care. That prophet from Judah points ahead to another Judean, of whom it was said, "but if any one does sin, we have an advocate with the Father, Jesus Christ the righteous . . ." (I John 2:1).

Amos 7:10–17
Preaching and Propriety

The clash between priest and prophet reported in this biographical section takes place at Bethel, the site of the chapel where the royal family worships. The comment that "the land is not able to bear" the words of Amos suggests that the prophet has been active for some time, long enough for his words to have made a considerable impact.

1. Prophet and Priest

Amaziah, the chief of staff at the royal chapel, has reported to the king that he has on his hands a person guilty of both conspiracy (cf. I Kings 16:9) and treason. Amos, the priest reports, has announced that the king will die and the people will go into exile (cf. 4:3; 6:7; 7:17).

In his report (7:11) Amaziah the priest misrepresents the prophet in two ways. He says, "Thus Amos has said. . . ." If anything is clear in the collection of the words of Amos, it is that Amos does not speak on his own but as the Lord's messenger. Also, the priest relays only a portion of Amos's message, the announcement of punishment. Nothing is said about the accusations which provide the reason for the announced punishment.

The persons involved here are identified by vocation. Amaziah is the priest and Jeroboam is the king (v. 10). What of

Amos? The priest addresses him as "seer" (vv. 12–13). The word does not necessarily have a negative tone. The editor of the book introduced Amos with the cognate verb, "The words of Amos . . . which he *saw* (author's italics). In II Kings 17:13 the words "seer" and "prophet" are used synonymously.

The priest's word to the prophet is unambiguous: "Go!" Amaziah threatens no punishment but only wants this seer, this "prophet," whatever and whoever he is, out of his hair. Let him peddle his wares elsewhere, preferably in Judah whence he is reputed to come! The doubled "there" (v. 12) makes the priest's concern quite clear: He does not want to have to deal with this person. Amaziah makes no judgment about the truth or falsity of the prophet's message. The only reason given for his ejection is that the kind of things Amos has been saying are just not appropriate for such an elegant setting as the royal sanctuary.

Amos's response to Amaziah begins by clarifying the matter of his own vocation, first in negative and then in positive terms. "I am no prophet," he says, "nor one of the sons of the prophets" (RSV margin). What did Amos mean with this two-fold denial? The "sons of the prophets" were groups of prophets who attached themselves to a particular master. These groups had headquarters at places like Bethel and Jericho (II Kings 2:1–5), and we read about them in the Books of Kings (I Kings 20:35; II Kings 4:1, 38). These were individuals for whom prophecy had become a profession. We also hear of bands of prophets roaming the countryside (I Sam. 10:5, 10; 19:20) and of groups of prophets on the royal payroll (I Kings 22:6, 10–12). Micah refers to prophets who tailor their preaching to the size of their salaries (Micah 3:5). By the time of Jeremiah, "prophet" seems to have become a tainted word, since those who bore that office were often ungodly and immoral (Jer. 23:9–22), lackeys, hangers-on, and yes-men who spoke only soothing words of comfort (Jer. 23:17).

It is against this background that we are to understand Amos's statement, "I am no prophet. . . ." "I am not," he meant to say, "one of those religious professionals, paid to make pious pronouncements at public occasions." He defines his vocation with a triple "I" (in the Hebrew) statement: "No prophet am I, and no son of a prophet am I, but a herdsman am I" (author's translation). The point has been made. Amos is not on the ec- **117** clesiastical payroll. He is, in fact, a lay person who makes his living by raising sheep and caring for sycamore trees.

After this denial, Amos defines his vocation in positive terms. The threefold "I" of verse 14 is balanced by a triple reference to the Lord in verses 15 and 16: "the LORD took me . . . the LORD said to me . . . hear the word of the LORD." It is not a matter of "thus Amos has said" (v.11) but of "thus says the LORD." The "Go!" of the priest is here countered with the "Go!" of the Lord.

A nuance in Amos's speaking is instructive: The Lord said, "Go, prophesy to my people Israel. . . ." This "my people" may be heard in the harsh announcements of punishment surrounding this biographical account (7:8; 8:2). In it may be heard the pathos, the suffering of a God who must punish his own (cf. Isa. 1:2–3 and Hos. 11:8–9).

The saying in verses 16–17 falls into the pattern of the announcement of judgment. The accusation quotes the words of the accused, a favorite technique of Amos (see on 1:1, part 1). The announcement of punishment is total and terrifying: Your wife will be forced into prostitution because of the difficult days ahead, your children will be killed, your land will be divided up by conquerors, you yourself will die away from home, and your people will go into exile.

With such a message, it is no wonder that the land was not able to bear what the prophet had to say.

2. A Jagged Edge

Amaziah is presented here as an expert in diplomacy and conflict management; no doubt such skills had helped him to attain his position as the number one person at the number one religious establishment in the country. When he reports the words of Amos to his superior, he conveniently avoids the disturbing charges about the social and economic situation in Israel and only relays what sounds like the words of a conspirator. In this way the priest would spare the king the pain of having to deal with what may have been called "the poverty issue," and Amos would appear as some sort of extremist. Jeroboam would certainly endorse his chaplain's recommendation that this fanatic be sent back to the south from where he came!

The priest tried to deal with the prophet's criticism of religion in the same way. This time it was what might have been called "the justice issue." Amos had attacked a one-day-a-week kind of religion which allowed a dichotomy between faith and daily life, saying that worship in the temple was nau-

118

seous to the Lord when there was no concern for justice in the courts and honesty in the shops. In another move designed to avoid conflict at any cost, the priest advised this bothersome rural eccentric to go back to where he came from. So Amaziah dealt with Amos. The king would no doubt send a memo to the priest, commending him for running a smooth operation at Bethel, and the priest would be spared any further embarrassment.

The criterion for what could be said at Bethel was quite clear: that which was proper, fitting, suitable for such a place as the royal chapel (v. 13). Propriety, in other words, determined the content of the preaching allowed there.

The Bible provides examples enough of religious types who speak for religion, who are yes-sayers, eager to endorse the views of those who support them (I Kings 22:10–12), whose words are always soothing even when they should be jarring (Jer. 23:16–22), who shape their sermons according to their salaries (Micah 3:5).

However, the aim of biblical religion has never been the avoidance of conflict at any cost. Jesus once said, "Woe to you when all men speak well of you, for so their fathers did to the false prophets" (Luke 6:26). I recall reading the journal of a well-known theologian and preacher. After hearing a sermon marked by eloquence and soothing charm, he wrote, "Lord, preserve me from eloquence . . . let my words have a jagged edge. . . ."

Authentic ministry, someone has said, ought to comfort the afflicted but also afflict the comfortable. Taken together, the biography and the vision reports in this part of the Amos book stand as a warning against letting propriety determine the content of proclamation and as an encouragement to criticism of both society and established religion, when that criticism is rooted in the word of God.

Amos 8:4–8
The Customer Is Always Wronged

Like the matching oracle in 4:1–3, the saying in 8:4–8 is addressed to a particular group within Israel. There it was the women; here it is the businessmen of the city, presumably Samaria or Bethel. The time is one when business is booming and the merchants are eager to capitalize on every opportunity to increase their sales. The comments in 4:1-3 note the similarities between these two sayings. Taken together they express the comprehensive accusations of Amos. Women and men, husbands and wives alike stand accused before the Lord.

1. Crime and Punishment

The first oracle against Israel in the Book of Amos charged the people with crimes against the needy, the poor, and the afflicted (2:6-7). This last oracle of judgment in the book makes the same complaint, again using a trio of Hebrew words for the poor (the Hebrew for "poor" of 8:4 is translated "afflicted" in 2:7).

After the initial "Hear this" call for attention, the prophet states the accusation against the merchants in general terms: They "trample upon the needy and bring the poor of the land to an end." The sense of "bring to an end" is to get rid of something, as one gets rid of leaven in a house at Passover time (Exod. 12:15) or as Josiah got rid of the idolatrous priests in Jerusalem by deposing them (II Kings 23:5). The meaning here is clear: The actions of Israel's business community are leading to the extermination of the poor.

The prophet continues his accusation by quoting what the accused have said (see on 1:1, part 1). The quotation is framed with a reference to "selling," indicating the first and last concerns of those addressed (vv. 5-6).

The first pair of charges (v. 5a) has to do with the insatiable greed of the merchants in the marketplace. Outwardly these people are careful to observe their religion, shutting their shops on the sabbath and on festival days (the "new moon" was also not a working day, cf. Ezek. 46:1). Though their shops were closed on such days, their minds were open to the concerns of their businesses, which would be operating at full tilt the minute the holy day came to an end.

The second pair of charges (v. 5b) identifies three ways in which the shopkeepers cheated their customers both in buying and in selling. The ephah was roughly the size of a bushel; by using an undersized basket in selling, the customer was cheated. The shekel was a weight placed on one of the trays of a scale when buying grain; when the weight was too heavy, the

120

customer was cheated again. Finally, the scales themselves were rigged. Downtown, the customer was always wronged.

Such dishonesty in buying and selling must have been a common problem in the eighth century. Both Hosea (12:7) and Micah (6:9–11) also speak of it. The legal materials in the Bible warn against having separate sets of weights for buying and selling (Deut. 25:13–16) and call for "just weights, a just ephah" (Lev. 19:35–37). Honesty in the marketplace was also a concern of Wisdom instruction (Prov. 11:1; 16:11; 20:10; 20:23).

The pair of charges in verse 6a balances the first accusation in the Amos book in 2:6a. The poor and needy are sold as slaves when they owe as little as the cost of a pair of sandals. With the final charge, "and sell the refuse of the wheat," the accusation comes to a conclusion. The number of complaints has now reached seven, the number of totality. This refers to the practice of mixing chaff and scrap materials with the wheat which was sold.

The accusation part of this saying makes clear that religion has to do not only with the sabbath and the sanctuary but also with the shops and the shekel. The same words for buying and selling are used whether the object of that activity is grain, wheat, trash mixed in with the wheat—or human beings. They, too, are "bought for silver." The poor and the needy are treated just like trash.

As was the case in 4:1–3, the announcement of punishment is introduced by the oath formula. In 4:2 the Lord swore "by his holiness." "Pride of Jacob" here must mean something similar; most likely it is a title for God (cf. I Sam. 15:29; Mays, *Amos,* p.145).

After the oath formula, seven verbs declare the totality of the coming disaster. The punishment will disrupt the normal relationships with the Lord (v. 7) and with the land (v. 8). The description of the earth trembling, heaving, and being tossed about again sounds like the announcement of a coming earthquake (cf. 2:13–16).

2. A Convenient Dichotomy

The long speech at the beginning of the Amos book came to an end with an accusation against Israel for oppressing the poor. The same charge is made in the middle of the book (4:1–3). Now, in this saying which introduces the final segment of the book, the charge of oppression of the poor is made once

121

again. From beginning to middle to the end of the Amos book, the prophet's accusation is the same: You have trampled, oppressed, and crushed the poor and the needy.

At issue here is the classic and convenient dichotomy between faith and life, between religion and everyday business. The businessmen Amos addressed have divided their lives into watertight compartments, one marked religion, the other business. They are scrupulous in closing down for the holy days. No doubt they are to be found among those thronging to the sanctuaries on the sabbath! During the rest of the week their religion is not involved, though, and the customers who enter their places of business are doubly cheated, when they buy and when they sell. Religion, after all, is religion and as for the rest—well, business is business! So the relatively wealthy merchants get richer and the poor get poorer, until they are crushed and trampled to death. The result of these practices will finally be to "solve" the poverty problem by the extermination of the poor.

"The love of money," the epistle writer once observed, "is the root of all evils" (I Tim. 6:10). It was that sort of love that once kept a young man from becoming a follower of Jesus (Matt. 19:16–22). It was the love of money and plain greed which was controlling the lives of these citizens of Israel. Their greed prevented them from finding either spiritual refreshment or physical relaxation on the holy days. All the while only one question persisted: "When will the day be over?" Then this greed impelled them to devise ever more clever ways to cheat and to treat their fellow human beings just like the trash that they sold with the wheat.

This prophetic word rejects that dichotomy between faith and life. Religion, it says, has to do with the whole of life, holy day and holy place, but also every day and every place. It also compels its hearers to examine their attitude toward possessions and wealth, with a reminder that in the ancient church one of the seven deadly sins was greed.

Finally, for the last time in the Amos book, this saying brings to attention the poor and the powerless. This prophetic word indicates that the Lord has heard their cry (Exod. 22:21–24). Other voices in the biblical tradition tell us that when none of the Lord's people are concerned about the powerless (Amos 6:6), the Lord will act as their Advocate (Prov. 22:22–23; 23:10–11; Isa. 3:13–15). The Lord's own people have been weighed in

the balances, which are just balances, and have been found
wanting. The Lord has seen their deeds and will not forget
(Amos 8:7).

Amos 9:5–7
This Is Your God

Amos 9:5–7 is the centerpiece of a collection of sayings in
8:11—9:15 arranged in a concentric or "ring" pattern. This
centerpiece invites attention as a summary of what 8:11—9:15
says about God, and indeed as a summary of the theology of the
Book of Amos as a whole.

1. The Centerpiece (9:5–7)

The hymn fragment in verses 5 and 6 tells of the majesty
and might of God "who touches the earth and it melts." Two
psalms speak the same language. Psalm 104 concludes: "who
looks upon the earth and it trembles, who touches the mountains and they smoke!" (v. 32). Psalm 144 contains the prayer of
a king asking for rescue: "Bow thy heavens, O LORD, and come
down! Touch the mountains that they smoke!" (v. 5). We have
seen that Amos 8:8 refers to an earthquake, describing the land
as trembling, rising, and falling, the inhabitants mourning. The
similar language in 9:5 appears to refer to the same thing; the
power of this mighty Lord who rules over nature is most evident when the Lord comes near the earth, touches it and it
quakes.

The remainder of the hymn fragment in verse 6 speaks of
God in more gentle terms. God is the builder, the Creator who
has constructed a dwelling place in heaven. The hymn pieces
in 4:13 and 5:8 indicate that while this God has also made the
mountains, the wind, and the stars, the Creator has not then
withdrawn from creation, retiring from any further involvement. The Lord maintains nature's great rhythms, calling for
the waters of the sea and returning them in the form of rain (cf.
4:13; 5:8).

The "Egypt" catchword links verses 5–6 with verse 7, but
there is a deeper connection between these two pieces. If
verses 5–6 describe the God of nature who is Creator but also

123

Blesser, verse 7 speaks of the Lord as the God who acts in history as Deliverer. Considered together these sentences provide a succinct summary of Israel's understanding of God.

Verse 7 consists of two rhetorical questions. The first one asserts the Lord's care for the Ethiopians, those fascinating, dark people, "tall and smooth" (Isa. 18:2). The next statement would clearly call forth a "yes" answer from the audience, as Amos once again (see 2:10; 3:1) sounds the central affirmation of Israel's catechism: "Did I not bring up Israel from the land of Egypt . . . ?" But the assertions that follow (in the form of continuing questions) are quite radical. The first two nations to be mentioned in the long speech at the beginning of the book were Israel's traditional enemies the Philistines and the Syrians (1:3–8). They were mentioned first precisely because they were enemies. Now the prophet speaks of the Lord delivering them in the same breath as he speaks of the Lord's deliverance of Israel! God acts, Amos is saying, in the histories of all nations, not just Israel's! God has delivered Israel, but God has also delivered the Philistines and the Syrians!

In sum, this centerpiece describes the activity of God in two ways. God is the builder of the universe and the maintainer of all the processes of nature, the one who creates and who blesses (Westermann, *Elements of Old Testament Theology,* Part III). Secondly, God is the engineer of history, controlling the movements of the nations of the world. The Ethiopians, the Philistines, the Syrians, and Israel are all mentioned together. Is there something special about the Lord's relationship to Israel? In this saying God speaks *about* the Ethiopians, Philistines, and Syrians, but when it comes to the people of Israel, it is "you" and "me." The last word in the Amos book expresses that you/me relationship from the side of the people: This mighty God of nature and history, it declares, is *your* God.

2. God of Nature and History (8:11—9:15)

The twin themes of this centerpiece are developed in the remainder of 8:11—9;15.

The sections immediately adjacent to the centerpiece (9:1–4, 8–10) both announce that the Lord who addresses his people as "you" has set his eyes upon them (9:4; cf. 9:8) for evil and not for good (9:4; cf. 9:10). God will punish Israel and this punishment will come first of all in history. At God's command

124

the enemy's sword will slay them (9:4, 10). The master of all history will shake the nations as easily as one shakes a sieve (9:9). Both of these balancing sections also speak about the Lord's actions in nature. The shaking of the thresholds (9:1) sounds like the result of an earthquake. Just as easily as an enemy army is commanded, the Lord will command the fearsome monster at the bottom of the sea (9:3). None will escape the Lord's resolve to punish, as 9:1–4 makes clear in the listing of seven acts of the Lord, describing the totality of the coming punishment: "I will slay . . . my hand take . . . I will bring them down . . . I will search out . . . take them . . . I will command the serpent . . . I will command the sword." The balancing section makes the same point with the figure of the sieve. The grain is put into the sieve so that it will fall through and the undesirable stones be caught. Here it is said that "no pebble shall fall upon the earth. All the sinners of my people shall die by the sword" (vv. 9–10). Thus these two sayings adjacent to the centerpiece describe the certainty of the Lord's judgment. Even though Israel believes that "Evil shall not overtake or meet us" (9:10), not a one of them will escape.

The next two balancing "in that day" sayings (8:13–14 and 9:11–12) emphasize the Lord's role as master of history. Those who worship gods other than the Lord "shall fall and never rise again" (8:13–14). Using the same two verbs, 9:11–12 announces that the Lord will "raise up" the kingdom of David which has "fallen." In contrast to the gods of Samaria, Dan, or Beersheba, who themselves fall down never to rise, Israel's God will act in the future to raise up and repair, raise up and rebuild Israel "as in the days of old" (9:11).

The "Behold the days are coming" sayings in 8:11–12 and 9:13–15 are at the extremes of the ring composition. Both speak of the Lord's action in nature and in history. While the mention of "famine" in 8:11 calls to mind a crisis in nature (cf. the drought in 8:13), the announcement is made that this will be a famine of the word of God, when the Lord will no longer communicate with his people. The balancing section tells of God's blessings mediated through nature in terms of astonishing fertility and productivity (9:13) and also of God's supporting actions in history, when the Lord will act to restore the fortunes of "my people" as they rebuild their ruined cities. Finally, the spheres of nature and history merge: Just as God's people will

125

plant their vineyards, just as the vineyards will grow and flourish and produce fruit, so will the Lord "plant" his people and they will flourish in the land he gives them.

The final messenger formula summarizes the theology of this section in the shortest possible way. Yahweh, the Lord, is the all powerful God. He is also *your* God, who continues to care for this people Israel. In contrast to the famine of the word announced in 8:11–12, here is a word of good news which brings the Amos book to a close.

3. What the Book of Amos Says About God

What the centerpiece in 9:5–7 says about God provides a concise summary for the theology which animates the entire Book of Amos.

First, the Lord is the God of nature. The pastures, the mountains react when the Lord speaks (1:2). The Lord has created the mountains, the winds, the stars, and continues to be active in maintaining the rhythms of darkness and morning, sunshine and rain (4:13; 5:8). The Lord is responsible when the vineyards are fruitful (9:13–14) or when the crops fail (5:11). The Lord can cause famine, drought, blight, plague, or epidemic (4:6–10; 7:1–2). The Lord can make the earth to quake or the sun to eclipse (8:8–9).

On the other hand, the Lord is not a fertility God to be identified somehow with the forces of nature. The Lord has acted and continues to act in the history of all the nations (1:3—2:16; 9:7, 9). The Lord has acted in Israel's history to deliver them from slavery and to give them a land (2:9–11; 3:1–2; 9:7). The Lord has communicated with Israel through the succession of prophets (2:11), but in the near future there will be no further prophetic word (8:11–12). In fact, Israel's God will raise up a nation to conquer them (3:9–11; 6:14) and deport them into exile (4:3; 5:27; 6:7). Finally, beyond that tragedy the Lord will act again, to rebuild the kingdom of David (9:11–12), to restore the good life of the people in their land (9:13–14), and indeed to identify himself to his people as "the LORD *your* God" (9:15, author's italics).

THE BOOK OF
Obadiah

Introduction

In this the shortest of the Old Testament books, the prophet Obadiah takes an older prophetic saying and applies it to his own situation. Since such a reapplying of older texts to new situations remains the task of the modern-day expositor and preacher, it is of interest to see how the prophet goes about his work. Beyond this, the Book of Obadiah brings an important message about oppressors and the oppressed, betrayers and those who have been betrayed. Arising out of a time of national crisis, it has a word for "innocent bystanders" and also for survivors.

Verse 1 introduces Obadiah as bringing a message from the Lord concerning Edom and identifies him as one with the people ("we") whom he addresses.

Verses 2–14 and 15*b* address Edom, the "innocent bystanders," in the second person singular (with the exception of vv. 6 and 8 which speak *about* Edom). The section from verse 1*b* ("We have heard . . .") through verse 4 is closely paralleled in Jeremiah 49:12–15; verse 5 is close to Jeremiah 49:9 and verse 6 expresses the same thought as Jeremiah 49:10. This material is the prophetic "text" upon which Obadiah's sermon is based. The function of this section is to announce punishment to Edom. The reason for the punishment is indicated in the general statement about pride in verses 3 and 4. Verses 10–14 and 15*b* continue to address Edom, providing detailed reasons for the punishment announced in verses 2–9. Verse 10 is a general statement, verses 11–14 tell of Edom's role at the fall of Jerusalem, and verse 15*b* returns to the announcement

of punishment with a summary statement. It appears that 15*a*
and 15*b* have been reversed in order during the transmitting
of the text.

Verse 15*a* plus 16–21 address Judah, the survivors, in the
second person plural. This section tells of the Day of the Lord
which is near. That day will be a time of punishment for the
nations (vv. 15*a*, 16), but for the Jews a time of deliverance and
of victory over Edom (vv. 17–18). Verses 19 and 20 expand upon
the "possess" theme of 17 and may be part of the later redac-
tional history of the book. Verse 21 rounds off the book, returning to the themes of Jerusalem, Edom, and the Lord with which
it began.

Obadiah 1:1
The Prophet Obadiah

This initial verse provides a lens through which to see what
the "vision of Obadiah" is all about. It introduces Obadiah and
the Lord, Edom and the Jews.

1. Obadiah

The name "Obadiah" means "servant of the Lord" and is
given to a dozen different individuals in the Old Testament,
including this prophet. In keeping with the brevity of the book,
the title tells nothing about the prophet beyond his name. From
a reading of the book, we may conclude that Obadiah was acquainted with earlier prophecy. Verses 1–5 are closely paralleled in Jeremiah 49:14–16, 9. Since the parallels are not exact,
it may be that both prophetic sayings are drawing upon a common source. Thus it appears that Obadiah was acquainted with
a stock of prophetic sayings upon which he drew for this particular prophetic message.

We also discover that Obadiah was a skillful and imaginative interpreter of the older prophetic tradition. We note some
of his rhetorical techniques: He uses the repetition of the word
"day" to build to a climax in 11–15. His imagery includes the
cup of wrath (v. 16) and the flaming fire (v. 18), both pictures
of the Lord's punishment. The saying in verse 15*b*, "As you

have done, it shall be done to you, your own deeds shall return upon your head," is explicated in verses 2–9. The book is framed with an inclusio, beginning and ending with a reference to the Lord, the Edomites, and Israel.

The use of the formula "thus says the LORD" further identifies Obadiah. He stands in the tradition of those prophets who are messengers from the Lord (see on Amos 1:3—2:16, part 1).

2. Edom

Immediately after naming the prophet and the Lord, Edom is introduced. A quick scan of the book indicates that Edom is its central concern: Verse 1 identifies the message as "concerning Edom." We have seen that the bulk of verses 2–15 addresses Edom; Verses 16–21 are addressed to Judah but the subject is still Edom. The final verse, like the first one, again speaks of the Jews, Edom, and the Lord. Thus it is obvious that to understand the Book of Obadiah we shall have to know something about Edom and the relationships between Edom and the Israelites.

The territory of Edom was situated to the south of the Dead Sea. Its western border was the mountain range overlooking the Arabah, that great rift running southward from the Dead Sea to the Gulf of Aqaba. The eastern and southern borders were the desert. On the north, the brook Zered separated Edom from Moab. The territory was small, roughly seventy miles from north to south and only fifteen miles from east to west. The most notable feature of this area is the reddish colored rocks and cliffs, which offers one explanation for the name "Edom," meaning "red region" in Hebrew. The modern-day visitor to Jordan may visit ancient Petra (Greek, "rock"), situated high in the cliffs and located at or near the site of the city of Sela (Hebrew, "rock"; Obad. 3, RSV footnote) and a few miles from the city of Teman (Obad. 9).

The Edomites had settled this territory about 1300 B.C., shortly before the Israelites arrived in the area. The history of relationships between the neighboring nations is a history of hostility. The Bible reflects this hostility at a variety of times. The struggle of the twins in Rebekah's womb is a symbol of the struggle between the two nations they represent, Israel and Edom (Gen. 25:19–34). At the time of Saul, the Edomites were among Israel's enemies (I Sam. 14:47). David subdued them (II

129

Sam. 8:12–14), and in the days of Jehoram of Judah (c. 850 B.C.) Edom revolted (II Kings 8:20–22). Most notorious in the history of relationships between these nations was the conduct of the Edomites at the time of the fall of Jerusalem in 587 B.C. (II Kings 25). Psalm 137:7 remembers how they mocked the Jews and encouraged the conquerors: "Remember, O LORD, against the Edomites the day of Jerusalem, how they said, 'Rase it, rase it! Down to its foundations!' " Ezekiel recalls their conduct at that time (Ezek. 25:12–14; 35:5–6) as does Lamentations (4:21–22). I Esdras 4:45 accuses them of burning the temple; it says to Darius, "You also vowed to build the temple, which the Edomites burned when Judea was laid waste by the Chaldeans." Edom is a favorite target of prophetic sayings: Isaiah 34; Jeremiah 49:7–22; Ezekiel 35; and Malachi 1:2–4. One has only to read through some of these chilling oracles to sense something of the enmity between Israel and Edom.

The most detailed description of Edom's conduct at the time of Jerusalem's fall is that found in Obadiah 1:11–14. Though the Edomites were relatives of the Jews, they acted just like their enemies (v. 11). They gloated and rejoiced (v. 12) and entered the city gate to participate in looting (v. 13). They handed over to the enemy refugees who were seeking sanctuary (v. 14). Such a betrayal could never be forgotten.

Soon after the return from exile, the fall of Jerusalem was remembered in a regular memorial service (Zech. 7:3; cf. II Kings 25:8 for the "fifth month," the time when the temple was burned down). The laments now found in Lamentations were heard at these services, much as they still are when Jews observe the event today. In order to understand the mood which Obadiah addresses, one should read through these laments, which begin, "How lonely sits the city that was full of people! How like a widow has she become. . . ." In the course of them, Edom was remembered and her punishment announced (Lam. 4:21–22).

3. The Jews

The "we" of verse 1 refers to the Jews, the people whom Obadiah addresses and of whom he is a part. What was the situation of these people when the prophet spoke to them? It is clear that he is speaking some time after the fall of Jerusalem in 587 B.C. Some have suggested that Obadiah's

130

prophecy is an example of the kind of preaching that took place at the memorial services for the fall of Jerusalem, as described above. He does "preach on" a prophetic text; whether such preaching took place at such a service may be left an open question. In any case, a date for Obadiah's activity soon after the return from exile in 539 B.C. seems reasonable.

Obadiah 1:2–14, 15*b*
A Word to the Bystanders

This section contains the elements typical to the prophetic word of judgment, namely an announcement of punishment (vv. 2–9 plus 15*b*), an accusation providing the reason for the announced punishment (vv. 10–14), and a messenger formula (v. 1; cf. vv. 4, 8; for further examples of the prophetic word of judgment, see Amos 1 and 2).

Obadiah believes that the old prophetic saying upon which he draws in verses 1*b*–6 is especially relevant for the situation in which he finds his people. That saying thus becomes the "text" for the sermon which he delivers. The suggestion that he is preaching to the gathered postexilic community at a service of memorial for the temple is an attractive one; in any case, it is important to remember that Obadiah is addressing a people who have already drunk the Lord's cup of wrath (v. 16), who have experienced the destruction of their city and temple, who have experienced deportation, and who are now trying to rebuild their lives. The word the prophet brings is a word about one of those enemies responsible for all that had happened to them.

Verses 2 and 4 are announcements of punishment which declare that the Lord will make Edom small and despised and bring that nation to its knees. The reasons for this punishment are given in verse 3: Edom's self-image is as elevated as the location of her capital city, high in the cliffs. This pride is an inward matter ("in your heart") which finds expression in words (the quotation in v. 3) as well as in acts, as the prophet will indicate in what follows.

131

The enemy that will attack Edom will be worse than an ordinary robber. Such thieves take only what they want; this enemy will totally destroy (vv. 5–6)! The parallel saying in Jeremiah expands the theme of Obadiah 1:6:

> "But I have stripped Esau bare,
> I have uncovered his hiding places,
> and he is not able to conceal himself.
> His children are destroyed, and his brothers,
> and his neighbors; and he is no more."
>
> (Jer. 49:10)

The prophet continues to speak of Edom's future, utilizing the "prophetic perfect" tense which speaks of future events as if they have already happened. Edom's friends will desert her and will drive her refugees to their borders and out of their lands (v. 7). Edom was noted for its "wise men" (Jer. 49:7; if Uz refers to Edom, as Lam. 4:21 indicates, then Job was from Edom, Job 1:1; cf. also Job 2:11 which indicates that Eliphaz was from Edom's capital city, Teman). One of the marks of "wisdom" in the ancient near east was a practical ability in military matters (Isa. 19:11–12). The prophet promises that neither this wisdom nor the manpower of the armies will be enough to deliver Edom from what awaits her (vv. 8–9).

Why should Edom be punished? Verse 10 gives a general reason. Although the Edomites were Israel's relatives (Deut. 2:1–8; 23:7), they have acted with violence toward their brothers! Verses 11–14 provide detailed reasons for Edom's punishment, with descriptions so graphic that they sound as if they come from an eyewitness. The reference is to the fall of Jerusalem in 587 B.C. First the Edomites stood by and did nothing. Then these "relatives" began to act just like the enemy! When the invading armies began to carry off both possessions and people (cf. Joel 3:3), the Edomites did not lift a finger to help (v. 11)! Verse 12 mentions the inner attitude of gloating which then expressed itself in rejoicing at the defeat of the Jews and in words of boasting. The Edomites poured in through the city gates with the conquerors and joined in the looting. When refugees sought help in Edom, the Edomites did not give them sanctuary but turned them over to the Babylonians (v. 14).

132

For all of this, says the prophet, there will be punishment, and the punishment will fit the crime! Wolff points out how the general statement, "As you have done, it shall be done to you, your deeds shall return upon your head," is illustrated in the earlier part of the prophet's speech: Those who stood by doing nothing when Jerusalem was conquered (v. 11) will themselves be deserted by their allies (v. 7). Those who gloated and boasted at the predicament of their neighbors (v. 12) will themselves be despised (v. 2) and will be humiliated (v. 4). Those who looted their neighbors (v. 13) will themselves be plundered (vv. 5–6). Those who would not give sanctuary to refugees (v. 14) will find no refuge with their own friends (v. 7). They who "cut off" the fleeing victims of war (v. 14) will be "cut off" themselves (v. 10) (Hans Walter Wolff, *Obadiah and Jonah,* pp. 56–7). Thus verse 15*b* is a summary of verses 2–14 and 2–14 are an explication of 15*b*.

Obadiah 1:15*a*, 16–21
A Word to the Survivors

Up to this point, the "you" of the prophet's speech had been addressed to Edom. Now the "you" of verse 16, a second plural form in Hebrew, is addressed to those Jews who had returned from exile and had settled on Mount Zion. This is a word addressed to the survivors.

In verses 11–14, the prophet had used the word "day" ten times in reference to the day of the fall of Jerusalem. That was the "Day of the Lord" which meant the Lord's punishment of his own people, the "day of his fierce anger" (Lam. 1:12; cf. Lam. 2:1). Now in verse 15*a* the prophet speaks of another "day" which will be one of punishment for the nations, but deliverance for God's people. The prophet Joel would also speak of this day (Joel 2:3–32; chap. 3).

With verse 16, Obadiah uses the traditional picture of the cup of the Lord's wrath (cf. Ps. 75:8; Jer. 51:7, used of Babylon as the Lord's cup). "You survivors," he says to those gathered on Mount Zion, "have already drunk of that cup." Now the other nations will taste the Lord's punishment as the cup is passed on to them. Obadiah is expressing a thought devel-

133

oped at greater length in Isaiah 51. There the Lord says to his people:

"Behold, I have taken from your hand
   the cup of staggering;
the bowl of my wrath
   you shall drink no more;
and I will put it into the hand of your tormentors. . . ."

                            (Isa. 51:22–23)

To this point the prophet has twice referred to Mount Esau, high in the rocky cliffs of Edom. Now he begins to speak of Mount Zion. The survivors gathered there will one day repossess the land which was rightfully theirs.

The prophet stops talking about punishment for the nations in general and focuses on Edom in particular (v. 18). Edom is the chaff and God's people are the fire that will consume them (for the image, cf. Exod. 15:7; Isa. 5:24; 10:17; 29:5–6; Mal. 4:1; Matt. 3:12). This is the final word about Edom, the saying concluding with a "for the LORD has spoken" formula which certifies it as a word from God.

Verses 19–20 pick up on the "possess, possessions" of verse 17 and spell out just what those possessions will be; these verses could well be an expansion of Obadiah's original words. The larger commentaries deal with the geographical details. We may note that verses 19–20 are framed with a reference to the Negeb, the southern part of the land, which borders on Edom. These sayings promise that the Jews will possess the land of their enemies Edom and Philistia as well as their own traditional territories of Ephraim and Samaria and Gilead in Transjordan. The northern border will be extended to Zarephath (cf. I Kings 17:9–10) and the southern into the Negeb.

The first word in verse 21 should be read, "those who have been saved," necessitating only a change of the vowels in the Hebrew text (cf. Allen, *Joel, Obadiah, Jonah, and Micah,* p. 163):

Those who have been saved shall go up to Mount Zion to
   rule Mount Esau;
and the kingdom shall be the LORD'S.

                            (author's translation)

134

The sermon preached to the struggling survivors ends with a promise that those on Mount Zion will rule over those on Mount

Esau, and with a reminder that the ultimate ruling power belongs to the Lord.

Obadiah 1:1–21
A Word for the Church

Obadiah's prophetic message has a word for the bystander and also for the survivor.

1. A Word to Bystanders

The Edomites were not responsible for initiating the destruction of their neighboring people the Jews. Their role is clear from Obadiah, verses 11–14. They began as observers, innocent bystanders, watching as foreign soldiers entered Jerusalem and carried off its treasures and its citizens. The Edomites gloated a bit, even rejoiced, and then finally joined in the looting themselves. When Jewish survivors asked them for sanctuary, they saw it as their civic duty to turn the refugees over to the occupying troops. According to the prophet, this was all wrong. They should have *stood with* their neighbor; they chose to *stand by*.

Obadiah suggests that there are no "innocent bystanders." When a neighbor suffers under an oppressor, the place of God's people is on the side of the neighbor. Jesus spoke of a final accounting, and of those who had failed to stand with the hungry and thirsty, the stranger and naked, the sick, and the imprisoned (Matt. 25:31–46). The prophet raises the question for the church: If the church has not often found itself in the role of the oppressor, has it too often played the role of the innocent bystander? If it has not often been guilty of robbing and plundering, has it too often chosen to avoid getting involved in the lives of those who are hurting, choosing rather to pass by on the other side (Luke 10:25–37)?

The other accusation against Edom is the charge of pride or arrogance (v. 3). This people had become quite self-confident as they settled back in the safety of their defense systems. Their symbol was the eagle, nesting high among the stars. Their own politicians assured them, "We're number one!"

Obadiah warns against this sort of national pride and

135

against the *power of arrogance.* Pride can deceive and beguile a nation as well as an individual into a false sense of self-reliance. The same word (deceive/beguile) is used to describe how pride got to Eve: "You will be like God" was the serpent's promise and Eve was beguiled (Gen. 3:5, 13). Obadiah warns a people of God against being deceived by pride and arrogance into thinking of itself as invincible and indestructible.

2. A Word to Survivors

The second part of Obadiah's message was directed to the survivors, that band of men, women, and children who had come back from exile to find that their homes and their dwellings as well as their hopes and their dreams were all shattered.

To those whose lives are a shambles, but who have survived, Obadiah says: Evil will be punished (v. 18). There will remain a people of God (vv. 17, 21). Finally, in the words of the hymn, "though the wrong seems oft so strong, God is the ruler yet" ("This Is My Father's World"), or in the prophet's words, "the kingdom shall be the LORD's" (v. 21).

Here the ancient prophetic word reaches out to the future, to the time when another prophet who also spoke of God's judgment as an unquenchable fire (Matt. 3:12) would say that the promise of the kingdom had been fulfilled. This prophet's word was "repent, for the kingdom of heaven is at hand" (Matt. 3:2).

The good news is that this invitation is issued to all who will hear it—to bystanders who have failed to stand by their neighbor in need, as well as to survivors who have been betrayed by their friends. There is room in God's kingdom for both.

THE BOOK OF
Jonah

Introduction

The first word in the Hebrew text of Jonah is *vayehi* which may be translated, "and it happened. . . ." In many instances, the King James Version translated it as, "Now it came to pass . . ." (Josh. 1:1; Judg. 1:1; II Sam. 1:1; Ruth 1:1; Esther 1:1). That word is important for understanding the Book of Jonah because it signals the beginning of a particular type of literature: a narrative or story (on biblical stories, see *Old Stories for a New Time,* by the author).

This introductory word which identifies that which follows as a narrative is unique among the prophetic books. Other books include narrative sections (Isa. 36—39; Amos 7:10–17), but only Jonah is exclusively a story about a prophet.

The story divides into five scenes:

1:1–3 In the land of Israel: the Lord and Jonah
1:4–16 At sea: Jonah and the sailors
1:17—2:10 In the fish: the Lord and Jonah
3:1–10 In Nineveh: the Lord, Jonah, the Ninevites
4:1–11 Outside Nineveh: the Lord and Jonah

The setting for the action of the story is clear. "Jonah the son of Amittai" is known as a prophet from the Northern Kingdom who was active in the days of Jeroboam II (786–746 B.C.; II Kings 14:25). During this period Nineveh was an important Assyrian city; from the time of Sennacherib (704 B.C.) it was the capital. The story of Jonah is thus set during the eighth century, during the time of the Assyrian empire.

The book provides no clue to the setting for the composition of the story. Various views have been proposed, ranging

137

from the eighth down to the fourth centuries. The vagueness of the reference to Nineveh, the exaggerated description of its size, which suggests it is viewed from a period long after its heyday (3:3), as well as vocabulary all suggest that the book should be dated some time in the postexilic period, most likely in the fifth century B.C. For full discussion of dating, see the commentaries of Wolff (who dates it in the fourth century), Allen (fifth or fourth century), and Fretheim (475–450 B.C.).

Jonah 1:1–3
The Runaway

The initial scene introduces the story by presenting the persons and places that will be involved in it.

1. Persons and Places

The Lord is the first to be named in this scene, in the formula, "Now the word of the LORD came to . . ." (cf. I Kings 17:2, 8–9; Hos. 1:1; Joel 1:1; Micah 1:1). The frequent mention of the Lord in the Jonah book indicates that God plays a major role in the story. "LORD" translating Yahweh is used twenty-five times, "God" thirteen times, "LORD GOD" once, for a total of thirty-nine references to the diety in the forty-four verses of the book. The atmosphere of this story is quite different from that of Ruth, for example, where the narrator mentions the Lord only at the beginning (1:6) and ending (4:13), or Esther, which makes no mention of God at all. This is a story about Jonah, but more precisely about the Lord and Jonah.

Jonah the son of Amittai is also mentioned in II Kings 14:25, which locates the prophet during the time of Jeroboam II (786–746 B.C.). This Jonah's home town was Gath-Hepher, just to the west of the Sea of Galilee. The traditional site of Jonah's tomb is located in this area (G. W. Van Beck, "Gath-Hepher," *Interpreter's Dictionary*, E–J, 356). The name Jonah means "dove." This figure is used for Israel a number of times (Hos. 7:11; 11:11; Ps. 74:19). Is there a hint here that "Jonah" is again a metaphor for the people Israel?

The other characters who will play roles in the story are introduced only by pronouns: "their wickedness" refers to the

138

people of Nineveh, while the "them" of verse 3 refers to the
sailors with whom Jonah set out to sea.

The first place to be named is *Nineveh.* It is a "great city"
(1:2; 3:2; 4:11), in fact an "exceedingly great city" (3:3). It is
described in quantitative terms, a three-day journey in breadth
(3:3) and having a population of a hundred and twenty thousand
(4:11). The population is also described qualitatively, as having
a reputation for wickedness (1:2), evil, and violence (3:8, 10). Yet
the people are commendable because they turned from their
evil ways (3:10). They are in fact a helpless lot for whom the
Lord has pity (4:11).

The site where Nineveh was located, on the river Tigris in
present-day northern Iraq, is a very old one. Archaeologists say
that it was occupied thousands of years before Christ. During
the eighth century B.C., the city was at its peak. Nineveh became Assyria's capital under Sennacherib (704–681 B.C.) and
remained the capital until the end of the empire. Ashurbani-
pal's famous library was located there (668–627 B.C.). In 612
B.C., Nineveh fell to the combined armies of the Medes and the
Babylonians. Archaeological handbooks refer to two mounds in
the present ruins of the city: the mound of Kuyunjik, "little
lamb," and the mound called Nebi Yunus, "the prophet Jonah,"
which contains a reputed tomb of Jonah.

To understand what Nineveh meant to those who heard
the story of Jonah, we must recall the reputation of Nineveh and
of the Assyrians as reported in the Old Testament. The Assyrians captured the Northern Kingdom in 722 B.C. and deported
its citizens (II Kings 17). They almost succeeded in capturing
Jerusalem some years later (II Kings 18—19). The Book of the
prophet Nahum announces the fall of Nineveh. That book
should be read as background for understanding the story of
Jonah. Note especially chapter 3:

> Woe to the bloody city,
>   all full of lies and booty . . .
> All who hear the news of you
>   clap their hands over you.
> For upon whom has not come
>   your unceasing evil?
>   (Nah. 3:1, 19)

Thus Nineveh, with its reputation for violence and terrorism,
was a symbol of all that opposed the Lord and the Lord's people.
Those whom the Book of Jonah addresses had memories of their

139

own ancestors suffering under the cruelty of Nineveh and the Assyrians. It is quite understandable that an Israelite prophet would be reluctant to accept a mission to that city. It would be as if a Jew who had lost family in the Holocaust were asked to undertake a mission to Germany just after the Nazi period. Nineveh was, as Nahum named her, "the harlot," the "bloody city," the center of violence and terrorism, the enemy.

While the location of Tarshish is still somewhat in doubt, most agree that the reference is to a site in modern-day Spain. The important thing to note is that when Jonah was told to go to Nineveh to the northeast, he chose to set out in the opposite direction, heading southwest toward *Joppa*, a seaport on the Mediterranean, which is the modern Yafo, a suburb of Tel Aviv.

2. The Impossible Escape

The story of Jonah begins with a command from the Lord to Jonah, "Arise, go to Nineveh. . . ." This sort of command is a typical one; the Lord said to Elijah, "Arise, go to Zarephath. . . ." That narrative continues, "So he arose and went to Zarephath" (I Kings 17:9–10). In fact, the Lord will later say to Jonah, "Arise, go to Nineveh" and the narrative will continue, "So Jonah arose and went to Nineveh" (3:2–3). Here the usual pattern is broken, for when he is told to arise and go to Nineveh and speak against its wickedness, Jonah instead arises and heads off in the opposite direction. Now begins a series of "descents" in the unfolding of the story: Jonah goes down to Joppa, then he goes down (RSV, "went on board") into the ship. A repetition indicates what is most important in this beginning of the story: Jonah was running away "from the presence of the LORD" (v. 3, twice).

In this way the story of Jonah is introduced by setting up a double tension. The reader or hearer wonders: What will happen to Jonah, who is running away from the task God has given him? What will happen to Nineveh, that great—but wicked—city?

The doubled expression, "from the presence of the LORD" invites reflection on the theme of running away from God.

The verb "flee" has the sense of running away from a relationship or a community. Thus Hagar flees from her mistress (Gen. 16:6, 8), Jacob flees from Laban (Gen. 31:20, 21, 22), Moses flees from the service of Pharaoh (Exod. 2:15), and Jephthah flees from his brothers (Judg. 11:3). The idea is to make a

140

break with past relationships and to begin a new life outside those relationships. It is possible to "flee" from a person or a community, but only of Jonah is it said that he intended to flee from the presence of the Lord.

Jonah discovered that it is *impossible to escape God's presence.* Psalm 139 puts the matter clearly:

> Whither shall I go from thy Spirit?
> Or whither shall I flee from thy presence?
> If I ascend to heaven, thou art there!
> If I make my bed in Sheol, thou art there!
> (Ps. 139:7–8)

Jonah's story illustrates the truth of the psalm. Whether in the depths of the sea, in the belly of the fish, or in the suburbs of Nineveh, Jonah never succeeded in running away from God.

The story of Jonah also indicates that it is *impossible to escape God's tasks.* Jonah tells why he was on the run: because he wanted no part of the task God had given him (4:2). His attempted flight cost him a good deal of money (a ticket from Joppa to Tarshish must have been expensive), a good deal of time, and it almost cost him his life. Yet he never escaped from the task. After a number of extraordinary experiences at sea, he finds himself seated somewhere on a sunny beach, and that task comes bouncing right back at him again: "Arise, go to Nineveh. . . ."

Finally, the story of Jonah teaches that it is *impossible to escape the love of God.* Psalm 139 had put it succinctly, declaring that neither height (heaven) nor depth (Sheol) nor travel to the east (the wings of the morning) nor to the west (the uttermost parts of the sea) could separate the psalmist from the Lord. "Even there thy hand shall lead me, and thy right hand shall hold me," he said (v. 10). Jonah discovered what that promise meant as he sank into the depths of the sea and was rescued.

The impossibility of escaping God's love was apparent to the apostle Paul, who himself had known what it was to be adrift at sea and near death (II Cor. 11:24–27). He wrote that no power, no place, no time can separate God's people from the love shown them in Christ (Rom. 8:38–39).

Jesus once told a story about a young man who could not wait to escape from the confining atmosphere of life at home. After he left, when his life had become a shambles, he "came to himself" and remembered his loving father. When he finally

141

arrived home, he discovered that he had never escaped his father's love. So it is, said Jesus, with the inescapable love of God (Luke 15:11–32).

Jonah 1:4–16
The Storm

1. The Story: Man Overboard!

Scene II in the story of Jonah takes place on board a ship traveling on the Mediterranean Sea from Joppa to Tarshish. As the scene opens, the Lord sends a great storm on the sea. Psalm 107 tells of a storm sent by the Lord and reports the reaction of the sailors:

> For he commanded, and raised the stormy wind,
>   which lifted up the waves of the sea.
> They mounted up to heaven, they went down into the
>   depths;
>   their courage melted away in their evil plight;
> they reeled and staggered like drunken men,
>   and were at their wits' end.
>
> (Ps. 107:25–27)

The storm worsens. The descriptions in the story intensify progressively, indicating the progressive worsening of the storm: "there was a mighty tempest on the sea" (v. 4), "for the sea grew more and more tempestuous" (v. 11), "for the sea grew more and more tempestuous against them" (v. 13). The storm becomes so violent that the ship threatens to break to pieces.

The major characters in this scene are the sailors. As we watch them, we discover that they are realistic, pious, and peaceful men. Their first reaction is an honest one: They are afraid. Their second reaction is to pray, each to his own god. These sailors, the story makes clear, were not Israelites, but worshipers of a variety of gods and no doubt citizens of a variety of countries. Their conduct illustrates the truth of the maxim, "Let him who knows not how to pray go to sea." Finally, they try to save the ship by jettisoning the cargo. "Pray as if it all depended on God; act as if it all depended on you," someone once said. Such appears to be the manner of these sailors.

142

At their head is the captain. Again, the storyteller wants to point out that the captain's religious preference is non-Israelite. The captain speaks to Jonah about "your god," not "our god." He too is a man of piety. When he finds Jonah sleeping, his first word is not "Why aren't you helping?" but rather "Why aren't you praying?"

The sailors are persons whose religion calls them to a healthy balance between prayer and action. They are also humane. When Jonah tells them to throw him into the sea, they refuse. They risk their lives and keep on rowing.

Finally they do throw Jonah overboard, but not without first praying to the Lord, lest they be guilty of shedding innocent blood (Deut. 21:8). When the sea stops raging, their great fear of the storm (v. 5) turns to a great fear of the Lord (v. 16). The storyteller portrays the sailors as exemplary in every way.

After the Lord and the sailors, we finally encounter Jonah. He arrives on the scene late and leaves early (Wolff, *Obadiah and Jonah,* p. 122). Jonah is the Israelite in the story, the representative of those people to whom the story was first addressed. His descent continues (see on 1:1–3) as he goes down into the hold of the ship (v. 5). His behavior is in sharp contrast to that of the sailors. They are on the deck working to save the ship; Jonah is down below sound asleep. They have prayed to their gods; we hear not one word of prayer from Jonah. The sailors are working to preserve life; Jonah gives up and prefers to die. They are men who act; Jonah only reacts, getting up when awakened, speaking when asked questions. The sailors worship the Lord; Jonah is running away from the Lord.

Noteworthy is the theological interest in this part of the story. The sailors, including the captain, are described in terms of their religion. Jonah too is described theologically, in that when pressed, he makes a statement about his own religious preference. His religion appears to be only word-deep, though, for while he can talk *about* God, unlike the sailors, he does not talk *to* God. He can prattle about theology (v. 9), but he does not pray. He can offer theological observations, but he does not obey. He is, after all, a runaway from his religion.

2. Insiders and Outsiders

We can imagine the sailors in this scene as rugged men **143** from a variety of backgrounds. No doubt some had chapters in their past which were not commendable, and one or two among them may have been a criminal. These sailors have a few things in common. They have great respect for a storm at sea. When one hits, they know just what to do: They pray, and they go into action. They also have in common the fact that they are not Israelities. Wolff alludes to a Jewish tradition that their company included representatives from all seventy nations which existed on the earth (Wolff, *Obadiah and Jonah,* p. 123). Not being a part of the people of God, these sailors represent the people of the world. In other words, they reflect the same mixed population as would be found in the city of Nineveh.

Jonah, on the other hand, represents the people of God. From the standpoint of the narrator and those who first heard the story, Jonah is an *insider,* and the sailors are *outsiders.* This story is a word to insiders concerning outsiders. To put it another way: It is a word addressed to the people of God concerning the people of the world.

This part of the story says some things about the people of the world which may be surprising to lifelong insiders. For one thing, these people are *humane.* Told that the only way to save their own lives is to sacrifice another who is a stranger to them all, they resist. They will do anything to avoid causing the death of a fellow human being, even one who is an admitted runaway. For another thing, these people are *pious* in their own way. Could they have recited a catechism-like statement summarizing their own faith as well as Jonah did for his? We do not know. One thing we do know. When they are in trouble, they pray. Though an insider would no doubt judge their prayers doctrinally deficient, let this be said for these outsiders: They do pray. They are also *practical.* When the crisis hits, they can be counted on to be out there, shoulder-to-shoulder, doing what they can. At such times, national, ethnic, or confessional differences matter little. What does matter is that there are concerned efforts to help one another. Finally, we see that these people are *open to theological growth.* Having learned something about the true God, they pray to the Lord and offer sacrifices. Did they continue in this new faith? Did they keep their vows? Again, we do not know. We do know that in this time of crisis, these humane, pious, and practical people prayed and worshiped the Lord.

144   Jonah is the insider. He is the one with whom the hearer of the story is to identify. He is our man on board the ship: Mr. Israelite or Mr. Lutheran, Mr. Methodist, Mr. Roman Catholic,

Mr. Presbyterian. And he, as well as the community he represents, does not come off well at all. He can "talk religion" but
does not seem to be much at practicing it. In an emergency, he
cannot be counted on to pray or to act; in fact, he just gives up.
In addition, of course, he is running away from God.

This scene asks the "insiders," those who count themselves
as part of God's people, to reevaluate their attitudes and preju-
dices toward "outsiders." It reminds them of that summary of
the gospel which says that God so loved the *world* (John 3:16,
author's italics), and that "the world" includes the teeming
cities of Nineveh, but also of Moscow, Teheran, Beirut, or Bei-
jing. It is a reminder of Jesus' own demonstrations of care for
the outsider. The story about the one who proved to be a neighbor, told to insiders, held up an outsider as exemplary (Luke
10:25–37). Jesus once surprised his disciples by conversing with
an outsider (John 4:7–9; 27). The leper who came back to say
"thank you," Luke points out, was an outsider (Luke 17:11–19).
Jesus said that he came for the sake of the outsiders, though the
insiders criticized him for it (Luke 15:1–2).

Finally, the apostle wrote that the categories insider/out-
sider are no longer valid since Christ. "For there is no distinction between Jew and Greek; the same Lord is Lord of all and
bestows his riches upon all who call upon him. For, 'every one
who calls upon the name of the Lord will be saved'" (Rom.
10:12–13; cf. Gal. 3:28).

Jonah 1:17—2:10
The Fish

Scene III consists of a prayer (2:2–9) framed by a narrative
introduction and conclusion (1:17—2:1; 2:10).

1. The Story: One Vast Kidney

Jonah had tried to run away from the Lord, was unsuccess-
ful, and was punished by being thrown into the sea. The story
could have ended here. Its point could have been: Do not diso-
bey God. Remember what happened to Jonah who did!

On the contrary, the story continues. Like scenes I and II,
scene III opens with an act of the Lord. This time the Lord

145

appoints a great fish to rescue Jonah from the sea (1:17). The setting for the psalm that follows is inside that fish. We have to imagine Jonah safe and sound, sitting inside that huge creature of the sea, singing praises to the Lord. Aldous Huxley paints the scene with imagination:

> Seated upon the convex mound
> of one vast kidney Jonah prays
> and sings his canticles and hymns.
> Making the hollow vault resound
> God's goodness and mysterious ways
> Til
> the great fish spouts music as he swims.
> ("Jonah," *The Cherry Tree*, p. 211)

The psalm in verses 2–9 may be classified as a psalm of individual thanksgiving or, to use Westermann's classification, of narrative praise of the individual. In psalms of this type, an individual praises God because of a deliverance from a specific situation of distress (see Claus Westermann, *The Psalms: Structure, Content and Message*, pp. 71–80). Comparison with Psalm 30, another psalm of the same type, is instructive:

	Psalm 30	*Jonah 2:2–9*
Introductory Summary	1–3	2
Description of Distress	6–10	3–6ab
Report of Deliverance	11	6c
Vow to Praise	12	9ab

These are the typical elements in the psalm of narrative praise of the individual. These two psalms both contain a further element:

Word to Congregation		
Based on the Experience	4–5	2a,7a,9c,8

In Psalm 30, the word to the congregation is a call to praise (v. 4) plus a reason (v. 5). In Jonah, these words are statements *about* the Lord, plus a proverbial saying. If we read the psalm as part of the book as a whole, we note that these statements apply the message of the book to the listening audience.

The psalm which Jonah sings provides his version of what had happened. Though it was the sailors who threw him overboard, Jonah knows that the Lord was behind it all (v. 3). In a

146

final "going down" (cf. 1:1–3, 5) Jonah describes his descent to the land of the dead (vv. 5–6*ab*). As he was plummeting down into the sea, however, Jonah had time to breathe a prayer (vv. 2, 4, 7). The narrative framework tells us that God answered the prayer by "appointing" a fish to rescue the prophet (1:17). At three points in the psalm itself, Jonah reports that his prayer was answered: "thou didst hear my voice" (v. 2), "and my prayer came to thee, into thy holy temple" (v. 7), "Deliverance belongs to the LORD" (v. 9).

Having recalled the *distress* and *God's deliverance* in a manner typical of such psalms, Jonah is now at the same point as the sailors described in scene II. They sacrificed and made vows. From inside the fish, Jonah promises to do the same (v. 9).

Finally, the Lord acts to deliver Jonah once again. After saving him from a watery death, the Lord now gives him a chance at a new life on the land. The Lord speaks to the fish, Jonah is vomited out, and there he sits, on the beach in the sunshine. With this, the third and most dramatic scene in the story comes to an end.

2. When the Bottom Drops Out

We have seen that the psalm fits well into the story of Jonah. It is also composed with an eye to the listening congregation, with a kerygmatic and didactic aim expressed in verses 2*a*, 7*a*, 9*c* and 8, as noted above. These statements point the way for contemporary appropriation of the psalm.

Two of these statements indicate that *the psalm has a word for those who are about to go under,* for those whose lives are in a state of crisis. In verse 2*a* the psalmist describes his situation as one of "distress." Verse 7*a* says, "when my soul fainted. . . ." "Soul" refers to one's whole life; the same expression is used of weary travelers in the desert, "hungry and thirsty, their soul fainted within them" (Ps. 107:5). The psalm uses other images to describe the extreme situation of the one praying. He is in "the belly of Sheol" or "the Pit" (vv. 2, 6). Both expressions denote the location in the underworld where the dead are found; cf. Psalm 16:10, where the terms are used in parallel. We have noted that the story tells of Jonah's continual descent: He went down to Joppa (1:3), then down to the ship (RSV, "on board," 1:3), then down into the hold (1:5). Now he goes down a final time, "to the land whose bars closed on me for ever" (2:6),

147

a picture of the realm of the dead from which there is no escape, where the gates are secured with heavy iron bars like those which secure the gates of a city (Deut. 3:5; Judg. 16:3; Neh. 3:6).

These statements about deliverance in verses 2*a* and 7*a* as well as the summary statement "Deliverance belongs to the LORD" in verse 9 indicated that this psalm intends to speak to those who are themselves in need of rescue or deliverance. They direct the message of the psalm to those whose lives have been shipwrecked, who are at the end of their rope, for whom the bottom has dropped out. They may have lost a loved one, lost a job, or experienced a breakup in their marriage or family. Like Jonah, the crisis they are experiencing may be of their own making. They are aware of that and do not need to be reminded of it.

The witness of this psalm is that in such a desperate situation *the only thing to do is to pray*. The psalm begins with a testimony of one whose prayer has been answered, such as one might hear at a gathering of Christians sharing their faith experiences: "I called to the LORD out of my distress, and he answered me." Verse 7 says the same thing: "When my soul fainted within me, I remembered the LORD; and my prayer came to thee. . . ." Other psalms are also prayers designed for situations of extreme distress, describing a situation where the psalmist is about to go under (Ps. 130; 42:7; 69:1–2, 13–15).

The third of the statements aimed at the listening congregation declares simply: *The Lord delivers* (v. 9*c*). That assertion is tacked onto the end of the psalm as a kind of slogan, just as one might tack a motto on the wall saying "God answers prayer" or "Jesus saves." It is as if within the excitement of the story the storyteller stops the action to make a direct statement to the hearers. He knows that he has their attention, because they are caught up in the story. His message is a simple one, only two words in Hebrew: *yeshuata leyahweh*, "deliverance/salvation is from the Lord."

The word for deliverance or salvation is *yeshua*. When the angel announced to Mary that she would have a son, he said, "you shall call his name Jesus [Hebrew, *yeshua*], for he will save his people from their sins" (Matt. 1:21). The Christian reader cannot hear this final statement of the psalm in Jonah without hearing the name of Jesus, which has meant salvation for the peoples of the world (John 3:16).

148

In placing this psalm here, the final composer of the Book

of Jonah has yet another point to make. This is expressed in the most clearly didactic statement in the entire book: "Those who pay regard to vain idols forsake their true loyalty" (2:8). The word translated "loyalty" is the Hebrew *hesed* which means covenant love (see on Hos. 6:4–6), and which is used for God himself, "forsake their true God."

Finally, the statement about deliverance coming from the Lord is given dramatic illustration. The Lord speaks to the fish, the fish spits the prophet out onto the beach, and Jonah is rescued once again.

Jonah 3:1–10
The City

We have seen that the tension driving the story of Jonah may be expressed with two questions: What will happen to a prophet who disobeys a command from the Lord? What will happen to the wicked city of Nineveh? Here the first question is answered: The Lord has maneuvered the prophet around to a position where he gets a second chance. Scene IV begins just as scene I did, "Then the word of the LORD came to Jonah. . . ." Now the story will focus on the matter of Nineveh.

1. The Story: The Second Time Around

As scene IV opens, Jonah is sitting on a Mediterranean beach, no doubt shaken by his recent extraordinary experiences. Then that same word from the Lord comes to him a second time: "Arise, go to Nineveh, that great city. . . ." This time Jonah responds as we expect a prophet to respond. Told to arise and go, "Jonah arose and went" (cf. I Kings 17:8–10).

The teller of the story was much impressed by the size of Nineveh. God himself names it "great" three times (1:2; 3:2; 4:11). The Hebrew idiom here describes the city literally as "great to God" (RSV, "exceedingly great"), just as Nimrod was described as "a mighty hunter before the LORD" (Gen. 10:9). How big was the city? The narrator says, "It was so big that it took three days to walk across it." This would be a very large city. In comparison with what is known of ancient Nineveh from history and archaeology, this appears to be a storyteller's

149

exaggeration, recalling a huge metropolis from the distant past. Wolff remarks: "The reader is not supposed to do arithmetic. He is supposed to be lost in astonishment . . ." (Wolff, *Obadiah and Jonah,* p. 148).

Jonah is pictured as carrying out his assignment without much enthusiasm. He only "begins" to go into the city and only goes part way. His preaching in Nineveh does not reflect creativity or imagination and consists of only five words in Hebrew: "Yet forty days and-Nineveh will-be-overthrown" (author's translation). If Jonah's preaching is successful, that success will surely not be credited to the homiletical or rhetorical skills of the prophet!

Surprisingly, Jonah's preaching is remarkably successful. The reaction of the people is amazing. They believe God, call for a fast, and dress in the clothes of mourning.

Now Jonah disappears from the scene and verses 6–9 provide a detailed report about what was summarized in verse 5. The king's behavior is exemplary. He humbles himself by divesting himself of his symbols of authority, his throne and his robe, and by putting on sackcloth and sitting in ashes. He calls for an all-inclusive fast extending even to the animals and admonishes all to turn from their evil and violent ways.

The king realizes that conducting a fast does not guarantee that the Lord will act favorably. The best that can be said is, "Who knows?" (cf. Joel 2:14). Like the captain on the ship, the king's overriding concern is for the welfare of his people (3:9; cf. 1:6).

The scene comes to an end with a report of God's reaction. Having seen the repentance of the citizens of Nineveh, God calls off the announced punishment. Now the question, "What will happen to sinful Nineveh?" finds its answer. The people have heard the prophet's message and repented, and the scheduled destruction has been called off.

2. Who Cares for the City?

The story of Jonah had its beginning because God cared about the city of Nineveh. "Their wickedness has come up before me," the Lord had said. The focus of the story up to chapter 3 had been on Jonah, the runaway prophet. Now it is on Nineveh, that great—and wicked—city.

Jonah's message was that in forty days Nineveh would be *overthrown.* That word is used in the Bible in connection with

Sodom and Gomorrah, the wicked cities upon which the Lord rained brimstone and fire, and which the Lord *overthrew* (Gen. 19:24–25; cf. 29). We have already noted the bad reputation of Nineveh. The prophet Nahum labeled it "vile" (Nah. 1:14), "the bloody city, all full of lies and booty" (3:1), comparing it to a den of lions (2:10–12) or a harlot (3:4–7), and announcing its fall in chilling terms (3:1–19). When Nineveh's end came, no one would feel sorry, "For upon whom has not come your unceasing evil?" (Nah. 3:19).

When Nineveh is first introduced in the story of Jonah, it is remembered for its size and for its wickedness (1:2). The story comments again on its size (3:2–3). As for its wickedness, the hearers would remember the Nineveh which had deported their ancestors in the Northern Kingdom, and the Nineveh about which Nahum had spoken. These listeners could no doubt easily identify with Jonah! If given an assignment which involved travel to Nineveh, they too may have preferred to go in the opposite direction! If forced to go to Nineveh, no doubt they too would go with reluctance! If compelled to preach, such sermonizing would no doubt be executed only in the most perfunctory manner, without passion or imagination.

Who cares for the city in the story to this point? Certainly not Jonah, the insider representing the people of God. The answer is that God does—and God has gone to great efforts to see that a prophet is sent to the people of the city.

Like the sailors of scene II, the Ninevites here are portrayed in a most positive manner. These citizens of the "bloody city" offer some surprises for the listening audience.

The preaching which the Ninevites heard did not come certified as a word from God. Nor did it make its appeal on reasonable grounds, by pointing out the sins of the people which therefore deserved punishment (cf. Amos 1—2). Out of the blue, Jonah announced the city's overthrow. Most hearers, one would think, would dismiss such words as the ravings of a religious fanatic.

In contrast, the people believed God, announced a fast, humbled themselves, and did something to clean up the terrorism and violence in their city. This was not the action of just a few, but involved everyone, including the animals! And what of the king? We have noted that his proclamation ended with a humble, "Who knows?" indicating that the king did not presume to control God. His is no mechanistic religion, expecting that repentance automatically guarantees rescue. The king is humble before God and concerned for his people, "so that we perish not."

As was the case in scene II, the people of God may be amazed by the behavior of the people of the world. The insiders are surprised by the outsiders. Hearing only a few words from a prophet, these outsiders have repented and cleaned up the violence in their city. The insiders had been listening to the words of prophets for centuries, and the record of their response to those words was not a happy one (cf. Matt. 23:37–39). The attitude of these people of Nineveh would be long remembered, and even held up as exemplary (Matt. 12:41).

Who cares for the city? The story of Jonah makes the answer to this question clear: God does. This is apparent at the beginning, when the Lord cares enough to send a prophet. It is clear in 3:10, where the Lord calls off the announced punishment. It is clear from the question with which the book ends.

Thus the word to insiders in this part of the Jonah story is again a hard one. It asks God's own people, those within the church, about their attitude toward the people of the great cities of the world. It asks them about the people of the Calcuttas, the Karachis, the Sao Paulos of our own day. It reminds the people of God that they exist for the sake of the people of the world and warns against an arrogant "insider/outsider" mentality. It speaks a word of criticism against a people who prefer huddling and cuddling (like Jonah in the hold of the ship) in the safety of their own groups to being about the task to which Jesus called them: "Go therefore and make disciples of all nations" (Matt. 28:19). It warns a people of God against the danger of forgetting that they are ambassadors, participating in the reconciling of the world to God (II Cor. 5:18–21).

The great images of the church remind God's people that they exist for the sake of the world's people. They are the salt of the earth, the light of the world (Matt. 5:13–16), the body through which the risen Christ accomplishes his work (Eph. 1:23; 3:6; I Cor. 12:12–31).

152 Who cares for the city? God does, says the story of Jonah. Addressed to insiders, it says one thing more: God's people should.

Jonah 4:1–11
The Question

As the story of Jonah began, it involved the Lord, Jonah, and "Nineveh, that great city" (1:1–2). Now as the story ends, the same three themes appear: Jonah, the Lord, and "Nineveh, that great city" (4:11).

This final chapter consists of a speech of Jonah framed by brief narrative statements (vv. 1–5) and a narrative plus a speech of the Lord (vv. 6–11). The speeches of Jonah at the beginning and of the Lord at the end balance each other, since each is exactly thirty-nine words (cf. Jonathan Magonet, *Form and Meaning: Studies in Literary Techniques in the Book of Jonah*, p. 56). The central impact is in these speeches. Jonah's includes a tightly packed creed-like confession of faith (v. 2*b*). The Lord's words are questions addressed to Jonah. Since Jonah represents the hearers/readers of the story, these questions give the conclusion a strong didactic flavor and point the direction for the ongoing appropriation of the story.

1. The Story: The Questioning

Jonah had disappeared from the story after the account of his preaching in the streets of Nineveh. Now we hear of his reaction when God calls off the destruction which Jonah had announced.

Jonah is very angry because Nineveh will not be destroyed (v. 1). The intensity of his anger is indicated by the repeated "displeased" in Hebrew (literally, "And Jonah was displeased with a great displeasure . . .") and also by the word "angry" which literally means "burned up" (cf. Gen. 44:18).

Earlier we heard a prayer of Jonah from the belly of the fish in which he praised God for saving his life (2:2–9). Now we hear another prayer from Jonah in which the prophet asks that the Lord end his life (vv. 2–3). What could cause this extreme reversal of attitude?

Jonah's prayer itself tells us. It begins with, "I told you so!" "Is this not what I said . . . ?" asks Jonah. The "this" here means

153

the repentance of Nineveh and God's calling off the punishment. Jonah does not want God's grace extended to these Assyrians! God, he seems to think, is soft on sinners!

Jonah's prayer includes a creedal statement which, like the one in 1:9, articulates some of the classic themes of biblical faith. Jonah knows that faith well! This statement in verse 2 has points of contact with a number of passages in the Old Testament: Exodus 34:6; Numbers 14:18; Nehemiah 9:17, 31; Psalms 86:15; 103:8; 111:4; 145:8. The closest parallel is the five-element creed in Joel 2:13. "Gracious" can be used on the human level to mean simple kindness, such as that shown to the poor (Prov. 14:31; 19:17; 28:8). When used of God, it refers to God's help for those in physical and spiritual trouble (Pss. 6:2; 25:16); it is often found in the cries of the lament, "be gracious to me" (Pss. 4:1; 6:2; 9:13; 25:16). This is the word used in the benediction of Numbers 6:25. The Hebrew root for the word translated "merciful" is *rehem*, which means "womb." The sense of this word may be understood as "motherly love," a love which surrounds the beloved with care and protection (cf. on "compassion" in Micah 7:19). "Slow to anger" is a human virtue (Prov. 14:29; 15:18; 16:32) and also a characteristic of the Lord. "Steadfast love" translates the Hebrew *hesed*, that love that endures (Ps. 136) and is a special characteristic of the Lord's relationship to his covenant people (cf. on Hos. 6:4–6). Additionally, the Lord is "good to all, and his compassion is over all that he has made" (Ps. 145:9; cf. "steadfast love" in v. 8). Jonah knew something of this love which knew no limits in time (Ps. 136) and which was not restricted only to God's people. Finally, this creedal statement says, "and repentest of evil." In Joel 2:13 the phrase refers to God and the Jews; here the reference is to God and the Assyrians, and that is what gets Jonah. If *they* are in on the love of God, then Jonah wants out. He would rather die than live!

The Lord speaks to Jonah with a question: "Do you do well to be angry?" (v. 4). Jonah responds with an action: He walks out. He finds a place to the east of the city where he sits to watch and see what will happen. He builds a shelter such as Jews build at the Feast of Booths (Lev. 23:39–43; Neh. 8:14–18). Jonah has dissociated himself from the city and now observes it in a detached manner (v. 5).

Jonah's words of complaint and request were matched by words of the Lord (vv. 1–4). Now his actions are matched by three "appointing" acts of the Lord. The prophet's mood swings from one extreme to the other. When the Lord appoints a plant to provide more shade, the prophet is "exceedingly glad." When the Lord appoints a worm to destroy the plant, and then a hot east wind, Jonah wishes he were dead. When questioned, Jonah again declares that he is justified in being angry enough to die (v. 9).

Before the Lord puts the final question to Jonah, he teaches the prophet by means of an example. "You pity the plant," he says, "for which you did not labor, nor did you make it grow, which came into being in a night, and perished in a night." The argument is of the "how much more" type (cf. Matt. 6:30; 10:31; 12:12; Luke 12:24). "Should I not pity Nineveh?" the Lord asks. The city is described quantitatively, in terms of its population, and then qualitatively, in terms of its needs: The people of the city are helpless (cf. Amos 7:2, 5), hardly able to distinguish right from left, and there are also many innocent animals there.

The verb translated "pity" has the literal sense, "the eye flows on account of" (cf. Ludwig Koehler and Walter Baumgartner, *Lexicon in Veteris Testamenti Libros,* p. 282). The picture is a touching one. The Lord sees Nineveh and is moved to tears of compassion not only for the people but for the cattle as well.

"Should I not pity Nineveh . . . ?" With this question the story ends.

2. Amazing Grace

In appropriating what this chapter has to say, we may consider Jonah, the people of Nineveh, and the Lord.

Who is Jonah? The answer to this question is essential for appropriating the message of the Jonah story. First of all, Jonah is clearly a believer. He is introduced as a prophet active in the days of Jeroboam II. He knows the historic faith in its creedal expressions (1:9; 4:2). He knows how to pray, whether the prayer be one of praise (2:2–9) or complaint (4:2–3).

Jonah is also a believer who is angry, literally "burned up" about something. It all has to do with the Lord's calling off the destruction of Nineveh, which Jonah had obediently announced. Was he irritated because his reputation as a prophet had been thrown into question by the sparing of Nineveh? Perhaps, but his prayer reveals a deeper reason for his anger. He had a hunch that, given half a chance, the Assyrians would repent. Then he suspected that God would forgive them. Therein lay the problem: If the Assyrians were in on the love of God, then Jonah wanted out.

Who is Jonah? The initial hearers would identify with neither the sailors nor the Ninevites in this story. Jonah is their man on the scene, their representative in the story. As the story winds down, the questions addressed to Jonah more and more become questions addressed to those listening to the story. Jonah, it becomes clear, is me! Thus the story asks its hearers: Do you recognize yourself in the figure of Jonah? Do you detect in yourself symptoms of the Jonah syndrome?

One can detect symptoms of that syndrome in two of the parables Jesus told. Those who had worked all day in the vineyard grumbled when those hired at the last hour received the same pay as they did. That parable ends with a question: "Do you begrudge my generosity?" the vineyard keeper asks (Matt. 20:1–16). The other is the story of the man with two sons. When the wasteful rebel comes home and gets a party, the older brother refuses to join the celebration. He stays outside sulking because of his father's generosity, thus exhibiting symptoms of the Jonah syndrome (Luke 15:11–32).

What about Nineveh? The people of Nineveh are the "people of the world," the "outsiders." We recall the exemplary behavior of the outsiders in this story. In times of crisis, the sailors pray and act, and the Ninevites repent and clean up the violence in their city. These favorable pictures of the people of the world suggest two things for the people of God. First, God's people could be instructed by the people of the world. Jesus once commended the resourcefulness of the "people of this world," concluding that his own followers could learn from them (Luke 16:1–13). Second, the report of this people's eagerness to hear a word from God is a reminder of the missionary calling of the church. Israel had been called to be a "light to the nations" (Isa. 49:6). Jesus spoke of the task of the disciples in the same language (Matt. 5:14). The picture of Jesus lamenting over Jerusalem is a reminder of God's love for the people of that city and that tradition (Matt. 23:37–39). The story of Jonah shows us a picture of the Lord with tears of compassion in his eyes for the people of the other great cities of the world.

What does this final chapter say about God? First, we hear the traditional creedal affirmations in Jonah's prayer of 4:2. The Lord is "a gracious God and merciful, slow to anger, and abounding in steadfast love, and repentest of evil." The story

156

illustrates these characteristics of God. Chapter 3 tells how God repents of evil (3:10). Jonah himself is quick to anger (4:1–3; 7–8), but the story shows how God is very patient with him, sending a storm, then a great fish, then giving Jonah a second chance, and finally appointing a plant, a worm, and a wind, all for the sake of Jonah's instruction. The other attributes are illustrated in the Lord's words about Nineveh which conclude the story. The Lord does not see in Nineveh only a great and wicked city. He also sees thousands of helpless people and innocent animals.

Jesus once said that God cared about the sparrows of Jerusalem (Matt. 10:29). The Book of Jonah tells of that amazing grace by speaking of the Lord's concern for the cows of Nineveh.

Finally, we remember that the story of Jonah ends with a question. Nahum is the only other prophetic book to end this way. That prophet was also concerned about Nineveh, but he announced its destruction and posed an accusing question to that city: "For upon whom has not come your unceasing evil?" (Nah. 3:19).

Now, at a later time, another prophetic book raises a different question about Nineveh. This time the question is put to the people of God, asking about their attitude toward the people of the Ninevehs, the great cities of the world. The question is put to each who hears the story, to those who may have discovered symptoms of the Jonah syndrome in their hearts. God asks it: Should my love not extend to the thousands, the millions of people in the great cities of the world? And even to the animals?

THE BOOK OF
Micah

Introduction

Words from this Minor Prophet have made a major impact on public life. When Jimmy Carter was inaugurated as President of the United States in January of 1977, he took his oath of office on a Bible opened to Micah 6:8 and quoted those words:

> He hath showed thee, O man, what *is* good; and what doth the LORD require of thee, but to do justly, and to love mercy, and to walk humbly with thy God (KJV).

In 1959, the Soviet Union presented to the United Nations a bronze sculpture of a man beating a sword into a plowshare, a symbol of the universal hope for disarmament and peace. On the base of the nine-foot sculpture are words paraphrasing Micah 4:3 and Isaiah 2:4: "We shall beat our swords into plowshares." Wherever English-speaking people celebrate Christmas, among the hymns which are sung is "O Little Town of Bethlehem" by Phillips Brooks, which picks up words from Micah 5:2, "But you, O Bethlehem Ephrathah, who are little to be among the clans of Judah . . .."

Justice, peace, and Messiah: Though the Book of Micah is itself little among the prophetic writings, it deals with these great biblical themes.

The Book of Micah falls into three major divisions, each introduced by the imperative plural, "Hear": chapters 1—2; 3—5; and 6—7 (cf. the similar introductory function of the "hear" imperative in Amos 3:1; 4:1; 5:1; 8:4). Within these broad divisions we can also note a pattern of alternation between sayings which announce doom and those which express hope: 1:2—2:11 (doom) plus 2:12–13 (hope); 3 (doom) plus 4—5 (hope);

6:1—7:7 (doom) plus 7:8–20 (hope; cf. the similar alternation in Hosea). The structure and movement of the book as a whole may be summarized as follows:

1:1: The title locates the prophet geographically (from Moresheth) and temporally (in the days of Jotham, Ahaz, and Hezekiah) and indicates the focus of his message (concerning Samaria and Jerusalem).

1:2—2:13: The initial saying in 1:2–7 calls all to *hear* the Lord's complaint against Samaria and Judah (vv. 2–5) and announces that punishment will come (vv. 6–7). With 1:8–9, the prophet describes his own reaction to the destruction ("for this") he has just announced. His grief is all the more intense as he contemplates the devastation that will reach into his own homeland. Verses 10–16 of chapter 1 describe the march of the conqueror through eleven cities and finally to Jerusalem. The reason for this announced conquest is stated in general terms as "transgression" (v. 13; cf. 1:5). The prophet calls upon the inhabitants of these cities to join him in mourning because their children will be taken into exile (v. 16).

Those hearing these words concerning Samaria and Judah would ask, "Why should all of this come upon us?" To this point the accusations have been general, in terms of transgression, sin, and idolatry (1:5, 7, 13). With 2:1–5, the prophetic critique becomes more specific. Using the form of the woe-oracle (see on Amos 6:1–7), the first half of this saying addresses that "why" question, identifying the greed of wealthy landowners as the problem (2:1–2). The saying continues by announcing that the Lord will punish these landgrabbers by taking their own property from them (2:3–5).

Such preaching would not win the prophet any friends among those property owners eager to expand their assets! The controversy-saying in 2:6–11 indicates the response that Micah's preaching evoked. "Do not preach!" they said. The prophet retaliates with further accusations (2:8–9) and the saying is concluded with a bitter observation about the kind of preaching these people really want to hear (v. 11).

At this point, the editor of the book inserts a short word of hope (2:12–13), indicating that the sending of evil (1:12; 2:3) is not the Lord's final work. Like a good shepherd, the Lord will one day gather a scattered people (v. 12). Like a victorious king, the Lord will deliver those who have been imprisoned (v. 13).

3:1—5:15: The *hear* formula signals a new section, again

160

organized on a doom (v. 3) plus hope (vv. 4–5) pattern. The beginning is connected to the end of the previous section with the "head/heads" catchwords of 2:13 and 3:1.

The charges against the people now become more specific, with three short sayings built on the accusation/announcement of punishment pattern: 3:1–4, 5–8, 9–12. Each saying speaks of justice (vv. 1, 8, 9) and each climaxes with an announcement about God's silence.

Sayings of a hopeful nature are collected in 4:1—5:15, arranged according to a concentric ring pattern. The central core is 4:9—5:6, made up of three oracles built on a distress/deliverance model. Moving out from that core, 4:6–8 tells of a future when the Lord will gather the scattered remnant of the people; the balancing section in 5:7–9 also speaks of a remnant. Micah 5:10–15 and 4:1–5 balance one another with words about a future that will bring disarmament and peace.

6:1—7:20: The final part of the book is again introduced with a call to *hear;* it falls into five subdivisions:

Micah 6:1–5 portrays God and people as participants in a legal process. The content of the Lord's complaint must be inferred from verse 3: The people say the Lord has "wearied" them. The charge is doubly rejected, the Lord reminding the people of the deliverance from Egypt (v. 4) and of the crossing of the Jordan (v. 5).

The previous section had emphasized the relationship between God and people (the doubled "my people" of vv. 3, 5) and had reminded the people of what God had done for them. An individual hearing this wishes to respond to what God has done and asks the questions of verses 6 and 7. The surprising answer is provided in verse 8.

After the reminder of what God has done (6:1–5) and the indication of the expected response (6:6–8), the saying in 6:9–16 accuses the hearers of not responding as they ought to have (vv. 10–12) and then announces punishment (vv. 13–15). Verse 16 summarizes, with an accusation (v. 16*a*) and an announcement of punishment (v. 16*b*).

Micah 7:1–7 is an individual lament, first expressed figuratively with the picture of one walking through a field and lamenting the lack of food (v. 1) and then literally with words lamenting the lack of uprightness in public life (vv. 2–4) as well as in the private circle of friends and family (vv. 5–6). Nevertheless, the one lamenting affirms faith in God (v. 7).

161

The book comes to a conclusion on a hopeful note with a liturgy designed to make the book usable in public worship (7:8–20).

The earliest material in the book comes from Micah, a prophet active in the latter half of the eighth century B.C., as 1:1 indicates (see below). Other materials became a part of the collection at a later time. The saying in 4:9–10, for example, addresses a situation just before the fall of Jerusalem and the exile to Babylon in 587. The concluding liturgy assumes that the walls of Jerusalem have been destroyed (7:11) and therefore originated some time after 587 B.C. The sayings about the gathering of the remnant in 2:12–13 and 4:6–7 assume that the people are scattered and thus address a situation after 587.

A number of clues indicate that in its present form the material in the Book of Micah has been shaped for use in public worship. At the conclusion of the "swords into plowshares" saying in chapter 4, the editor has placed a rubric which allows the listening congregation to respond with a "we" statement (4:5). The imitation of an entrance liturgy in 6:6–8 would lend itself to use in public worship with two different speakers taking part. The liturgy in 7:8–20 includes portions to be spoken by the congregation (the "us/our" of vv. 19–20). Thus the prophetic message was remembered, collected, updated, and reshaped for use in the assembly of the community for worship, so that later generations could also hear in these words a word from God.

The expositions which follow will deal with those sections of the book which seem especially promising for preaching and teaching. Each section should be understood in the context of the movement of the whole book, as sketched above.

Micah 1:1
The Prophet Micah

1. Micah of Moresheth

The name Micah is an abbreviated form of the Hebrew "Micayahu" which means "Who is like Yah(weh)?" A declaration of praise at the end of the Book of Micah uses the same Hebrew elements "mi" and "ca," thus concluding the book with a play on the prophet's name, "Who *(mi)* is a God like *(ca)* thee . . . ? (7:18).

The name, also spelled Micaiah, was a common one in the Old Testament period (Judg. 17—18; I Kings 22). The prophet Micah is not identified in relationship to his parent (cf. Hos. 1:1; Joel 1:1) but rather in connection with his hometown of Moresheth, or Moresheth-gath (Micah 1:14). Little is known of that town; even the location is not certain. It is most likely the Gath mentioned in Second Chronicles 11:8 as one of the defense cities which Rehoboam had built to protect Jerusalem, located about twenty-five miles to the southwest of Jerusalem. Tekoa, the hometown of Amos, was also a part of that defense network (II Chron. 11:6).

We can infer some things about the prophet by careful attention to the sayings in the book. Micah has poetic and rhetorical gifts, making use of similes and metaphors. When the Lord comes, the mountains will melt like wax or flow like water (1:4). The prophet's lamenting will be like that of the jackal or ostrich (1:8); the nation itself is compared to a person mortally wounded (1:9). The leaders of the nation are described as butchers, cannibalizing their people (3:1–3). Micah uses the technique of quoting the words of his audience against them (3:11; cf. Amos 1:1, part 1). His most dramatic rhetorical device is a series of puns on city names in 1:10–16.

Behind the sayings of the prophet we discover a person of great sensitivity, grieving over the message of doom which he must bring (1:8). We also detect a sense of solidarity with fellow citizens who are being oppressed and who are identified as "my people" (1:9; 3:2, 3).

One saying provides a hint of Micah's own understanding of his vocation. After describing "prophets" who trim their oracles to the size of their fees (3:5), he tells of his own qualifications and of his task:

> But as for me, I am filled with power,
> with the Spirit of the LORD,
> and with justice and might,
> to declare to Jacob his transgression
> and to Israel his sin (3:8).

2. The Days of Jotham, Ahaz, and Hezekiah in Judah

163

The editor of the book dates Micah's activity in the administrations of Jotham (750–735), Ahaz (735–715), and Hezekiah (715–687), kings of Judah in the second half of the eighth century B.C.

The prophet Amos was active just before 750 B.C., in a period which may be described as the calm before the Assyrian storm. The Book of Hosea gives some indications of the effects that storm had on the Northern Kingdom. The Book of Micah gives evidence of the effects of that Assyrian storm on both Israel in the north and Judah in the south.

After the death of Jeroboam II in 746 B.C., the situation in the northern state of Israel began to disintegrate rapidly. The political anarchy of the last decades of Israel's existence is reflected in the Book of Hosea and is described in the comments on Hosea 1:1. The first oracle in the Micah book concerns Samaria, and is thus to be dated before Samaria fell to Assyria in 722 B.C. (Micah 1:2–7).

The peace and prosperity enjoyed in Judah under Uzziah (783–742) seems to have continued into the time of Jotham (coregency from about 750–735). However, when Ahaz took the throne in 735, he was immediately faced with a national emergency. Israel and Syria were invading from the north, seeking to force Judah into a coalition against Assyria. Ahaz refused to join, and appealed to the Assyrian emperor for help. This appeal precipitated the Assyrian invasion into the west, which eventually resulted in the fall of both Damascus and Samaria. Ahaz was thus freed of the Israel-Syria problem, but at the cost of selling out Judah's freedom and becoming a vassal state of Assyria (II Kings 16:5–9). Political subjugation also meant acknowledgment of Assyrian gods (II Kings 16:10–18), and the time of Ahaz is thus remembered as a time of apostasy (II Kings 16:1–4).

When Jeremiah was on trial for his life in 609 B.C., Micah was remembered as active in the time of Hezekiah (Jer. 26:18). Hezekiah, king from 715–687, sought to reverse the policies of his father Ahaz both in regard to international politics and to religion. When a new emperor came to the Assyrian throne in 704 B.C., Judah rebelled (II Kings 18:7). In 701 the Assyrians invaded, breaking through Judah's defense cities, and coming up to the city of Jerusalem itself. Hezekiah was forced to pay a huge tribute (II Kings 18:13–16). The biblical narrative tells of a miraculous deliverance of Jerusalem from the Assyrians, as announced by Isaiah (II Kings 18:17—19:37). Whether this account refers to events in 701 or to a supposed later invasion of the Assyrians in 688 remains a matter of debate (see Bright, *History,* pp. 298–309). The lament of Micah in 1:8–9, describing the wound of Judah which "has reached to the gate of my people, to Jerusalem," refers to this 701 invasion of the armies of Assyria.

A careful reading of Micah's oracles gives some clues to the immediate situation the prophet addressed. Social and economic injustices abound. Wealthy land owners lie awake at night devising new schemes for increasing their accumulation of property at the expense of the small farmer (2:1–2). Women and young children belonging to the social group with which Micah himself identifies ("my people") are evicted from their homes (2:9). The political leaders are cannibals who destroy and then devour those over whom they have power (3:1–3). They engage in building projects in Jerusalem that are executed only with the exploitation of labor and at the cost of human lives (3:10). The courts, where those oppressed should have a chance at righting the wrongs done to them, are infected with bribery (3:11).

The religious situation which Micah addresses is equally corrupt. Like Hosea, Micah denounces the worship of pagan gods in Israel (1:6–7). The "prophets" of the land are in their vocation only for pay, and priest and prophet alike have sold out to greed (3:5, 11). When a prophet who brings an authentic word from the Lord does appear, that prophet meets opposition (2:6–11). Those religious leaders who ought to know better have the audacity to say to their people, "Is not the LORD in the midst of us? No evil shall come upon us" (3:11).

Micah of Moresheth, "filled with power, with the Spirit of the LORD," had something quite different to say about his nation's future.

Micah 1:2–16
When the Lord Comes

1. Something for Everybody (1:2–7)

165

The saying concerning Samaria (1:2–7) opens with a summons which invites all people to hear. This "all" makes the message inclusive, even extending to those who would hear these words in later generations. The Lord, says the prophet, has a legal complaint to make. What is this complaint, and against whom will it be made?

Before those questions are answered, the prophet describes the coming of the Lord (vv. 3–4). The description of this coming or "theophany" follows the form typical of such, consisting of (1) an announcement of the Lord's coming and (2) a description of the effects of that coming upon nature. Note these elements in the description of the Lord coming to help Israel battle the Canaanites:

> (1) LORD, when thou didst go forth from Seir,
>   when thou didst march from the region of Edom,
> (2) the earth trembled,
>   and the heavens dropped,
>   yea, the clouds dropped water.
> The mountains quaked before the LORD,
>   yon Sinai before the LORD, the God of Israel.
>   (Judg. 5:4–5; cf. Isa. 64:1–3; Hab. 3:13–15)

Micah 1:3 announces the Lord's coming and verse 4 indicates the effects: the mountains melt and the valleys are split open.

With verse 5 comes a shock. In most theophany texts, the Lord comes to rescue his people from distress (Judg. 5; Isa. 64; Hab. 3). This time the Lord is not coming to answer the prayers of a people in need (cf. Isa. 64); this coming is occasioned by Israel's sin and transgression. In fact, the prophet uses these words to describe his task, "to declare to Jacob his transgression and to Israel his sin" (3:8).

"But why should this be?" those hearing these words would ask. What wrongdoing could bring about such a terrifying intervention of the Lord? Verse 5 gives a partial hint: The wrongdoing is centered in the capital cities of both the north and the south.

Now, in verses 6–7, the prophet speaks as the Lord's messenger, announcing the punishment to come. The beautiful city of Samaria, built by King Omri (876–869) as the new capital of the north, will be destroyed. All that will remain is a "heap" (the same word is used for the destruction of Jerusalem in 3:12). The carefully laid stones will be thrown about in the valleys below and the site will revert to a field. Tourists visiting the area will find only the bare foundations of what had once been a showpiece city.

Again, the hearer asks, "But why?" Verse 7 continues to fill in the answer: because the city is full of idols. Samaria's fascination with idols is described with the same imagery as is used by Hosea (Hos. 4:10–15). The nation has played the harlot with the Lord, and the moneys gained from such whoring have been used to erect the images of pagan religions. This was the message for Samaria.

The prophet who has had to deliver this message grieves deeply over what he has had to say. Israel, he knows, is sick unto death. The illness has not been contained at the border; it extends to Jerusalem as well (vv. 8–9). The next segment, verses 10–16, expands upon the statement in verse 9, "to the gate of my people, to Jerusalem." The prophet describes the path of a conqueror (v. 15) rolling southward through the small towns and cities which serve as Jerusalem's defense network. These words find their fulfillment in Sennacherib's campaign of the late 700's B.C., when his armies did proceed to the gate of Jerusalem (II Kings 18:13–16). The roll call of the cities ends with a call to join the prophet in mourning, because the hearers are going to see their own children deported from their land (v. 16).

2. Maranatha

The message of Micah begins with the words, "the LORD is coming" (1:3). The coming announced in chapter 1 was one which occasioned lamenting, wailing, and mourning on the part of God's people. Samaria fell to the Assyrians in 722 B.C., and the citizens were deported. The Deuteronomic historian interpreted the event as the Lord's judgment upon the city and nation because of their worship of other gods (II Kings 17:1–8). The coming of the Lord meant the near end for Jerusalem, when the Assyrian armies trapped King Hezekiah in the capital city "like a bird in a cage," as the Assyrian records put it. The coming of the Lord announced in the opening of the Book of Micah is terrifying news to the people of God who hear it.

Yet the Bible also knows of an announced coming of the Lord which is good news for God's people. We have seen that such was the case with the majority of the theophany accounts in the Old Testament. The central message of the New Testament is that a unique sort of theophany has occurred: the Lord has come in the person of Jesus of Nazareth, the Messiah. The

167

Messiah Jesus, says the New Testament, came into the world to save sinners (I Tim. 1:15).

This coming of the Lord was a joyful occasion, celebrated with song (Luke 2:13–14). One of the Christmas hymns of the church describes this coming with the same two-part structure that we have noted in the biblical theophanies: an announcement of coming, followed by the effects of that coming on nature:

> Joy to the world, the Lord is come!
>   let earth receive its king . . .
> And heav'n and nature sing,
>   And heav'n and nature sing.

The congregation in which I grew up was regularly visited by missionaries, usually from China or Africa. On the occasion of such a visit, the custom was to sing a favorite missionary hymn which began:

> Lost in the night doth the heathen yet languish,
>   longing for daylight the darkness to vanquish . . .

At the end of each stanza came the haunting refrain,

> He is coming soon, he is coming soon.

This coming was also good news, referring to the taking of the gospel to lands where it had never been heard before.

The church looks forward to yet another coming of the Lord. Like the one announced in Micah, this will take place before all nations and will involve a judgment, which means that it will be a terrifying occasion for some and a joyful time for others (Matt. 25:31–46). For God's people who have been called out of a variety of darknesses into God's marvelous light, this final coming can only be good news.

Karl Barth wrote the following in connection with Christ's final coming:

> If we wish to understand aright here, we must from the start repress certain pictures of the world-judgment, as far as we can, and make an effort not to think of what they are describing. All those visions, as the great painters represent them, about the judging of the world (Michael Angelo in the Sistine Chapel), Christ advancing with clenched fist and dividing those on the right from those on the left, while one's glance remains fixed on those on the left! The painters have imagined to some extent with delight how these damned folk sink

into the pool of hell. But that is certainly not the point. Question 52 of the Heidelberg Catechism asks: "What comfort hast thou by the coming again of Christ to judge the quick and the dead?" Answer: "That in all my miseries and persecutions I look with my head erect for the very same, who before yielded Himself unto the judgment of God for me and took away all malediction from me, to come Judge from heaven. . . ." A different note is struck here. Jesus Christ's return to judge the quick and the dead is tidings of joy (*Dogmatics in Outline*, p. 134).

The final coming of the Lord is a teaching of comfort, as the catechism says. For this reason the early Christians prayed, "Maranatha," "Our Lord, come!" (I Cor. 16:22). The New Testament itself ends with the promise and the prayer,

"Surely I am coming soon!" Amen. Come Lord Jesus!
(Rev. 22:20)

Micah 2:1–11
The More You Have, the More You Want

Since the woe-saying in 2:1–5 and the controversy saying in 2:6–11 are linked as prophetic preaching and people's response (see Introduction), the two will be considered together here.

1. You Shall Not Covet (2:1–5)

To pronounce a "woe" upon someone meant to announce their funeral (see on Amos 6:1–7). Those upon whom the woe is pronounced are described here as lying awake on their beds at night, thinking up ever more creative and corrupt schemes for increasing their own property at the expense of others less powerful. Who were these people? Wolff has suggested that they were the military and government officials who populated the small defense cities like Moresheth (II Chron. 11:5–12 lists some other defense cities; Hans Walter Wolff, *Micah the Prophet*, p. 48). They may also have been the moderately well-to-do who lived in Jerusalem, but who wanted some property for weekends and vacations in the country, with fresh air, a few horses, and a marvelous view.

169

Whoever they were, these individuals were dangerous to the health of Judean society because their schemes for acquiring more and more real estate were dishonest. What makes them all the more dangerous is that they have power: "because it is in the power of their hand" (v. 1). They have the money and the connections to get what they want, no matter who is hurt along the way.

One word in verse 2 gets at what is behind this striving to accumulate more and more property: "covet." Here is where it all starts and what keeps it going. "The engine which drives the enterprise is covetousness" (Mays, *Micah,* p. 63). The Bible devotes the last of the Ten Commandments to this issue: "You shall not covet your neighbor's wife, or his manservant, or his maidservant, or his ox, or his ass, or anything that is your neighbor's" (Exod. 20:17).

These individuals, however, do covet the houses of their neighbors—or in any case the small acreages of the farmers who live in the countryside near Jerusalem. There were laws in Israel that protected the holdings of the small farmer; the land was an inheritance and was not to be sold (Lev. 25:10–13, 23, 34). In spite of this, there were ways to get around these laws. Ahab and Jezebel devised one (I Kings 21). These clever, covetous citizens of Judah no doubt invented many others. In so doing they were guilty of oppressing their fellow citizens and wrongfully taking the inheritance which rightfully belonged to another family.

The messenger formula in verse 3 identifies that which follows as a message directly from the Lord. Have these people been lying awake nights, devising ever more ingeniously crooked schemes? The Lord, who neither slumbers nor sleeps (Ps. 121), has been doing some "devising" too, says the prophet—devising evil against them! The punishment will fit the crime. These people *devise* wickedness and work *evil* (v. 1); in return the Lord will *devise evil* against them (v. 3). They covet *fields* (v. 2), but the Lord will give those *fields* to others (v. 4). The exact nature of the "evil" which the Lord is devising is not specified. Those accused by the prophet will have to submit to a yoke which they will not be able to remove—the picture is of political bondage—and they will have to listen to the taunting songs of those who are their neighbors. These schemers will be saying, "We are utterly ruined . . . among our captors he divides our fields" (v. 4). The land which they had coveted and taken will in turn be taken from them, to be divided up among the armies of occupation.

2. Your Kind of Preacher (2:6–11)

Prophetic preaching was not simply monologue. This saying provides a sample of the give and take in which the prophet found himself engaged. Micah himself reports the reception his words received: "Do not preach," they said. Then the prophet gives the reason for this advice, "one should not preach of such things!" This statement has a familiar ring: the preacher should stick to talking about religion, about prayer, about church matters, and not meddle in such issues as the economy or politics or business! Then another statement from Micah's opponents: "Disgrace will not overtake us." Like an individual who is diagnosed as having an incurable disease but who denies the diagnosis, the reaction of these people to Micah's diagnosis is denial: "The Lord won't let such a thing happen to us!" Amos also had to deal with this sort of misplaced security (Amos 5:14; 9:10).

The Revised Standard Version translation of verse 7 does not make good sense as it stands. Mays suggests the following, which results from only minor adjustments in the Hebrew text:

> Is the house of Jacob accursed?
> Is YHWH impatient,
>   or are these things his deeds?
> Do his acts not benefit
>   the one who walks uprightly?
>   (Mays, *Micah*, p. 66)

Thus these people's objections to Micah's preaching were grounded in theology, a theology which assured them of the Lord's perpetual blessing, of his long-suffering and patience, and of his mighty acts on behalf of his people.

Something is wrong, says the prophets, with that theology which knows only of blessing and protection and success. He turns to his hearers and addresses them straight on: "But you rise against my people as an enemy" (v. 8)! Here Micah, the man from the rural town of Moresheth, identifies himself with the small farmers who are being oppressed: These are "my people," he says, "and you fellow Judeans who happen to have some wealth and some power are treating your own people as enemies!" The charge is illustrated concretely: Innocent people, peacefully going along their way, are robbed, even of their

171

clothing! Women are forced out of their comfortable homes! Children are also evicted! Again, the motivation behind such acts is covetousness and greed, which first expressed itself in clever schemes, then in cruel acts, and finally in the oppression of the men (v. 2), women, and children of Judah. The prophet delivers the eviction notice given to these displacers about to be displaced themselves: "Arise and go . . ." (v. 10).

The atmosphere must have been highly charged as the prophet spoke to these influential citizens of Judah in this way. It must have become all the more so as he returned to the "preach" theme which had set him off in the beginning. He knew what these middle-class, mid-life folks who like to talk about a theology of blessing and success were really interested in, and he suggested that they ought to have a preacher who catered to their interests. Such a preacher, he proposes, would chat about expensive wines and exotic liquors, mixed in with a lot of hot air and downright lies (v. 11)!

3. Whatever Happened to Covetousness?

Preaching about covetousness, one suspects, is no more popular today than it was in Micah's time. The word itself has to be explained before it can be effectively used. It has a musty, antique air about it, and seems totally out of place in a society which glitters with BMWs, Hobie Cat sailboats, and four-bedroom ramblers with three-car garages.

Still, covetousness, self-centered greed which longs for that which belongs to another, is a theme which runs through the Bible. The commandment says, "You shall not covet your neighbor's wife. . . . " The story of the tawdry affair between aging King David and a young soldier's wife who lived in the neighborhood is commentary enough on that sentence (II Sam. 11). ". . . Or anything that is your neighbor's," the Decalogue continues. The account of Jezebel and Ahab's scheming to get their neighbor's property for a vegetable garden comments on that commandment (I Kings 21). In both narratives the sequence is the same: Coveting leads to a scheme, the scheme is put into action, more and more duplicity is involved, and finally an innocent person is dead. The same pattern is found in Micah. A piece of property is coveted, schemes are devised late into the night, the property is seized, and innocent families are left homeless.

The motto stamped on each box of the confection of my childhood days called "Cracker Jack" was, as I remember it, "The more you eat the more you want." The prophets discovered the same insatiability among their fellow citizens who were obsessed with increasing their real estate holdings: The more you have, the more you want. Micah's contemporary Isaiah once pronounced a woe on those with such an obsession:

> Woe to those who join house to house,
>   who add field to field,
> until there is no more room,
>   and you are made to dwell alone
>   in the midst of the land.
>   (Isa. 5:8)

Two texts from the New Testament offer insights into the nature of covetousness. In the letter to the Colossians the apostle writes, "Put to death therefore what is earthly in you: immorality, impurity, passion, evil desire, and covetousness, which is idolatry" (Col. 3:5). The last phrase, almost an aside, identifies the real nature of covetousness. That person or thing so strongly desired becomes an obsession, a matter of ultimate concern, and thus displaces God and becomes a god, an idol. In this way, the last of the commandments reaches back to the first, "You shall have no other gods before me."

The other text is the well-known one in the letter to young Timothy, which speaks positively about godliness and contentment and then identifies "the root of all evils":

> There is great gain in godliness with contentment; for we brought nothing into the world, and we cannot take anything out of the world; but if we have food and clothing, with these we shall be content. But those who desire to be rich fall into temptation, into a snare, into many senseless and hurtful desires that plunge men into ruin and destruction. For the love of money is the root of all evils; it is through this craving that some have wandered away from the faith and pierced their hearts with many pangs (I Tim. 6:6–10).

It may be that the theme of covetousness is so rarely preached on because the preacher knows that these commandments or prophetic words speak directly to him or her. We have seen that Micah was addressing the "haves" of his time, those who had the money, the property, and the power. Most of us know that we must identify with these people in our text, rather than with the "have nots" who are dispossessed of clothing and displaced from homes.

This prophetic saying places a special responsibility on those persons within the people of God who have been given much. It would call us to lie awake at night once in a while devising plans to help the hungry, the hurting, the homeless in our neighborhoods and our world. It also points us to the parable about the faithful steward, which concludes, "Every one to whom much is given, of him will much be required . . ." (Luke 12:41–48).

Micah 3:1–12
The Silence of God

The similarity in both structure and theme suggests that all three sayings in this chapter be considered together.

1. No Answer (3:1–4)

The prophet is addressing the leadership of "Jacob" and "the house of Israel." Though these terms were used to refer to the Northern Kingdom in 1:5, the reference here is to the leaders of Jerusalem, as 3:9–10 indicates. The address reminds these officials who they are: those responsible for "Jacob/Israel," the ancient name for the whole people of God.

After the "Hear!" call for attention, the prophet engages the participation of his audience by means of a rhetorical question: "Is it not for you to know justice?" The obvious response to that question is yes, as the prophet assumes the leaders whom he addresses agree that the establishing and maintaining of justice is their proper task. What is meant by "justice," though, this word which is of central importance in all three of these sayings? The remainder of the accusation (vv. 2–3) helps to answer that question by describing a situation where justice is *not* being maintained. These officials are accused of hating good and loving evil; maintaining justice thus involves loving good and hating evil. A saying from Micah's contemporary Isaiah is illuminating at this point. As Isaiah speaks to the leaders of Jerusalem (Isa. 1:10), he concludes his speech with an exhortation:

174

"Cease to do evil,
  learn to do good;
seek justice,
  correct oppression
defend the fatherless,
  plead for the widow."
    (Isa. 1:16–17)

Here is described what is expected of responsible leaders. The statements are all approximately synonymous. Thus to "seek justice" means in general terms to stop doing evil and start doing good, the same terms used in our Micah text. More specifically, to seek justice means to correct oppression. Even more to the point, seeking justice means to take up the cause of the orphan and the widow, to pay special attention to the powerless. The biblical notion of justice is best described in verbal terms. Amos had used the image of a churning, roaring stream (Amos 5:24). Micah 6:8 speaks of "doing justice." In this context we could describe justice as the state of order and fairness ("equity," 3:9) in a society which results when oppression is eliminated and when the powerless are properly attended (Cf. James Luther Mays, "Justice," in *Interpretation* 37:5–17 [Jan 1983]; *The Prophets and the Powerless,* by the author, chapter 6).

Those to whom the prophet is speaking have not done their job, however. They hate the good and love the evil. Micah describes their actions with a metaphor that is both coarse and shocking. These leaders, he says, tear, eat, flay, break, and chop "my people" as one would slaughter an animal to be eaten. The passion behind this charge is reflected in its structure: The statements are jammed together, piled up without regard to logical sequence, the prophet talking about eating before speaking of cooking (v. 3).

In comparison with the accusation, the announcement of punishment is brief (v. 4). The language is reminiscent of the individual laments, those prayers coming from people in deep distress. An example:

Hear, O LORD, when I cry aloud,
  be gracious to me and answer me!
Thou hast said, "Seek ye my face."
  My heart says to thee,
"Thy face, LORD, do I seek."
  Hide not thy face from me.
    (Ps. 27:7–9)

When these leaders cry to the Lord in the midst of the distress which is coming their way, there will be no answer. When they seek the Lord's face, he will not turn toward them, beaming with blessing and grace (Num. 6:24–26), but will hide. Why? The final sentence returns to the "evil" theme with which the saying began and restates the reason for the Lord's silence: "because they have made their deeds evil."

2. A Passion for Justice (3:5–8)

In the second saying (vv. 5–8) the pattern of accusation (v. 5) and announcement of punishment (vv. 6–7) continues, though in this case the announcement of punishment is developed further, and an autobiographical statement appears at the end (v. 8). The saying as a whole has to do with the religious leaders, the theologians of Micah's day, identified as prophets, seers, and diviners. Micah's accusation against the prophets asserts that they are infected with the greed which appears to be epidemic in Judean society (cf. 2:2; 3:11). The content of their messages is not determined by what they have heard from the Lord (cf. Jer. 23:18) but by what they are paid by their people. When their salaries are up, they speak about peace and prosperity; when they are not, they threaten holy war. These leaders are misleaders, says Micah, unfaithful shepherds who take their trusting flocks into the wilderness, rather than into green pastures (cf. Jer. 50:6).

The punishment announced in verses 6 and 7 fits the crime. A variety of methods of receiving revelation from God are named here without making judgments about their validity. The "vision" was one of the classic sources for prophetic revelation (Isa. 1:1; Obad. 1:1; Nah. 1:1). "Divination" could be practiced in a variety of ways. The Book of Numbers tells of Balaam, a famed diviner from Mesopotamia, who received revelations during the night (Num. 22:9–12) but also by means of highly complex technical procedures (Num. 23:1–10, 13–24). Other methods might involve the use of arrows or the observation of a liver (Ezek. 21:21). No matter what the method, says the prophet, the result will be the same: There will be no answer from God. There will be seers who see nothing, diviners with no sign from the Divinity, prophets with nothing to preach. The theologians will be professionally disgraced, publicly shamed, and personally broken in spirit (vv.

176

6–7). They will cover themselves like those who mourn (Ezek. 24:17, 22).

How could this happen? We can be sure that these theologians had extensive (and probably expensive) training. One did not learn the elaborate techniques of divining without considerable instruction and apprenticeship! The same could be said for those trained as priests. Try as they may, though, they will not receive a word from God says the prophet. The antennas may be up, the receivers tuned in, the switches thrown, but there will be no signal. The prophet's reason for this is simple. Like the public officials of their time, the theologians have sold out their integrity. They have become more greedy than godly (vv. 5, 11). They may be slick professionals, but we hear nothing of a passion for justice on their part. Their only passion, it would seem, has to do with their paychecks and pocketbooks.

These words about the theologians can be transposed into another key. Once again, the antennas may be up, the receivers tuned in, the switches thrown. To put it in other words, the lexicons have been consulted, the commentaries and concordances lie strewn around the desk. Yet even with the mastery of the techniques of form and redaction criticism, not to mention the sophistications of the word processor, it is possible that the theologian may sit alone at night gazing into the darkness with no vision, no word from God (v. 6).

Micah's diagnosis warns that it is still possible for a theologian to become more concerned about fees than faith, about honoraria than honor. The response of God may then be the same: silence. The theologian experiences a burn-out or flame-out, with no more fire, no more steam, no more passion for justice or for God. Then the theo-logian has broken with his or her vocation. There is no contact with *theos,* and thus no longer an authentic *logos,* and the preacher is left with nothing to preach.

In sharp contrast stands the prophet from Moresheth, who now makes a rare statement about himself. "But as for me, I am filled with power, with the Spirit of the Lord, and with justice and might." Micah has been preaching passionately about justice; both the message and the power to preach it, he says, came from the Lord. In a final statement the prophet describes his task: to declare to the people of Israel their transgression and sin (cf. 1:5). These declarations are what we hear in the "accusation" segments of his words of judgment.

177

3. The Silent City (3:9–12)

The third saying begins like the first, again addressing the leaders of Jerusalem. Once more, the central concern is justice. These leaders "abhor" justice. The word means to consider something totally repulsive, for cultic or moral reasons; thus one abhors the food from unclean animals (Deut. 14:3) or sexual perversions (Lev. 18:22; Deut. 22:5) or idols (Deut. 7:25–26). These leaders abhor *justice!* To "pervert equity" means to twist, to make crooked, that which should be straight. The remainder of the accusation hints at the specifics of this charge. While those listening to the prophet were in the midst of the beautiful capital city of Jerusalem, the prophet's eye saw something else behind the artfully cut wood and the carefully hewn stone. He knew something of the human cost of these buildings. Perhaps some of his own countrymen from Moresheth had been involved in forced labor assignments or as workmen who were not paid a fair wage. Micah knew that the city had been built "with blood" and "with wrong." These leaders were exploiting labor, and this too was to "abhor justice."

The accusation continues (v. 11) with complaints against three groups of the city's leaders. Public officials, priests, and prophets alike are charged with selling out their professional integrity for money. Those responsible for the courts accept bribes. The clergy have made religion into a business, motivated by a love for money. Despite this perversion of their vocations, these community leaders mouth pious cliches and assume that they will be forever secure: "Is not the Lord in the midst of us? No evil shall come upon us."

The brief announcement of punishment in verse 12, which concludes the saying and also concludes the series of three sayings, is remarkable for three reasons. First, the sharp and direct switch to "because of *you* (author's italics)." The prophet had been speaking *about* priests, prophets, and politicians in the third person. Now, for the first time, he turns to his audience and addresses them directly: "because of *you.*" Second, there is no mention of God here. The previous two sayings announced God's silence (vv. 4, 7). Other sayings make clear the Lord's involvement in judgment (1:6; 2:3). Here, the prophet makes no mention of God, saying simply, "Zion shall be plowed . . . Jerusalem shall become a heap." Even the temple is called "the house" rather than "the house of the LORD" (contrast 4:1).

178

Micah has had enough of public and religious officials making pious pronouncements about "the LORD" (v. 11). His language is nonreligious, earthy, and unambiguous, as befits the horrible event it announces. We hear nothing of God here. It is as if after the destruction of the temple, God is absent. The third remarkable thing about this statement is the shocking totality of the destruction it announces. We can imagine the scene: Standing in an open place in Jerusalem, in full view of the architectural achievements which were hundreds of years in the making, the prophet wheels on his audience and says, "because of *you*" (author's italics). "Because of you all of this will be leveled, like I level a field with a plow. And the temple? (Can we think of him looking toward it, maybe pointing at it?) In the place where the temple is standing, you'll see only a plowed field, with just a few trees growing."

The first two sayings in this chapter announced the silence of God (vv. 4, 7). This statement in 3:12 is a triple conclusion. It concludes the saying, concludes the chapter, and in fact is marked in the Hebrew Bible as concluding the first half of the Book of the Twelve, the Minor Prophets. It announces another kind of silence. The noise of buying and selling in the marketplace, the sounds of children laughing and playing in the streets, the songs of lament and praise in the temple—all will be stilled. The silence of the living God will be matched by the silence of a city which has died.

Micah 4:1–5
Peacemaking

This prophetic saying is duplicated almost exactly in the second chapter of Isaiah. Consideration of the two texts together will suggest the direction for appropriation of this saying in preaching and teaching.

1. One Saying, Two Settings

The portions of the two texts which are nearly identical are Isaiah 2:2–4 and Micah 4:1–3, which we shall label as the *core saying.*

In the Isaiah book, the core saying has been provided with

179

an editorial introduction and conclusion (Isa. 2:1, 5). Isaiah 2:1 introduces a major subcollection in the Isaiah book, running from chapters 2—12. The placement of this core saying at the beginning of the collection testifies to the editor's estimate of its significance. The conclusion which the editor provided in Isaiah 2:5 is addressed to those who will hear the core saying in a congregational setting, as the Isaiah book is read to them as Scripture. Verse 5 is an exhortation, encouraging those who hear to take action.

The editor of the Book of Micah did not provide the core saying with an introduction. He has, however, placed it at a point in the book where it has maximum dramatic impact, just after the announcement of the destruction of Jerusalem. The contrast is total. Instead of ruin and humiliation, we now hear of rebuilding and exaltation. Instead of the awful silence of the desolate mountaintop, we hear the joyful sounds of people from all nations on their way to worship. The reference to the temple testifies to God's presence. Instead of the "mountain of the house," this saying speaks of the "mountain of the house of the LORD."

Several features suggest that the Micah version is later than the one found in Isaiah. The grammar is smoother; in the Hebrew, the participle "established" in Micah 4:1 is in a position which improves the parallelism. The Micah version is longer, with the additions of "strong" and "afar off" in verse 3 and the addition of verse 4. (On the relationship of the two texts, see Mays, *Micah*, pp. 95–96.)

One effect of the longer Micah version is to extend the core saying in two directions. It is more universal, with a broader horizon including nations "strong" and "far off" and taking into consideration the religions of the world (v. 5). It is also more individual, spelling out the implications of world disarmament for each citizen (v. 4). Finally, the Micah version is also identified more strongly as a word from God, with the closing formula, "for the mouth of the Lord of hosts has spoken" (v. 4).

The way in which the core saying is handled in each prophetic book can aid in the application of that saying. In neither Isaiah nor Micah does the saying conclude with the vision of international disarmament and peace, magnificent as that vision may be. The congregations hearing the core saying are encouraged ("let us walk"; Isaiah) or led to make a resolution ("but we will walk"; Micah) to engage in action leading toward the realization of the vision of peace. Thus the direction for preaching and teaching has been staked out. The vision in the core saying should be placed before the hearers with imagination and clarity, but the interpretation will not stop there. The hearers will be challenged to work toward the realization of that vision, to "walk" toward it, or will be given an opportunity to resolve to do so.

2. A Vision and a Resolution (4:1–5)

The text falls into two sections, the vision portraying peace in verses 1–4 and the response expressing the resolve of the hearers in verse 5.

As is typical for such portrayals of salvation (cf. Isa. 11:6–8), the language is not literal but figurative. The beating of swords into plowshares and spears into pruning hooks is a figurative way of describing a program of international disarmament. The elevation of Mount Zion should not be understood as a reference to future cataclysms or earthquakes in the Middle East, but rather as an expression of the central significance of Jerusalem as the place from which the word of the Lord will go forth.

"In the latter days" places the time of the realization of the vision in the distant future. First to be sounded is the *word to the nations* theme. Once Torah or instruction (translated "law" in v. 2) went forth from Mount Sinai for Israel alone (Exod. 20). In the future here envisioned, the word of the Lord will go forth from Mount Zion and it will be for all peoples and "strong nations." This Torah is not simply head knowledge, a body of dogma or doctrine. It is intruction, a word from the Lord which calls for a response resulting in a new way of living for those who hear it, here described as walking "in his paths" (v. 2; cf. the resolve to "walk" of v. 5).

The climax of the saying comes in verses 3 and 4 with the *peacemaking* theme. As background for understanding what is said here, we call attention to the prophetic "call to battle." This is a type of saying which summons to fight. The following, for example, calls the armies of Judah to do battle against Egypt:

> "Prepare buckler and shield,
>   and advance for battle!
> Harness the horses;
>   mount, O horsemen!
> Take your stations with your helmets,

> polish your spears,
> put on your coats of mail!"
>
> (Jer. 46:3–4)

Other examples may be observed in Jeremiah 51:11 and Isaiah 21:5.

Of special interest is the call to battle in Joel 3:9–10, which summons all nations to a great conflict at the end of time:

> Prepare war,
>   Stir up the mighty men . . .
> Beat your plowshares into swords,
>   and your pruning hooks into spears . . .

There is obviously a connection between this call to beat plowshares and pruning hooks into weapons and the vision of precisely the opposite in the Isaiah/Micah texts. How might the two be related? The immediate answer would be to say that Joel reversed the Isaiah/Micah saying, since that prophet was active in the fourth century B.C. It has also been suggested that the saying in Joel is the older form and is understood as a typical call to battle (see Robert Bach, *Die Aufforderung zum Kampf und zur Flucht im alttestamentlichen Prophetenspruch,* p. 72, note 1). Such calls are indeed ancient, and this one could have been passed on for centuries until it found written expression in Joel. This would mean that the promise that one day nations would "beat their swords into plowshares" would be a reversal of a well-known wartime slogan. The effect would be dramatic. Consider, for example, the battle cries, "Remember the Alamo" or "Let's remember Pearl Harbor." Think of the effect of a speaker describing a future time of peace, saying about Texas and Mexico, "In that day they will forget the Alamo!" Or a speaker saying about Japan and the United States, "At that time they will forget Pearl Harbor!"

Another biblical portrayal of international disarmament uses some of the same language as that of our core saying. Here is said of the Lord:

> He makes wars to cease to the end of the earth;
>   he breaks the bow, and shatters the spear,
>   he burns the chariots with fire.
>
> (Ps. 46:9)

182

The portrayal of disarmament in the psalm is different from that in Isaiah/Micah. In the psalm it is the Lord who is the subject of the verbs. *He* breaks the bow and shatters the spear. In the prophetic texts, the nations are the subjects of the action. It is *they* who transform weapons of war into instruments of peace.

We have noted that Micah 4:1–5 is balanced by the saying in 5:10–15. This latter text also speaks of disarmament, but in a manner closer to that of Psalm 46. According to Micah 5:10, it will be *the Lord* who destroys the chariots and horses needed for war and who dismantles the defense systems.

With verse 5, the congregation is given an opportunity to respond to the vision of peace. First, they acknowledge that the vision has not yet been realized; the world still knows a variety of religions (v. 5*a*). Then, picking up the "walk" theme from verse 2, the congregation resolves to *do* something, but as for *us* (the Hebrew is emphatic), "we will walk in the name of the LORD our God for ever and ever."

3. Talking the Talk, Walking the Walk

The vision portrayed in this saying was to be realized in the future, "in the latter days." The New Testament announces that these "latter days" have already begun with the coming of Jesus the Messiah. Peter's Pentecost sermon, for example, declares that the gift of tongues is a sign that the "last days" announced by the prophets are now at hand (Acts 2:16–17 and context).

The New Testament also announces that the *word to the nations* dimension of the vision is beginning to be realized. Matthew's Gospel ends with a charge to proclaim the good news about Jesus, to baptize and to teach "all nations." As this task is carried out, the vision of the word of the Lord reaching the nations begins to become reality. This dimension of the vision also comes to expression in Acts 1:8, which announces the program for the earliest Christian mission. The Book of Acts tells how that program is carried out, reporting the spread of the good news from Jerusalem "to the end of the earth." Thus for the Christian, the "latter days" announced in the prophetic vision have already begun. The word of the Lord, the Torah, has been going out from Jerusalem, though the task of bringing it to all nations is not yet complete.

What about the churches and *peacemaking?* First of all, 183
we note that the picture of international disarmament is in the context of words about the word of the Lord going out to

the nations. Sometimes the question is asked: Ought the church to be concerned with evangelism or with peacemaking? According to this text, the church should be concerned about both. There is a connection between the word of gospel and Torah which goes out to the nations and the actions which lead to disarmament and peace. Secondly, neither the Isaiah text nor this text from Micah allows hearers to be content with affirming, admiring, even applauding the vision of world disarmament and peace that is portrayed. The Isaiah text challenges the congregation to get involved in action leading toward the realization of the vision (Isa. 2:5). The Micah text gives the congregation an opportunity to resolve to engage in peacemaking activities (Micah 4:5). Neither text allows those who hear it simply to talk about peace and disarmament. Both are a call not only to "talk the talk" but also to "walk the walk" which leads toward international reduction of arms and toward peace.

Some in the church will take the attitude expressed in Psalm 46 or Micah 5:10. They will want to wait for God to act in a miraculous way to shatter the weapons of war and to destroy both offensive weapons and defense systems. In these prophetic texts, while the believer will continue to pray for God to act, the subject of the actions is *they,* the nations themselves. This means that those who wish to "walk the walk" of peacemaking will use their energy and imagination to help nations themselves to bring about disarmament. These texts are a call to be involved in political processes, to work from within existing structures, to invent new structures, all for the purpose of bringing about the realization of the vision.

The impact of these twin texts on the imaginations of the world's peoples has been powerful. On a wall at the United Nations headquarters in New York, these words are inscribed:

> They shall beat their swords into plowshares. And their spears into pruning hooks. Nation shall not lift up sword against nation. Neither shall they learn war any more.

In this new setting, at this gathering place for "many peoples ... strong nations afar off," this ancient prophetic word in both literal and sculptured form continues to call the nations of the world to walk the walk that leads toward disarmament and toward peace.

Micah 5:1–6
Messiah

The promise in Micah 5:2 about the ruler who will come from Bethlehem is one of the most well-known texts from the Old Testament. It is cited in Matthew 2:6 in connection with the birth of Jesus, and may be heard throughout the world each year whenever the Christmas story is told.

1. Distress and Deliverance: 4:9–10, 11–13; 5:1–6

The central core of 4:1—5:15 is made up of three sayings which follow a distress/deliverance pattern (see Introduction). Each saying begins with "now," which describes a present distress. The first addresses a people about to be taken out of the city to deportation camps in the country, and then to exile in Babylon (4:9–10*a*). The Lord will rescue them as he once redeemed them from Egypt (v. 10*b*). The second saying in 4:11–13 describes the distress of the "now" time in terms of nations surrounding Jerusalem (v. 11) and then promises that the Lord will strengthen Jerusalem's armies so that the enemies will be defeated (vv. 12–13).

In 5:1–6 the reference to the distress is very brief (v. 1), while the deliverance is described at length (vv. 2–6). The footnote in the Revised Standard Version indicates that the Hebrew of the first line of 5:1 is obscure, but the remainder of the verse is clear. It describes two aspects of the situation of distress, a distress which the speaker is also experiencing ("against *us*," author's emphasis). The city is under siege and the king has been publicly humiliated. More than a "slap in the face" (cf. I Kings 22:24), this was a public shaming with a club. The king is called the "judge of Israel" (RSV, "ruler") in what appears to be an ironic contrast to those heroic figures in the Book of Judges. They delivered God's people, now the leader himself is in need of deliverance (cf. Mays, *Micah,* pp. 114–115).

The Hebrew of the first line reads, "Now slash yourselves, daughter of slashers" (author's translation). This is apparently an ironic call to the inhabitants of the besieged city, inviting

185

them to engage in self-mutiliation in appealing to the deity (cf. I Kings 18:28), as if such would do any good in this extreme situation! "Daughter of slashers" may be a derogatory title contrasting to the "daughter of Zion" of the other two sayings, verses 10 and 13.

In sharp contrast to the description of a people under siege and a humiliated leader, verses 2–4 portray one who rules in strength over a people living in security. The focus is now upon "Bethlehem Ephrathah." Ephrathah is the name of the clan of people who lived in the area of Bethlehem; the family of Elimelech and Naomi are described as "Ephrathites from Bethlehem" (Ruth 1:2; see also I Sam. 17:12). The double identification is necessary to distinguish the town from Bethlehem in Zebulon (Josh. 19:15). The New Testament remembers the Bethlehem of these times as a "village" (John 7:42) and Christian tradition recalls it as the "little town of Bethlehem." This stress on its smallness finds support in the Micah text. In contrast to Jerusalem with its magnificent buildings (Micah 3:10), this country village is "little to be among the clans of Judah." Bethlehem had a fame of its own, however, as the home of Jesse, David's father, and the birthplace of that greatest of the kings of Israel (I Sam. 17:12). The coming ruler will be from Bethlehem; in other words, that ruler will be a new David. The same idea is expressed in Isaiah 11:1, which promises a shoot from the stump of *Jesse*, thus again pointing to a new David.

We recognize a biblical theme here: God's choice of the least likely, the littlest, to accomplish God's purpose. Thus Gideon declared himself to be from the weakest clan, and the youngest in his family (Judg. 6:15). Saul described his tribe as the "least" of those in Israel (I Sam. 9:21). The Lord chose David, the youngest, over his brothers (I Sam. 16:1–13). The theme finds climactic expression in the announcement that the Messiah and Savior of the world is the baby lying in the manger (Luke 2).

Micah 5:3 reads like a parenthesis between the description of the ruler in verse 2 and the picture of that ruler in the midst of his rule in verse 4. "He shall give them up" means that the Lord is letting the people of Israel suffer for a time at the hand of their enemies. That time will be limited, however. The first limit is expressed with the picture of a woman experiencing labor pains (cf. Micah 4:9–10). Those pains are intense, but they will be over. The second limit is expressed in terms of the return of the exiles. This parenthetical verse seems to be a comment inserted in an older saying to explain the delay in the appearance of the promised ruler (cf. Mays, *Micah,* pp. 116–117; Wolff, *Micah,* pp. 106–107).

Micah 5:4 returns to the theme of the future ruler announced in verse 2. A literal translation would read, "And he shall stand and be a shepherd . . ." (author's translation). The picture of a ruler as shepherd is a common one in the ancient world (for example, Ezek. 34). The shepherd can also be a figure for the Lord (Isa. 40:11; Ps. 23). Here the ruler is the Lord's representative, ruling "in the majesty of the name of the LORD." Under this ruler, the people will dwell in security (the verb is the same as that translated "sit" in Micah 4:4), because the ruler's dominion will extend to the "ends of the earth." This last expression is known from the royal psalms, which describe the future rule of the ideal Davidic king in such terms (Ps. 2:8; 72:8).

Finally, verses 5–6 appear to be an originally independent piece placed here by the book's editor. The theme of the whole is peace. That peace will be brought about by the people of Israel themselves. "When the Assyrians come into our land," they say, "we'll drive them out and rule over them!" This phrase is repeated like a refrain at the end of the saying. As the material now stands, it describes what the coming ruler will do. "And this one shall bring peace" is the sense of the beginning of verses 5–6, and it ends, "And he shall deliver us from the Assyrian" (see RSV footnote).

2. From the Little Town of Bethlehem

This saying has always been considered one of the central Messianic promises for the Christian church. In its context in the Micah book, it is one in a series of three sayings which promise help to a people in distress. The first saying promises that God will rescue a people in exile (4:9–10). The second declares that God has a plan, that God is operating in history using other nations even though they may not be aware of it (4:11–13). The third saying comforts a people in distress with the promise of a ruler from Bethlehem who will bring peace (5:1–6). With the expectation of a future individual who will deliver from distress, the text links up with the other messianic promises in the Old Testament.

Fundamental to understanding messianic expectation are

187

those psalms which were originally used in connection with some event in the king's life, the royal psalms (2; 45; 72; 110; and others). These psalms describe one called the anointed one or messiah (2:2; 45:7). He will rule all nations (2:8–9; 72:8–11) and his throne will endure forever (45:6; 72:5). He will rule with righteousness and justice and will bring shalom (72:1–3, 7). This king will be a defender of the poor and needy (72:4, 12–14) and is identified as God's son (2:7) or God's right-hand helper (110:1). Such hopes were expressed for king after king. "It was a magnificent purple robe which the royal psalms laid on the shoulders of each young successor to the Davidic throne" (Gerhard von Rad, *Old Testament Theology* I, 323–324). As king after king took the throne and did not measure up to these extravagant expectations, the portrayal of the ideal king was pushed into the future. In this way the royal cult in Jerusalem became the "seedbed from which sprang Israel's expectation of a messiah" (Bright, *History,* p. 227).

The prophet Isaiah, who lived in Jerusalem, drew upon these themes as he spoke about a coming deliverer. That one will bear titles which hint at his power, the length of his rule, and his bringing of peace (Isa. 9:6). His administration will be marked by justice and righteousness and will last forever (Isa. 9:7). This coming ruler will be a new David, a new shoot from the family tree of Jesse (Isa. 11:1). He will have special concern for the poor and needy (Isa. 11:3–5) and will bring about shalom (Isa. 11:6–9).

It is in the context of this chorus of expectations for a future anointed one or Messiah that this saying about the ruler coming from Bethlehem should be heard. We hear the familiar themes about his greatness among all nations (Micah 5:4), about deliverance from enemies (v. 6), and about the peace that will result from his rule (vv. 4, 5).

The unanimous testimony of the New Testament is that this Messiah, this Christ (the Greek-based equivalent for Messiah), has come in the person of Jesus of Nazareth. Peter says, "You are the Christ"; the Good News Bible rightly translates, "You are the Messiah" (Mark 8:27–30; Matt. 16:13–20; Luke 9:18–21). With the coming of Jesus, the New Testament sees all the old promises fulfilled. His birth in Bethlehem fulfills the word from Micah (Matt. 2:5–6). He begins his ministry in the north, fulfilling the promises of Isaiah (Isa. 9:1–7; Matt. 4:12–17). A hymn which picks up themes from the royal psalms an-

188

nounces that Jesus will be called the Son of the Most High and will rule on David's throne forever, over a kingdom with no bounds (Luke 1:32–33).

One could go on listing passages. Practically every page of the New Testament is permeated with the conviction that Jesus of Nazareth is the long awaited Messiah of whom the psalms, the prophets, and the whole of Scripture spoke (Luke 24:27, 44–47).

Some did not agree with all of this. Their hearing of the royal psalms and the prophets led them to look for a military victor and a politically powerful ruler Even those closest to Jesus seemed to be waiting for him to restore Israel to the political greatness which it had in the days of David (Acts. 1:6). Such was not the program of Jesus. "My kingship is not of this world," he said to a Roman governor (John 18:36). The New Testament and almost 2000 years of Christian believers have confessed that this Jesus was the Messiah. According to the New Testament, he was also the Servant of the Lord, seeing the pattern for his work in those other prophetic passages which spoke of a mission to be accomplished through suffering and death, and finally, victory (Isa. 42:1–4; 49:1–6; 50:4–9; 52:13—53:12; cf. Matt. 12:15–21; Acts 8:26–35; Phil. 2:4–11).

The trilingual sign on the cross sums up what the New Testament says about Jesus. The one hanging there—the one suffering—was the Messiah, the King (John 19:19).

Micah 6:6–8
What Does the Lord Want From Me?

The call to "do justice, and to love kindness, and to walk humbly with your God" at the climax of this saying captures some of the essential themes of the prophets and indeed of biblical religion.

1. Entrance Liturgies

The first thing that strikes one in hearing this text after hearing Micah 6:1–5 is the change in speaker. The "I" of that previous saying is the Lord, represented by his messenger, the prophet. Here the "I" is an individual asking questions *about*

189

the Lord. This "I" is emphasized in the first part of this saying, indicating the personal involvement of the speaker: "I come before," "myself," "I come before," "I give," "my first-born," "my transgression," "my body," "my soul." The second part of the saying emphasizes the second-singular "you": "he has showed you," "of you," "your God." This is the text for a dialogue between two persons, one asking questions, the other giving an answer.

In what sort of situation might such a question (vv. 6–7) and answer (v. 8) dialogue take place? Two psalms provide clues. Both psalms present entrance liturgies, rituals used for entering the temple area. We are to imagine a pilgrim making the long journey from some outlying point to Jerusalem, perhaps for one of the annual feasts (Deut. 16:16). The pilgrimage psalms (120–134) reflect the moods: While the journey is anticipated with joy (Ps. 122:1), it was also dangerous, and thus the traveler stood in need of the Lord's protection (Ps. 121). Anticipation of the delight of worshiping with old friends sustained one on the long trek (Ps. 133). Upon arrival, we can imagine a pilgrim putting a question to the person at the gate of the temple area:

> O LORD, who shall sojourn in thy tent?
> Who shall dwell on thy holy hill?
> (Ps. 15:1)

The priest there would give the answer:

> He who walks blamelessly, and does what is right,
> and speaks truth from his heart. . . .
> (Ps. 15:2)

Alternatively, the worshiper might ask:

> Who shall ascend the hill of the LORD?
> And who shall stand in his holy place?

And the answer would be:

> He who has clean hands and a pure heart. . . .
> (Ps. 24:3–4)

The Book of Isaiah also contains an entrance liturgy (Isa. 33:14b–16).

This question-answer dialogue in Micah parallels such entrance liturgies. The saying may have originated with Micah who was then imitating the form of such an entrance liturgy; the "justice" theme was a concern of his (Micah 3), and the

190

juxtaposition of cult and concern for justice is characteristic of the eighth-century prophets (Isa. 1:10–17; Amos 5:21–24; Hos. 6:6).

2. Who, Not What (6:6–8)

"With what shall I come before the Lord?" To ask such a question assumes that God wants some thing from me. The worshiper's next question would then be, "What is it that God wants?"

The worshiper recites a series of possible answers to that question. "Burnt offerings" were those in which the whole animal was consumed in the fire, with none of it saved for eating. Calves could be sacrificed when they were eight days old (Lev. 22:27); those a year old would obviously be of much more value (Lev. 9:3). The series takes a quantitative leap with the question about "thousands of rams." Such an offering was still within the realm of possibility, with David reported to have offered "a thousand bulls, a thousand rams, and a thousand lambs" (I Chron. 29:21), and Solomon a thousand burnt offerings (I Kings 3:4). The use of oil for offering is mentioned in Exodus 29:40 in the amount of a hin, or about a quart; Numbers 15:9 speaks of using half that much. At this point in the series the suggested sacrifices escalate beyond the realm of reality with the talk of "ten thousand rivers of oil."

These four suggestions in question form have exhibited a step-by-step escalation. The next two questions stay on the same level. They are parallel, stating the final suggestion twice for emphasis: "Shall I give my first-born for my transgression, the fruit of my body for the sin of my soul?" Now the series takes a qualitative leap, from the offering of things or animals to the sacrifice of human life. The old story about Abraham and Isaac (Gen. 22) had made clear that the Lord did not want human sacrifices. While Israel's neighbors continued the practice (II Kings 3:27), and while it even took place in Judah in certain extreme situations (II Kings 16:3; 21:6), human sacrifice was never allowed in Israelite religion and the prophets spoke sharply against it (Jer. 19:5; Ezek. 16:20; see also Deut. 12:31; 18:10).

What does the Lord want from me? This was the worshiper's initial question, and the suggested responses ranged from burnt offerings to a beloved child. The answer to the question is given in verse 8. Now a different voice speaks. As the

191

Micah book was used in public worship, we could imagine another voice reading at this point. The answer begins by saying there will be no surprises! "He has showed you ... what is good." The Lord had already made known what was expected from the Lord's people; one thinks of the whole tradition of the commandments and also wisdom directives, long known in Israel. The question is restated: "What does the LORD require of you?" Then comes the answer, which turns out to be something of a surprise: no *thing* at all! The worshiper's question had been based on the false assumption that God wanted some *thing*. The answer makes clear that what God does want is *me!* "It's you, not something, God wants" (Mays, *Micah*, p. 136). In response to what God has done (v. 5), God would have from God's people a certain way of living, sketched in broad outline in the three statements which follow.

3. Doing, Loving, Walking

The first aspect of this way of living picks up the thematic word from the prophet Amos and emphasizes the social dimension: "to do justice." The notion is a dynamic one; justice is something one *does*. This matches Amos's comparison of justice to a flowing, churning stream (Amos 5:24). The Micah book has already provided a number of examples of the failure to do justice: The powerful oppress the powerless (2:1-2, 8-9; 3:1-3, 9-10), laborers are exploited (3:10), courts are corrupt (3:11). To do justice means to work for the establishment of equity for all, especially for the powerless.

Second, "to love kindness." Here is the thematic word for Hosea, *hesed*. This word is especially rich in meaning, as the variety of its translations indicates. When used of human relationships, it means love with a strong element of loyalty, such as that between a husband and wife (Hos. 2:19 "steadfast love") or between two friends (I Sam. 20:14, "loyal love"). When used of the human relationship to God, it again means love-loyalty (Hos. 6:4, "love" and 6:6, "steadfast love"; see the commentary on these texts).

Third, "to walk humbly with your God." This expression stresses the theological dimension of the sort of life God wants. The word translated "humbly" has more the sense of "circumspectly, carefully," than humility (cf. NEB, "wisely"). The important word is "walk," which is used to describe the whole

192

orientation of one's life in 4:2 and 4:5; it has the same sense in 6:16. In Judaism the word for ethics is *halacha* which means "walking"; the idea is that the task of ethics is to describe how one ought to walk one's day-by-day life. This call to "walk" is similar to the call of Jesus, whose most characteristic invitation was not "believe" but rather "walk" or "Follow me." One who so walks with God will not be exempt from the dark places of life. That person does have the assurance though that this walk is not taken alone: "Even though I walk through the valley of the shadow of death, I fear no evil; for thou art with me . . ." (Ps. 23:4).

The reminder of what God has done in 6:1–5 prompts the hearer of those words to ask, "How should I respond? What does God want from me?" That is the question. The answer given here describes a step-by-step living with God and living for others, acting as advocate for the powerless and showing care for those who are hurting and who need help.

Micah 7:8–20
Who Is a God Like Thee?

The name Micah means "Who is like Yahweh?" The final segment of the book is introduced with a question which is a pun on the prophet's name: "Who is a God like thee . . . ?" (7:18). This concluding hymnic piece is in the context of a liturgy which makes the materials in the Micah collection suitable for use in public worship.

1. A Liturgy (7:8–20)

This liturgy includes parts for the people and for the priest leading the worship. In verses 11–13, the people are addressed, presumably by a priest or the voice of a leader in the worship. The people themselves speak the words in verses 8–10, 14–17, and 18–20. The liturgy assumes a situation when the people have fallen and are in darkness (v. 8), when enemies mock (v. 10), and when the city walls have been destroyed (v. 11). This points to a time after the fall of Jerusalem in 587 B.C., perhaps late in the exilic or early in the postexilic period, when the

193

sayings of Micah were being arranged and the book put into final form. The liturgy falls into four parts:

The People (vv. 8–10). Those gathered for worship described themselves as fallen and as sitting in the darkness. They have experienced the mocking and ridicule of enemies. The situation which comes to mind is the treatment which the citizens of Judah received from Edom at the fall of Jerusalem, as reported in Obadiah 12. Despite the darkness of the situation, the worshipers express confidence that the Lord will be their light (cf. Ps. 27:1–6).

The congregation recognizes the situation in which it finds itself as a result of "the indignation of the LORD" (v. 9). The punishment is acknowledged as deserved, "because I have sinned against him." The prophet had declared that his task was to point out sin (3:8); here each person in the gathered congregation has a chance to acknowledge sin before God and fellow worshipers.

With verse 9*b* comes a turning point. Now the Lord is pictured as the advocate in a law court who takes up the cause of the people so that they are declared innocent. Then the liturgy returns to the themes of light and deliverance, the latter word recalling the "saving acts" of God to which 6:5 referred.

The somewhat vindictive tone of verse 10 must be understood in the context of a people whose capital city has fallen, who are living in the darkest hour of their history, and who have experienced the mockery of their neighbors. A quick review of Obadiah 11–14 will portray the mood and aid in understanding the very human sentiments here expressed.

A Priest (vv. 11–13). Here a different voice speaks, presumably that of a priest addressing the congregation. The people who have been expressing their trust in God are encouraged with words of hope. The speaker describes a time in the future when the broken city walls will be rebuilt, the boundaries of the nation enlarged, and the deported population brought home.

The People (vv. 14–17). Now the congregation speaks again, this time asking the Lord to "shepherd" them. The picture of God as shepherd recalls the same imagery in 2:12 and 5:4; thus this imagery occurs in each of the three "hope" sections of the Micah book. The people describe themselves as living in isolation, in a "forest." The same word occurred in 3:12, the most terrible announcement of doom in the book.

There it was translated "wooded height" and referred to the future desolation of the city. The people's prayer is that they may again "feed in Bashan and Gilead," the best of Israel's pasture lands (Num. 32:1; Jer. 50:19; Sol. 4:1; 6:5).

Verse 15 recalls the deliverance from Egypt. As the sentence reads in the Revised Standard Version, the speaker is the Lord. With but a slight adjustment to the Hebrew, it can be understood as continuing the words of the people, "As in the days when you came out (that is, "when you led us out") of the land of Egypt, show us marvelous things."

The topic of verses 16 and 17 is "the nations," a theme of obvious urgency for those for whom this material was originally composed. The anticipated deliverance will be such that the nations will be astounded (cf. the reaction of the nations in Isa. 52:14—53:1).

The People (vv. 18–20). The final portion of the liturgy is a hymn of praise with two parts. The first describes God as God is (v. 18) and the second declares what God will do in the future (vv. 19–20). The hymn begins and ends with address to God in the second person, "thee . . . thou."

Since few passages in Scripture speak so eloquently of God's grace and forgiveness, these concluding words of the Book of Micah suggest themselves for exposition toward preaching and teaching.

2. Who Is a God Like Thee? (7:18–20)

This is of course a rhetorical question, to which the answer is, "There is no God like thee!" The question expresses marvel at what God has done and continues to do.

The same question is asked in other parts of the Bible. In the Song of Moses, the occasion for the question is God's miraculous deliverance at the sea:

> "Who is like thee, majestic in holiness,
> terrible in glorious deeds, doing wonders?"
> (Exod. 15:11)

The same reaction to the power of God displayed at the Exodus gives rise to the question, "What god is great like our God? in Psalm 77:13. Other psalms also raise the question in reaction to the Lord's power (86:6–9; 71:18–19).

Who is a God like thee? In the psalms, that which provoked this question was God's power over nature and history. In this Micah passage, the cause for marvel is of a different sort. The Book of Micah had opened with a thundering announcement of the Lord's coming to punish both Israel and Judah. Now it concludes with a hymn that marvels at the Lord's grace and forgiveness in a series of seven assertions. The first four use traditional language and describe God as God is; the final three use fresh imagery to tell what God will do in the future:

1. God is the one who *pardons iniquity.* This first picture for forgiveness is drawn from the ritual of the scapegoat as described in Leviticus 16:20–22. The priest lays both hands on the head of the goat and confesses the iniquities of the people of Israel. Then the goat is sent into the wilderness to "bear all their iniquities upon him to a solitary land." This picture is developed further in the poem about the servant who "bore the sin of many" (Isa. 53:12) and in the person of Jesus, in whom the servant figure finds embodiment.

2. God is the one who *passes over transgression.* The Hebrew word behind "transgression" has the sense of rebellion, such as the rebellion of a child against parents (Isa. 1:2). God "passes over" such rebellion. The same language, translated as "overlook an offense," is used of the person who is wise in Proverbs 19:11.

3. God *does not retain his anger forever.* The preaching of Micah had announced the anger of the Lord, before which the mountains melt and the valleys split open (1:4). Fortunately, the ratio of God's anger to his mercy is as three to a thousand (Exod. 20:5–6; Wolff, *Micah,* p. 130). The psalm declares that "his anger is but for a moment, and his favor is for a lifetime" (Ps. 30:5; cf. 103:9).

4. The next statement provides the basis for all that has been said thus far: *"because he delights in steadfast love"* (author's italics). "Steadfast love" translates *hesed,* that love that keeps on loving, no matter what (see on Hos. 1—3).

The next three statements focus on the future and depart from traditional language with fresh imagery.

5. The liturgy becomes more personal, involving the congregation with the first-plural "us." The people say, "He will again have *compassion* on us . . . " (author's italics). The root meaning of the word translated "compassion" is softness or gentleness; the Hebrew noun means "womb." The notion is illustrated with the picture of a mother's love for her child:

196

"Can a woman forget her sucking child,
    that she should have no *compassion* on the son of her
      womb?" (Isa. 49:15, author's italics).

The same is also used to describe a father's love for his children,
translated "pities":

As a father *pities* his children,
    so the LORD *pities* those who fear him.
         (Ps. 103:13, author's italics)

The imagery here anticipates the picture of the waiting father
in Luke 15:11–32.

6. Next, "he will *tread our iniquities under foot*" (author's
italics). This time the plural of "iniquity" introduced in verse 18
is used. The word "tread" is used of the trampling of the enemy
in warfare (Zech. 9:15); the picture is of iniquities being
stamped out, trampled under foot.

7. Finally, "Thou wilt *cast all our sins into the depths of the
sea*" (author's italics). The word for "sin" here has the sense of
missing a target, as in the report about the seven hundred
left-handed slingshotters from the tribe of Benjamin who
"could sling a stone at a hair, and not *miss* (Judg. 20:16, author's
italics). The image is of an action well intended, but which ends
up being off target. The hymn says the Lord will not miss the
target—which is a very large one—when he picks up all our sins
and throws them into the depths of the sea.

After these seven pictures for sin and forgiveness, the final
sentence of the liturgy reaches back behind the exodus (v. 15)
to the time of the ancestors. The picture behind the word *faithfulness* is that of rock-solid reliability. A word from the same
Hebrew root denotes the solid pillars, the doorposts which supported the doorway of the Jerusalem temple (II Kings 18:16).
The hymn ends with another reference to God's steadfast love
or *hesed,* which God will continue to show to God's people,
here named Jacob and Abraham.

In few places does the Old Testament reach out to the
gospel message of the New Testament as dramatically as it does
here. The totality of God's forgiveness is expressed with seven
statements; Jesus once said that his disciples should forgive
"seventy times seven" times (Matt. 18:21–22). The hymn describes God's forgiveness in the language of parental compassion (v. 19); Jesus used the picture of the waiting father to
illustrate this same kind of radical love (Luke 15:11–32).

INTERPRETATION

Central to the earliest Christian preaching was the good news of forgiveness of sins (Acts 2:38; 3:19; 10:43; 13:38). The New Testament then begins to develop its own set of pictures to describe this forgiveness, most of them drawing upon Old Testament imagery: redemption, expiation, justification (Rom. 3:23–26), reconciliation (II Cor. 5:16–21). All of these pictures seek to express what was accomplished through the Lamb of God who has taken away the sin of the world (John 1:29), or, as our hymn would put it, who has cast all our sins into the depths of the sea.

BIBLIOGRAPHY

1. For further study

ALLEN, LESLIE C. *The Books of Joel, Obadiah, Jonah and Micah*, THE NEW INTERNATIONAL COMMENTARY ON THE OLD TESTAMENT (Grand Rapids: Eerdmans, 1976).

BRIGHT, JOHN. *A History of Israel*, Third edition (Philadelphia: The Westminster Press, 1981).

CRAIGIE, PETER. *Twelve Prophets*, Vol. 1, THE DAILY STUDY BIBLE (Philadelphia: The Westminster Press, 1984).

FRETHEIM, TERENCE E. *The Message of Jonah* (Minneapolis: Augsburg Publishing House, 1977).

HESCHEL, ABRAHAM J. *The Prophets*, Vol. 1, HARPER TORCHBOOKS (New York: Harper and Row, 1969).

LIMBURG, JAMES. *The Prophets and the Powerless* (Atlanta: John Knox Press, 1977).

———. *Old Stories for a New Time* (Atlanta: John Knox Press, 1983).

———. "Sevenfold Structures in the Book of Amos," *The Journal of Biblical Literature* 106:217–22 (1987).

LUTHER, MARTIN. *Luther's Works*, Vols. 18, 19. "Lectures on the Minor Prophets," I and II, edited by Hilton C. Oswald (St. Louis: Concordia Publishing House, 1975, 1974).

MAYS, JAMES LUTHER. *Hosea* (Philadelphia: The Westminster Press, 1969).

———. *Amos* (Philadelphia: The Westminster Press, 1969).

———. *Micah* (Philadelphia: The Westminster Press, 1976).

VON RAD, GERHARD. *Old Testament Theology*, Vol. II, translated by D.M.G. Stalker (New York: Harper and Row, 1965).

WESTERMANN, CLAUS. *Elements of Old Testament Theology*, translated by Douglas W. Stott (Atlanta: John Knox Press, 1982).

WOLFF, HANS WALTER. *Hosea*, translated by Gary Stansell and edited by Paul D. Hanson (Philadelphia: Fortress Press, 1974).

———. *Joel and Amos*, translated by Waldemar Janzen, et al. and edited by S. Dean McBride, Jr. (Philadelphia: Fortress Press, 1977).

———. *Micah the Prophet*, translated by Ralph D. Gehrke (Philadelphia: Fortress Press, 1981).

———. *Obadiah and Jonah*. translated by Margaret Kohl (Minneapolis: Augsburg Publishing House, 1986).

2. Literature cited

ALLEN, LESLIE C. *The Books of Joel, Obadiah, Jonah, and Micah*, THE NEW INTERNATIONAL COMMENTARY ON THE OLD TESTAMENT (Grand Rapids: Eerdmans, 1976).

ANDERSEN, FRANCIS I. and FREEDMAN, DAVID NOEL. *Hosea:* THE ANCHOR BIBLE (Garden City: Doubleday, 1980).

BACH, ROBERT. *Die Aufforderung zum Kampf und zur Flucht im alttestamentlichen Prophetenspruch* (Neukirchen: Neukirchener, 1962).

BARTH, KARL. *Dogmatics in Outline,* translated by G.T. Thompson (London: SCM Press, 1949).

BONHOEFFER, DIETRICH. *The Cost of Discipleship,* translated by R.H. Fuller (New York: Macmillan, 1958).

BRIGHT, JOHN. *A History of Israel,* Third edition (Philadelphia: The Westminster Press, 1981).

CAMPBELL, EDWARD F., Jr. *Ruth:* THE ANCHOR BIBLE (Garden City: Doubleday, 1975).

CRAIGIE, PETER. *Twelve Prophets,* Vol. 1, THE DAILY STUDY BIBLE (Philadelphia: The Westminster Press, 1984).

FORELL, GEORGE. *Faith Active in Love* (Minneapolis: Augsburg Publishing House, 1954).

FRETHEIM, TERENCE E. *The Message of Jonah* (Minneapolis: Augsburg Publishing House, 1977).

——. *The Suffering of God* (Philadelphia: Fortress Press, 1984).

HESCHEL, ABRAHAM J. *The Prophets,* Vol. I, HARPER TORCHBOOKS (New York: Harper and Row, 1969).

HUXLEY, ALDOUS. "Jonah," *The Cherry Tree: A Collection of Poems,* edited by Geoffrey Grigson (New York: Vanguard, 1959).

JEREMIAS, JÖRG. *Der Prophet Hosea,* DAS ALTE TESTAMENT DEUTSCH (Göttingen: Vandenhoeck & Ruprecht, 1983).

KOEHLER, LUDWIG and BAUMGARTNER, WALTER. *Lexicon in Veteris Testamenti Libros* (Leiden: Brill, 1958).

LIMBURG, JAMES. *The Prophets and the Powerless* (Atlanta: John Knox Press, 1977).

——. *Old Stories for a New Time* (Atlanta: John Knox Press, 1983).

LUTHER, MARTIN. *Luther's Works,* Vol. 35. "Word and Sacrament," edited by E. Theodore Bachmann. (Philadelphia: Muhlenberg Press, 1960).

MAGONET, JONATHAN. *Form and Meaning: Studies in Literary Techniques in the Book of Jonah* (Bern: Herbert Lang, 1976).

MAYS, JAMES LUTHER. *Hosea* (Philadelphia: The Westminster Press, 1969).

——. "Justice," *Interpretation* 37:5–17 (1983).

——. *Amos* (Philadelphia: The Westminster Press, 1969).

——. *Micah* (Philadelphia: The Westminster Press, 1976).

POPE, M.H. "Seven, Seventh, Seventy," [pp. 294–295]. *The Interpreter's Dictionary of the Bible R–Z* (New York and Nashville: Abingdon Press, 1962).

VON RAD, GERHARD. *Old Testament Theology,* Vols. I, II, translated by D.M.G. Stalker (New York: Harper and Row, 1962, 1965).

RÖLVAAG, O.E. *Giants in the Earth* (New York: Harper and Row, 1927).

RUDOLPH, WILHELM. *Hosea,* KOMMENTAR ZUM ALTEN TESTAMENT (Gütersloh: Gütersloher Verlagshaus Gerd Mohn, 1966).

SAKENFELD, KATHARINE DOOB. *Faithfulness in Action* (Philadelphia: Fortress Press, 1985).

SMITH, GEORGE ADAM. *The Book of the Twelve Prophets,* Vol. II, THE EXPOSITOR'S BIBLE (New York: A.C. Armstrong and Son, 1902).

THIELICKE, HELMUT. *The Waiting Father,* translated by John W. Doberstein (New York: Harper and Brothers, 1959).

VAN BEEK, G.W. "Gath-Hepher," [p. 356]. *The Interpreter's Dictionary of the Bible E–J* (New York and Nashville: Abingdon Press, 1962).

WESTERMANN, CLAUS. *Elements of Old Testament Theology,* translated by Douglas W. Stott (Atlanta: John Knox Press, 1982).

———. *Basic Forms of Prophetic Speech,* translated by Hugh Clayton White (Philadelphia: The Westminster Press, 1967).

———. *Blessing in the Bible and the Life of the Church,* translated by Keith Crim (Philadelphia: Fortress Press, 1978).

———. *The Psalms: Structure, Content and Message,* translated by Ralph D. Gehrke (Minneapolis: Augsburg Publishing House, 1980).

———. *Genesis,* BIBLISCHER KOMMENTAR: ALTES TESTAMENT (Neukirchen-Vluyn: Neukirchener Verlag, 1977).

WIESEL, ELIE. *Night,* translated by Stella Rodway (New York: Avon, 1969).

WOLFF, HANS WALTER. *Micha,* BIBLISHER KOMMENTAR: ALTES TESTAMENT (Neukirchen-Vluyn: Neukirchener Verlag, 1982).

———. *Obadiah and Jonah,* translated by Margaret Kohl (Minneapolis: Augsburg Publishing House, 1986).

———. *Joel and Amos,* translated by Waldemar Janzen et al and edited by S. Dean McBride, Jr. (Philadelphia: Fortress Press, 1977).

———. *Hosea,* translated by Gary Stansell and edited by Paul D. Hanson (Philadelphia: Fortress Press, 1974).

———. *Amos the Prophet,* translated by Foster R. McCurley and edited by John Reumann (Philadelphia: Fortress Press, 1973).

———. *Micah the Prophet,* translated by Ralph D. Gehrke (Philadelphia: Fortress Press, 1981).